YOU WIN
or
YOU DIE

'A fascinating guide to the shadows of antiquity that loom behind *Game of Thrones*, written by someone who really knows her stuff.'

YOU WIN
or
YOU DIE

THE ANCIENT WORLD OF
GAME OF THRONES

Ayelet Haimson Lushkov

I.B. TAURIS
LONDON · NEW YORK

Published in 2017 by
I.B.Tauris & Co. Ltd
London • New York
www.ibtauris.com

ISBN: 978 1 78453 699 2
eISBN: 978 1 78672 213 3
ePDF: 978 1 78673 213 2

A full CIP record for this book is available from the British Library
A full CIP record is available from the Library of Congress

Library of Congress Catalog Card Number: available

Text designed and typeset by Tetragon, London
Printed and bound by CPI Group (UK) Ltd, Croydon, CRO 4YY

CONTENTS

LIST OF ILLUSTRATIONS

NOTE ON SOURCES

BOOKS IN THE *A SONG OF ICE AND FIRE* SERIES, BY GEORGE R. R. MARTIN

GT: *A Game of Thrones*
CK: *A Clash of Kings*
SS: *A Storm of Swords*
FC: *A Feast for Crows*
DD: *A Dance with Dragons*

ANCIENT SOURCES

Ancient texts are divided into books rather than chapters, and then into sections (for prose works) or lines (for poetry). Some works have only one book, so their only subdivision is into sections or lines, but more usually they'll be made up of many books. The *Iliad*, for instance, has 24 books. Livy's history of Rome came to 142. This means that, in order to understand the references in this book, you'll have to understand the standard citation practices, which are fortunately very easy:

If a work has book divisions, the first number will invariably be the book number, and the second will be line numbers. So, '*Iliad* 19–22' means '*Iliad*, Books 19–22,' while '*Iliad* 1.1–10' means '*Iliad*, Book 1, lines 1–10.' The same holds for prose: 'Caesar, *The Gallic War*, 1.3–10' means 'Caesar, *The Gallic War*, Book 1, chapters 3–10.' Some older editions have further subdivisions, marked in

Roman numerals, but the newer editions invariably go for the more streamlined style.

For those works that do not have book divisions (here mostly Greek tragedies), the citation simply refers to line numbers; '*Helen* 30–6,' for example, does not mean 'Books 30–6 of Euripides' *Helen*,' but rather 'lines 30–6.'

In this book, all line numbers, no matter what format of citation, refer to the text of the cited translations, as opposed to the original Latin or Greek.

PREFACE

The world of *Game of Thrones* is vast, but what makes it bigger still is the multiplicity of connections to our own world – not just our present, but also our historical and literary past. This book presents one way of approaching *Game of Thrones*, which pays close attention to the points of contact with the ancient Greek and Roman world, of which there are many. Specifically, the book shows what happens in one reader's mind as she reads and views the series through the lens of a professional classicist. What this book is not, however, is a definitive guide to the Greco-Roman classics in Westeros: I have no special knowledge, for instance, of what goes on in the head or the library of George R. R. Martin, nor behind the scenes at HBO, nor any other venue that produces official versions of the franchise, except in cases where they state so explicitly (like Martin on Hadrian's Wall, for instance). And despite being the work of a professional classicist, this book isn't a compendium of every single similarity or reminiscence of the ancient world in Westeros. However large and complex *Game of Thrones* seems, the classical world is far larger, and classicists don't all focus on the same things when we study what the ancient Greeks or Romans thought, said, or did. What this book is, therefore, is one reader's view of how the classical world resonates with the world of Westeros, what similarities are of particular interest, and how these connections deepen the experience of reading, watching, or thinking about *Game of Thrones*. At the heart of the book is the idea that the *Game of Thrones* saga can usefully be read as a prose epic – that is, a combination of epic motifs, ideas, and storytelling techniques with material more commonly treated in prose histories: politics, domestic scheming, ethnographies, and so on.

Precise readers will already have noticed that I use *Game of Thrones* to mean more than the first book of the *Song of Ice and Fire* series. Indeed, throughout the book I use it both to refer to the whole series and to its first book. I have tried to make it very clear when I am referring to the single novel and when to the series (most instances refer to the latter). The rationale for risking potential confusion was to simplify what otherwise is a mouthful, and to use what has come to be the standard and popular name for the book and television series. To those readers who find their teeth set on edge by my usage, I offer apologies at the outset. In general, this work takes its cue from the books, with the HBO adaptation used to supplement rather than as the focus – so when I say *Game of Thrones* unspecified, I mean the books or a narrative on the show that is modeled so closely on the books as to make no significant difference.

Like *Game of Thrones*, the word 'classics' or 'classical world' is a shorthand that covers a multitude of sins. The classical world proper is the entire inhabited globe, with chronologies for 'the classical' changing for each specific culture: numerous civilizations – Greco-Roman, Indic, Chinese, etc. – retrospectively identify a classical moment in their history, or have one identified for them by successors or outsiders. Hence, the field of the 'classical,' even the very word, is as vast as it is contested. What I mean by 'the classical,' however, is much more confined and functions almost like a technical term in Western culture: it is the world of the ancient Mediterranean from about 800 BC to 400 AD (give or take a few centuries either way), and with a particular focus on the cultures of Greece and Rome and their empires. From this definition are excluded the Mediterranean cultures of the Phoenicians and the Carthaginians, and the Northern European tribes, except where they come into contact with Greece and Rome. This scope isn't exactly commensurate with the academic discipline of classics, which can range much further in time and space, but it does represent the core of the material we study.

My particular emphasis is often on the literature rather than the history, not least because it is the writings of Greek and Roman authors that have exerted the strongest and clearest influence on the subsequent tradition of literature and art, down to *Game of Thrones* itself. For this reason I include – indeed often focus on – the famous Trojan War, an event which, whether or not it really happened, is traditionally dated to roughly 1200 BC. Stories about the Trojan War circulated in all sorts of ways, especially oral performance, long before the two main epic poems, the *Iliad* and *Odyssey*, were set down in writing. The epics as we know them are a multilayered creation, and even after being written down evolved through the work of editors down to the Hellenistic period of the third century BC. Nor is this our only source of knowledge about the Trojan War: I'll also frequently turn to the representations in Athenian tragedy of the fifth century BC and Vergil's famous Roman epic, the *Aeneid*, in the first century BC. But besides the Trojan War there will be many other myths, histories, and monuments that we encounter over the course of the book. One thing that will emerge very clearly from all these works is just how much our understanding of the ancient world is mediated through its representation in texts and by the motivations of their authors. That sense of personal, and inevitably partial, point-of-view is equally crucial to understanding *Game of Thrones*, especially a book series defined and structured by individual characters' perspectives on events, and a fantasy world about which we can never hope to have complete information.

It's impossible to write a book like this without giving away spoilers. For my part, I've tried to avoid disclosing too much of the plot, not least because there is much yet to be resolved. There are, however, many spoilers in this book, and their severity depends on how far you've gotten in your reading or watching. I assume that you're familiar enough with *Game of Thrones* and its world not to need explanation or introductions, and that you've followed the series up to and including *A Dance with Dragons*, or the sixth season of the TV adaptation. As the two versions diverge, I discuss them less and less, and there are few spoilers for the most recent HBO season or for *A Dance with Dragons*. If you do learn a plot detail from this book you'd have rather not known, remember that classical myth was regularly told to people who already knew the end – yet they still read works and attended the theater with enthusiasm, and we're still fascinated by the same old stories two thousand years later. Nevertheless, *caveat lector*.

As with all books, I owe many thanks for help and encouragement with its composition. I started reading *Game of Thrones* after a casual recommendation by Taha Hasan – blame for anything that follows can be placed squarely at his well-shod feet. Three years of teaching this material to first-year students at the University of Texas at Austin has shown me how versatile the material is, and how no two people relate to it in quite the same way. The best encouragement came from two sources: Alex Wright, my editor, and his team at I.B.Tauris, who kept me from flagging during a dizzying journey to publication; and my students and colleagues, whose enthusiasm for the project has been boundless and heartwarming. David Welch offered invaluable help with matters pragmatic, and kept a keen eye on detail. He has saved me from many mistakes, and any that remain are entirely my own. The greatest thanks, however, go, as they always do, to my husband, Pramit Chaudhuri, without whom this book, and its author, would be much the worse off.

1. The Mountain and the Viper

INTRODUCTION

Ser Waymar Royce: 'And how did you find the Wall?' (GT 18)

W here is the ancient world in *Game of Thrones*? This isn't an easy question to answer, because Westeros and the other continents that make up the world created by George R. R. Martin have many histories, some their own and some that are borrowed from the mythologies and histories of our world. Not only does the fictional world, with its dragons and magic, look very different from ours, but its chronologies are different too: it has elements that correspond to what we think of as ancient or medieval or early modern, but not in any fixed order, and not in any fixed place. The ancient world I'm looking for is the one lived in the Mediterranean, especially in Greece and Italy, from about 1200 BC to the collapse of the Roman empire in the fourth century after Christ. This is a world that influences and animates many of the ways we think, talk, and describe our own world, and one that has been taken up by each successive generation from Homer down to us. It isn't just a historical world, it's also a world of stories and narratives, some fictional, some not, and the influence it has had on subsequent periods is as much a product of those stories as of the peoples and empires of antiquity. The classical world, as Greco-Roman antiquity is often known, is made up of epic mythologies like the *Iliad* as much as historical wars, cities, and kings – and those mythologies are often more influential than any historical event has ever been. *Game of Thrones*, however, doesn't immediately look very classical; it might seem more British, or medieval, or, in some cases, strikingly modern. It's all of those things, true, but it is also resoundingly classical, both in the way it tells its stories as well as in numerous aspects of its culture, myth, history, and indeed geography.

Just as in our world, traces of antiquity are scattered about Westeros, Essos, and the former Valyria, an empire that resembles Rome's influence and reach. High Valyrian, for instance, survives after the Doom as the language of culture and refinement, taught to well-educated young nobles, just as Latin thrives to the present day in elite education and institutional settings like the Catholic Church. Valyrian roads still run across the length and breadth of Essos: straight, true, and long-lasting, they are the equivalent of one of Rome's proudest achievements, its network of roads.

Roman roads spread from Rome itself and reached nearly every corner of the empire. They carried Rome's armies, as well as Rome's trade, customs, language, architecture, laws, coin, and grain- and

2. A Roman road in Algeria

tax-collectors. Roads were not only the arteries of the empire, they were also one of its most durable legacies, and many survive either in their original form, or provide the track and primary foundations for modern roads. Architecture across Essos also has strong ancient resemblances. Gladiatorial arenas, like the one Tyrion sees in Meereen, take their cue from the Colosseum, the gigantic arena built by the Flavian dynasty to host lavish and cruel entertainments for the masses.

The Titan of Braavos, an enormous statue bestriding the port, comes to us from the Colossus of Rhodes, one of the seven wonders of the ancient world, which no longer survives. The bronze figure depicting the sun god Helios was dedicated by the Rhodians after a great military victory, and took 12 years to complete. It stood by the harbor entrance (not bestriding it, as the medieval chronicles thought) until it collapsed in an earthquake some 60 years later. The Rhodians, told that they had offended the god, declined to rebuild, and the ruins remained in place for another 800 years, where tourists like Pliny the Elder could marvel at their size and artistry.[1] The history of Valyria recalls Rome too: just as the Romans apocryphally did to Carthage, the Valyrians raze to the ground

3. The Colosseum

the capital of their long-standing rivals, the Ghiscari, and sow the ground with salt (*SS* 311).

There are other classical traces in Essos, as well. The Free Cities, for instance, are a loose cluster of city-states, a model which goes back to the city-states of medieval Italy, but also further back to ancient Greece. Unlike Rome, the Greek world was a much more fragmented one before the Roman conquest. Topography as well as political ideology dictated the emergence of *poleis* or city-states, where citizens were drawn from small native communities and ran their cities according to a variety of political systems. Athens and Sparta are the most famous instances, and both came to have increasing spheres of influence – an empire of sorts – as other city-states made treaties and alliances with them, or were forced into submission.[2] As time wore on, loose collections of city-states, called leagues, solidified. Some were based on political power, like the Delian League dominated by fifth-century Athens. Some were based on expediency, like the Aetolian League in the fourth century. Others were grouped together simply by geographical proximity, or by having a shared culture, like the islands of Greece, or the cities of Ionia, a set of Greek settlements on what is now the Turkish shore. Some of these groupings were organized around a great temple, which was not just a holy place but often also a bank, protected by the gods. Braavos with its Iron Bank and flowing canals reminds us of Venice, but its position among a set of Free Cities with whom it shares culture and location makes it also like the cities of Ionia, a natural bridge between West and East.

The physical remains of the ancient world can be found scattered throughout Essos, but it is Westeros that boasts what is perhaps the most resonant echo of antiquity: the Wall. George R. R. Martin himself has said that he modeled the great ice wall on Hadrian's Wall, which bisects northern England between the Tyne and the Solway Firth.[3] There a Roman soldier might stare into the dense forest beyond and wonder what dangers rustled in the forest. There he might protect his fellow soldiers and the citizens of Britain from the threat of marauding Picts, and there too, in places like Vindolanda, he might live out his life. Westeros' Wall is, of course, bigger and more fantastic than Hadrian's Wall; nor did Roman soldiers abstain from marriage or swear to take no part in the politics of the land. Quite the contrary. The Roman army settled where it went, took local women for wives, and remained an important force in the service of any emperor or aspirant to the throne. But the wall at the end of the world, whether in the frigid north of Britain or the heat of Ctesiphon in the Fertile Crescent, still holds a special emotive power. Walls, after all, demarcate here from there, us from them, safety from danger, and civilization from wildness and barbarity.

In the case of Westeros, the Wall is something more: it is also a repository of knowledge, the last great library that might contain the secret of defeating the White Walkers. The Wall is also one of the few buildings in Westeros for which we have a date – it is 8,000 years old (*DD* 783). As such, the Wall is also a place of history and of learning, a boundary between saving knowledge and doomed ignorance. In fact, the Wall makes an unlikely pairing with the other place of learning in Westeros, the Citadel deep in the southwest of the Reach, where maesters earn the links in their chain by mastering

4. Hadrian's Wall

branches of knowledge. Both the Wall and the Citadel are manned
by what we might call a monastic order, men who have pledged
their lives to their work and disavowed either political interest or
domestic fulfillment. But on the Wall, the quest for knowledge is
conducted not with books or incantations, but with toil and courage.
The maesters of the Citadel expand their knowledge right where they
are; the Rangers of the Wall expand theirs by going out and having a
look. Autopsy and research therefore bracket Westeros, leaving the
middle ground empty for knights and kings and Sparrows to battle
out their lives. Still, the two cannot exist without each other; Sam's
Citadel learning will prove crucial to the fight, as history plays out
across the Seven Kingdoms. In the end, however, it is the Wall that
matters most, the Wall where the crucial battle must be fought and
the crucial questions answered. There is the clash not only of ice and
fire, but also of ideology, religion, and the entire game of thrones.

What would the Romans have made of the Wall? To many, especially those living or serving on the edges of the empire, the Wall
would have been simply a more fantastic version of the extensive
fortification systems that marked the limits of Roman expansion.
But its sheer scale can't be overestimated. The Roman system of
fortifications, called *limites*, were much simpler structures. They
generally consisted of low walls, ditches and trenches, and watch
towers and camps spaced along the fortification lines.

Roman *limites* were also deliberately more porous, and designed
not to stop massive invasions of barbarian tribes, but rather to
manage the regular traffic of traders, tourists, migrants, and other
people whose lives straddled the peripheries of the Roman sphere
of influence. And although these lines could not stop an invading
barbarian horde, they could serve as an early warning system when
such invasions were only beginning, as well as deter small-scale
raiding, thereby protecting Roman settlements near the border. The
limites also meant that there was a constant presence of organized
Roman military units spread out across any danger zones. These
units could be summoned quickly to hold the line against any attack,

5. Reconstruction of Roman *limes* near Saalburg

at least until larger forces could arrive from elsewhere in the empire. And because service in the Roman forces could frequently stretch to 20 years, many units simply settled where they were, bringing with them Roman customs and language, and in some cases normalizing Roman presence in the area. In other instances, of course, the presence of the legions was a constant irritant to the local population, just as the crows of the Night's Watch were an endless affront to the Free Folk on the other side of the Wall. The Romans would therefore have found some aspects of the Wall deeply familiar: the distribution of fortifications, the presence of a military order, and the reliance on faraway lords and kings to relieve the stretched resources of the Watch. What the Romans might have marveled at, however, was the audacity of its size, and the assurance that the Wall itself could stop the invading hordes in their track.

Indeed, they would have marveled at the Wall itself, just as Tyrion does when he comes to visit it, and just as any new arrival seems to do. Walls, like all large structures, inherently demonstrate a central authority in command of considerable resources: quarries for rocks, roads for transporting materials and workers, human and natural resources, and the military might to back up both the construction and the finished products. Walls declare sovereignty, and they draw a clear mark across any geography: we are here on this side, while the enemy or the unknown lingers over there. As such, walls have strong symbolic value. When the invading Persian army burned the Acropolis in Athens and forced the mass evacuation of its people in the fifth century BC, Themistocles, the leader of the Athenian forces, made a startling statement: 'the city is its people,' he said, 'and the walls of Athens are its battle ships.'[4] This view of the city as a portable unit was new to the ancient world, despite the fact that armies stationed away for a long time instinctively mimicked the way that life was lived back home even when far away. Incidentally, the idea of roving bands of men without walls became much more popular in the following century, when mercenary armies – the ancient equivalents of the Golden Company and their ilk – lent their services to the highest bidder. Many of these companies grouped together men who came from the same cities, and those bonds of origin exercised some power even at a time where loyalty was being transferred from small city-states to the much larger kingdoms of the Hellenistic rulers. In this way, one of the big questions antiquity invites us to ask about the Wall is what its symbolic significance was. The Wall was clearly meant to protect against an outside menace, but it was built by a Stark, Brandon the Builder, and was never meant to keep together the people of the Seven Kingdoms, nor even of the North, as does, perhaps, the fortification wall at Moat Cailin. The brothers of the Night's Watch, too, are not quite in the mold of Roman soldiers, and arguably have much more in common with either a monastic order or even a mercenary troop: they recruit voluntarily, swear an oath of allegiance, and take no part in politics except to the extent that political actors might donate soldiers or money. Once Jon Snow, together with Stannis Baratheon, subdues Mance Rayder and the Free Folk, can the strength of the Wall be recruited to win the Iron Throne?

Brandon the Builder, who erected both the Wall and Winterfell, the two main structures associated with the Starks, recalls again some of the mythical wall-builders of antiquity. Building a wall was a big task, and some ancient walls were imagined to have been built by the gods themselves. Poseidon and Apollo, for instance, built the walls of Troy, which could not be breached even after ten years of incessant warfare. The walls of Thebes were built by the musician Amphion, who charmed the stones to arrange themselves with his miraculous singing. And the walls of Rome were built by the city's founder, Romulus, the son of the war god Mars.[5] Those walls, quickly made useless by the rapid growth of the city, are at the very heart of the Roman foundation story, because they are the reason for the earliest instances of civil war the Romans knew in their own history. There are a few versions of this famous story, but they all recount how Romulus killed his twin brother Remus for mocking his nascent wall. 'So perish all who breach my walls!' shouts Romulus over the corpse of his brother, establishing both his own sovereignty and the Roman penchant for blood-soaked civil strife in one fell swoop.[6] To undermine the wall, whether by words or siege, was to attack the city's very being, and it's for this reason that the Romans frequently remember the greatest threats to their city as threats to the city walls. For several centuries the wild tribes of Gaul were the only enemy to actually penetrate the walls and sack the city early in the history of Rome, while Hannibal notoriously failed in his attempt to breach the walls, a failure that came to symbolize a turning point in the war against Carthage and the eventual ascendancy of Rome as the premier Mediterranean power. World history can turn on what happens at a wall.

Rome's first walls ran along the *pomerium*, the city's sacred boundary, and they were extended a few times as events demanded it. The *pomerium* was a religious as well as military boundary, and while it too required extending as the empire grew, it was only the very greatest sons of Rome who won that honor. The greatest of them, the emperor Augustus, extended the *pomerium* in 8 BC, but he was much more concerned with establishing clear boundaries for the Roman empire, even as his poets celebrated the Roman *imperium sine fine* – their empire without end. Augustus was also concerned with reminding the people of who they were and where they came from, a sense of national and personal identity he felt was lost in the midst of the brutal civil war that shook the Roman state in the 50 years before Augustus came to power. As part of that program, Augustus commissioned the first public library in Rome. In charge of it was an antiquarian scholar named Varro, whose many works accomplished exactly what Augustus had hoped: bringing the Romans back to themselves, whereas before they were foreigners in their own land, ignorant of its traditions and customs.[7] This feeling of alienation at home seems very much alive in Westeros: Sam feels it on the Wall until he finds its hidden library; Bran feels it as he travels from the ravaged Winterfell; and Theon Greyjoy feels it when he comes home at last to the Iron Islands only to find himself rejected and cast out. And Daenerys Targaryen feels it perhaps most of all, longing for a homeland she has never set foot in, and exiled not only from Westeros but also from the Dothraki she has taken as her own. Theon deals with his alienation by trying to take Winterfell as his own, while Dany attempts to learn what she can of home through books and stories. But can the last of the Targaryens, or indeed the last of the Starks, remind Westeros of its former rulers and resolve the horrors of civil war, or will they, like Romulus before them, have to do so over the corpse of their nearest kin?

The Wall and its counterpart at Moat Cailin are not the only topographical features to define the North. As the only area left in the Seven Kingdoms where the Old Gods are still worshipped, the North, and especially Winterfell, is also characterized by its dark and gloomy godswoods with the weirwood tree at their heart. So characteristic are these trees, in fact, that the godswood is where we first encounter Ned Stark on his own, as he cleans his greatsword, Ice, but it is also one of the features picked out for the striking animation that opens the television show, an organic growth from the otherwise mechanical models of cities.

The Greeks and Romans did not themselves worship trees, although the Romans knew that the Druids of Gaul held the oak tree in special reverence. In fact, the word *druid* might derive from the Greek word for tree, *drus*. Nevertheless, ancient mythology is full of tree-stories, myths that give specific trees an origin by animating them with human spirit. The most famous, perhaps, is the story of Apollo and Daphne, wherein the nymph Daphne, chased by the god, was turned into the laurel tree to protect her virtue.

The tree remained sacred to Apollo, and its leaves were used for religious ceremonies as well as to make victory wreaths for the winners of poetic competitions. Other trees were considered sacred to the gods by virtue of their locations: the oak trees of the precinct of Dodona, for instance, were used as oracles; worshippers who came to look for divine advice would listen to the rustle of the leaves, which were then interpreted by the priests. And other trees still were sacred not by themselves but as a sacred grove, which granted asylum for those who sought refuge in it. Rome had such a grove, which offered sanctuary for one man. When a new seeker arrived, he had to kill the previous incumbent to take his place. It was to there that the radical politician Gaius Gracchus escaped when

riots brought down his ambitious program of political change, and when it seemed that his aristocratic rivals had gotten the better of him. Gracchus did not last long, asking his slave to kill him when he finally realized all was lost.

But the grove that comes nearest to the dark wood in Winterfell is a fictional grove, depicted by the poet Lucan. The grove is described as being of great antiquity, spared by generations seeking wood for heat, building, or war. It is dark and ominous, and gods are worshipped there in foul rituals. There is water

6. Bernini's Apollo and Daphne

there, flowing in dark streams, and the images of the gods are only crude blocks hewn from fallen tree trunks. They are old, and rotting, and they strike terror in the hearts of men. Birds fear to perch there, and storms do not touch these trees, nor does light come in between their boughs. It is a place of darkness, and antiquity, and so obviously sacred that even the Roman legions who arrive to desecrate it refuse their orders, sure that their axes will rebound from the trees to strike off their own limbs. It requires the personal example of their general, the infamous Julius Caesar, to get them going. Wielding an axe, Caesar strikes the first blow on an ancient oak, and tells his soldiers not to worry: any divine anger will now fall on his own head:

> Then all the throng
> obeyed his orders, not free from fear with dread removed,
> but weighing in the scales the wrath of gods and Caesar.
> Down fall the ash-trees, the knotty holm-oak is overthrown;
> and Dodona's wood and alder, more fit for the waves,
> and cypress, witness to no plebeian grief,
> then for the first time shed their tresses and, robbed of foliage,
> let in the daylight: and thrown down on its packed timber
> the falling grove supports itself.[8]

Unlike this Gallic grove, the godswood of Winterfell survives even when the fortress changes hands and suffers considerable physical damage. Other, less numinous groves suffice to offer Sansa some kind of sanctuary even in her most difficult moments. But the tension between the sacred and profane that animates Lucan's grove-felling scene spells out some of the live tensions of Westeros as well: the old religion versus the new, the contemplative versus the active life, contrasting qualities of leadership, and the consequences of war for the environment. Indeed, one of Lucan's main themes in his poem, which tells the story of the bloody civil war between Caesar and Pompey (49–46 BC), is that civil war destroys not only the political state, but affects society at every level of its existence.

It pits fathers against sons and brothers against brothers, a story which replays itself across Westeros, but it also drags into its violent orbit the physical world itself: pools of blood, storms, ruined fields, and starvation all attend on civil war – as both Rome and the Seven Kingdoms find out to their cost.

One of the early details of characterization George R. R. Martin gives us about Ned Stark is his sense of personal responsibility as a key component of leadership: he who passes the judgment should wield the sword. Ned is willing to overlook this in his friend Robert, and this ethical failure is part and parcel of the general abandonment of leadership that characterized the Baratheon years, and even more so Joffrey's short and brutal reign. It is, therefore, appropriate but also ironic that Ned becomes both the Hand of the King, the primary mechanism by which Robert can avoid his responsibilities and delegate his authority, and the victim of Joffrey's first crime in office, but not at Joffrey's own hand. Joffrey passes the sentences, but cannot wield the sword. Indeed, after Ned, none can wield Ice, and it is broken into two smaller swords by Tywin – an apt metaphor for the unwieldy and fragmented state of the North after the collapse of the Starks.

This kind of personal responsibility – leading from the front – was a key part of the Roman ideology of generalship, though many generals fell short of the mark. A good general was expected to mingle with his troops before battle, inspire them during, and fight in the most dangerous spot if things went wrong. Julius Caesar, one of Rome's most illustrious and successful generals, worked hard to fit just such a mold. In his own writing, he always appears as the very model of a Roman general, swooping to the rescue when things go badly for his legates and always having a clever word for his troops to get them over the line. On some memorable occasions, when the Romans were badly pressed, he took the legionary colors and threw them beyond the enemy lines; since losing the colors was the height of shame to the legions, they stopped at nothing to retrieve them, and the battle was won.[9] The same story is told of many other generals, so whether or not Caesar actually did it is in some doubt, but the point is that Caesar cared very deeply about embodying an ideal image of generalship. In this, he was quite successful. The image stuck, and we see it even in Lucan's poem, albeit distorted by the poem's generally hostile, or at least very ambivalent, view of Caesar's legacy. 'Any divine anger will come to me: none of you need fear to strike now!' he cries out, ostensibly taking on exactly the kind of leadership espoused by the Roman code and by Ned Stark. He who passes the sentence should wield the sword, after all. But Lucan gives it all a rather more chilling aspect: Caesar is not afraid to take on even the gods, and his determination to conquer stops at nothing, even the utter desecration of his enemies' religious sites and traditions. What makes this all seem ever more pointless is that Caesar doesn't even stick around to see out the battle for which the grove was being cut down; full of impatience, he heads off to Spain and other more urgent tasks, leaving his army to build a fleet and fight a gruesome naval battle.

The Battle of Massilia, which follows the grove-felling, is one of the set pieces of Lucan's poem. It's a battle taken to the extreme, with men suffering wounds the likes of which had never been seen before in epic poetry. Not only that, but the battle makes fathers, sons, and brothers commit atrocities against each other, sometimes knowingly, and at other times discovering their opponent's identity only at the moment of death. The deaths themselves are emphatically grotesque, with bodies caught, torn, and destroyed by weapons, the prows of ships, the ferocity of battle, and the waves below. One soldier, the first of many on whose demise Lucan dwells, dies as follows:

> As a grappling-iron was fastening its grasping hooks on to a ship,
> it pierced Lycidas. He would have been submerged in the deep
> but for his comrades, who held on to his legs as he swung.
> He was torn and split apart and blood did not spurt out
>   as from a wound;
> slowly from his broken veins it falls everywhere,

and as the stream of life passed into his separated limbs
it was intercepted by the waters.[10]

The violence of even this short passage – and Lucan's poem is a
veritable catalogue of the various ways in which a human body can
be destroyed in extreme conditions – is a direct predecessor of the
notorious violence that is everywhere in *Game of Thrones*. Lucan is
possibly even more graphic than *Game of Thrones*, which tends to
prefer realistic violence over the elaborate contortions characteristic
of the epic; Lucan's poem is certainly more gratuitous than any other
ancient epic that survives today. Such violence seems to be part of
the aesthetic sensibility of the time, when, under the emperor Nero,
the Romans developed a pronounced taste for the shocking and the
spectacular, whether in their poetry, their plays, or their entertainments in the gladiatorial arena. There is a clear line connecting the
cruel executions and fights in the gladiatorial games and the amount
of blood pouring from the pages of Roman literature.

Battle is where Lucan chooses to highlight the horrors visited
on humans by civil war, but while the War of the Five Kings brings
suffering almost everywhere in the Seven Kingdoms, we get to
witness very few actual battles. And one of the more impressive
ones, as it happens, is the battle on the Blackwater Rush, the only
'proper' naval battle Westeros sees up until this point. The battle
is narrated from the point of view of Davos Seaworth, who tells us
already at the outset that the battle is practically doomed to failure,
since the poor tactics of the highborn generals nullify the strategic
advantage Stannis' larger force might have had. What wins the
battle at the end, however, is not any tactical maneuvering on the
river, but rather Tyrion Lannister's building of the chain and use
of wildfire, the green fire created by King's Landing's alchemists.
Davos, a sailor rather than a poet, sees the ships in the water rather
than their individual crew members, and the whole battle quickly
becomes nearly industrial, with both fleets reduced to cinders and
dead men clogging the water. Still, what is apparent is the horror

unleashed by the unnatural fire, which is compounded by Joffrey's launching captive spies over the walls, and Cersei's plan to use the noble women as hostages or as victims in a murder-suicide. What both battles show us clearly, then, is the madness brought on by civil war: the deformation of family or hospitality bonds, a growing willingness to inflict pain on fellow humans, and a tremendous price paid by non-combatants – and indeed by the very environment in which the war takes place. Lucan's trees come down; King's Landing's river burns.

Some of the classical items I've so far discussed, like Hadrian's Wall or gladiatorial games, have become familiar in contemporary culture as markers of the grandeur of Rome. Others, like the Trojan War, which I'll discuss at more length later, still reverberate with the glory of Greece. Recent movies like *Troy* or *Gladiator* have brought the ancient world to new audiences, while the academic discipline of Classics has continued to study what has survived of the ancient world, both unearthing new evidence and discovering new ways of looking at antiquity. This book and the kinds of reading it exemplifies are necessarily only one person's way of understanding *Game of Thrones*. That way, of course, is my own, and it's shaped by my own interests and scholarly preoccupations. But the ancient world is both large and diverse, and different classicists will have different ways of interpreting the same objects, whether *Game of Thrones* or the classical texts and artifacts I discuss in correlation with it.

At the center of my own approach is literature, and specifically Roman literature, and it is through this lens that I read the *Game of Thrones* books, or watch the TV show. But focusing on literature means both that I'm more interested in how *Game of Thrones* interacts with the narratives of the ancient world than with its material culture, *and* that I'm more interested in the version represented in George R. R. Martin's books than in the TV series. This doesn't mean that I ignore either ancient history or HBO, but to my mind *Game of Thrones* is a modern prose epic of sorts, and one of the ways I've most enjoyed reading it is through spotting what the books do with the traditions and conventions of ancient epic. In some cases, like the gruesome violence, *Game of Thrones* inherits the convention. In others, like Lucan's political allegory of the body, *Game of Thrones* manipulates it, so that the treatment looks both ancient and modern in different respects. In other cases still, *Game of Thrones* modernizes or adapts ancient conventions for its particular needs, but in all cases there are deep and influential layers of ancient precedent buried beneath the medieval trappings and modern prose, and the most important of those layers, to my eyes at least, is the language and style of the great ancient epic poems.

My focus on epic and on literature more generally also acknowledges that *Game of Thrones* started out as a literary work – that is, as words written on a page and collected in a book. As such, it is susceptible to methods of literary criticism, which largely consists of the art of careful reading and thinking about what a text can say to us about events, phenomena, and other texts – in other words, about human life and the human condition. This isn't to say that the HBO adaptation doesn't reflect on those things or have its own artistic merit – in fact, its parallel existence makes for a great study in how multiple stories and media can interact, some examples of which we'll encounter in this book – but it is to say that *for me*, words on a page always do more than images on a screen. This might be different for you, in which case the main payoff of reading this book may lie in the way you come to interpret the TV show, since visual images are as susceptible to 'literary' criticism as text is. You can apply to the HBO adaptation many of the same ideas I demonstrate with reference to the books – and if you do, it will inevitably enrich your viewing as well as your reading! As the books and the show increasingly diverge, there are some intriguing consequences for the development of the plot(s). For that reason, although the books take precedence for me, I've tried to focus especially on the early volumes, where there's less divergence between the two narratives.

7. Joffrey Baratheon

CHAPTER 1

FEASTS AND FAMILIES

Unlimited meat and sweet wine.

HOMER, *ODYSSEY* 9.557

The world of *Game of Thrones* is one of visceral, sensual experience. Across the Seven Kingdoms, the extreme conditions of war and coming winter reduce a once prosperous society to basic human impulses: food, sex, killing, and for the well-to-do, the scheming required to obtain, disperse, or withhold any of the above. What food, sex, and murder all have in common is a basic sense of transgression: they all involve the importation of foreign objects into the body, and they are experienced first and above all by the body and the senses. They are also each important in the formation and maintenance of alliances: marriage and rape both characterize two sides of victory in war, or, as often in the convulsed world of Westeros, provide a reason to go to war. Food, meanwhile, is a measure of success; in a world where winter lasts for years and years, prosperity, as the Tyrells demonstrate, is a matter of agriculture.

This chapter is about food, and while we'll come back to food as plain comestibles at the end of the chapter, the bulk of it is concerned with food in a very specific setting: the feast or heroic banquet. The word 'feast' conjures up visions of vast halls, a multitude of guests, and food spectacular in both quality and quantity. But feasts can be had in more humble circumstances, where hunger makes the best condiment. Crucial to all these occasions is the idea of communal eating, which consistently invites us to think about where the meal is happening, with whom, and how much of the food each person is getting. Feasts, as any bride planning her wedding can tell you, are a microcosm of society: some people get the best food at the best table and earlier (while it's still fresh and hot), while others settle – or are forced to settle – for less and later, when the best bits are gone, cold, or rotten. Food also needs to be sourced and acquired, and this too holds up a mirror to society: who can afford to buy what and in what quantity, and conversely, who has it in surplus to sell? Who hunts, and who gathers? Who eats meat, who eats fish, grain, or nothing at all? Feasts, especially when food is scarce, as it was in antiquity and as it increasingly becomes throughout the wars in Westeros, are a matter of politics and economics, and the places where people sit to eat together tell us a lot about that place and its values. Nor are these just questions that we impose as readers or as students of antiquity: the characters within *Game of Thrones* are acutely conscious of the semantics of food and eating.

In the prologue to *A Clash of Kings*, a feast is held on Dragonstone. For Stannis and his bannermen the feast is just another part of being a nobly born lord, but for the aged Maester Cressen, it is the end of a long day, in which the infirmity and indignity of his old age as well as the family drama of House Baratheon have been weighing heavily on his mind. The keep has recently been assigned a new young maester, come to aid Cressen in his duties, and Cressen says he does not mind. But it is at the feast, where he finds Pylos sat in Cressen's own seat, that he feels the final indignity, and where Stannis turns from a just lord to a cruel one, forcing the old man to wear a fool's motley helmet. The feast emphasizes Cressen's fall from grace in other ways too. The whole prologue is, for Cressen, a long and tiring trek down one tower and up another, a distance he is forced to traverse to be close – and therefore useful and important – to his lord. In the world of the court, proximity is everything. Tired by the effort, Cressen takes a nap before the feast, but is allowed to oversleep, and arrives at the hall only after festivities have begun. As he stands at the doors, he thinks, '*They did not summon me*. He was always summoned for feasts, seated near the salt, close to Lord Stannis' (*CK* 22). Salt was a precious commodity in antiquity as in the Middle Ages. Salt was important for many reasons in antiquity, chief among which was the fact that it allowed the ancients to preserve their meat for long durations of time. A contributing factor to the city of Rome's importance throughout the history of the Roman empire was its position along the *Via Salaria*, the 'Salt Road,' which was one of the major Western trading routes for this most precious of commodities. In fact, Pliny the Elder, in his *Natural History*, says that the Latin word *salarium*, from which we get the English word 'salary,' originally came from their word for salt, *sal* (Pliny, *Natural History* 31). Westeros seems to follow suit, since sitting by the salt here clearly implies sitting alongside the high and mighty, and especially near the lord himself.[1] Indeed, Stannis and his bannermen are seated at an elevated high table, while knights and sellswords are sat at the lower tables, further and further away from the center of power. The feasting is only a small part of the chapter, but even so it offers a perfect snapshot of the situation on Dragonstone: the lord is at the center, with his followers spreading out beneath him. The only intruder is Melisandre, and her presence dislodges the old maester just as her religious ideology aims to dislodge the Faith of the Seven.

But this feast also has a sinister side to it, as Cressen attempts to reveal Melisandre for the evil he thinks her to be. Under her influence, we are led to imagine, Stannis changes from what he once was, and allows Cressen to be humiliated and eventually sacrifice himself in vain by sharing a poisoned cup with Melisandre.

Feasts aren't just a convenient site for poisoning, they're also a site for knowing the people and world around you, whom you can trust and whom you cannot. In fact, the very act of eating is one of trust: you're more vulnerable when seated, when your hands are full, when you're distracted by drink and entertainment; above all, you're placing your trust in the various people – largely out of sight – who prepare and serve your food, as well as those sitting nearby. As we shall see, classical mythology frequently deals with the themes of testing and trust involved in feasting, from the consumption of polluted food to the murder of a victim caught unawares. It's at a banquet, appropriately enough, that Odysseus punishes the greedy suitors of his wife, who don't realize who he is until it's too late. Feasting, knowledge, power, and revenge come together in the myth of Atreus, too: the king of Mycenae gets the better of his brother – and secures his royal power – by tricking Thyestes into eating his own sons. Although the act of feasting might seem like a simple celebration, an opportunity for a writer to engage us with descriptions both luxurious and grotesque, the occasion is also a microcosm of society, when we find ourselves among a diversity of people and interests, and we have to use our wits to navigate the social and intellectual challenges that face us both in the moment and throughout our lives.

Nor do feasts always have to end in tension or tragedy; they're also sites of conviviality, comedy, and bonding. The first book of Homer's *Iliad* ends with two diametrically opposed scenes of feasting: up in Olympus the gods – all one family – lay aside their quarrels to eat a grand banquet, and together they laugh at the lame god Hephaestus bustling around serving them (in a way that strikes our modern ears as strangely cruel). Whereas the banqueting gods enjoy music played by their fellow Olympian Apollo, earlier in the same book the Greeks have to sacrifice to Apollo, singing his praises to appease him following a devastating plague sent by the god. Two scenes of eating, on earth and in heaven, and two utterly contrasting moods among two extended families: the Greeks – the collective descendants of Danaus – are vulnerable and divided following an argument between their leaders and the subsequent plague; the gods, on the other hand, are immortal and harmonious even after a marital row between Zeus and Hera (who are siblings as well as husband and wife). The Homeric example teaches us to be on the lookout for comparisons and contrasts between various occasions of feasting, the moods that bubble to the surface and lurk underneath, and the myriad ways in which one episode can illuminate another.

Besides the feast itself, as even a cursory glance at the examples above reveals, this chapter is also about family, the context in which food is most often consumed and produced. Occasions for feeding and eating are also occasions which visibly demonstrate the choices we make and the feelings we have about family, as the macabre myth of the brothers Atreus and Thyestes neatly illustrates. The two concepts of food and family are not always directly connected: as we'll see later on, Jon Snow's complicated feelings about brotherhood have nothing to do with the way Jon likes his meat cooked or his wine diluted. But the *presentation* of these feelings is organized – made simple and visible – through the medium of the formal feast, which requires that his family behave and arrange themselves in a particular way. At the feast in Winterfell, Jon must behave like the bastard son that he is, which means that he can also view his family differently than in his day-to-day interactions with them, and differently again from the way he remembers them during his new life at the Wall. The Starks in turn, like their Baratheon and Lannister guests, must behave more formally and structurally because of the special occasion. Dinner, as every viewer of a soap opera will attest, throws people together, and thereby offers a perfect stage for domestic dramas. When the family in question is lordly or royal, however, as is the case with the protagonists of *Game of Thrones* or almost every mythical story in antiquity, the domestic is necessarily also political and global.

SCENES OF EXCESS

Highly structured seating arrangements reveal a lot about the way
a society sees itself. In ancient Rome and Athens, two societies
which organized themselves according to an ideology of equality
among certain classes of citizen, communal eating took a rather
different form, with everyone (of that class) reclining together to
eat and drink. In the classical Athenian symposium, for instance,
aristocratic men participated in after-dinner conversation about
politics or philosophy, while in Rome elaborate dinner parties were
used not only to entertain friends but also to bribe voters before
elections, show off wealth, and distribute largesse. In both cases, the
private area in which the dinner party took place, the home of the
host, was also a public space – or put differently, a place where elite
men showed off their power or wealth or influence for an audience.

The classical *symposium* was characterized by an ideology of
self-restraint, something that was central to the way the aristocracy
of both Athens and Rome imagined themselves. This self-restraint
was expressed in many ways, but one of the main ones was the
moderate consumption of wine. Ancient wine was much stronger
than its modern counterpart, and the wine was therefore mixed and
measured out carefully. At the center of an Athenian symposium,
for instance, was the wine vessel (the *krater*), in which the wine was
mixed with water and from which the diluted wine was dispensed to
the guests. Each symposium had a host, or master of ceremonies, a
person charged with achieving the balance of levity and solemnity,
fun and seriousness, that was the aim at these events. This host
both directed the topic of conversation – often philosophy or some
other refuge from the immediate affairs of the state – and, crucially,
determined how many *kraters* would be drunk and at what ratio of
dilution. Drinking unmixed wine, by contrast, was the marker of
a savage, and invariably led to a bad end.

Being able to drink moderately in the symposium showed off not
only manly virtue (the ability to control oneself) but also civic virtue

(in remaining sober enough to participate in the exchange of ideas among equals). There is little doubt that this was more an ideal than a genuine glimpse of reality. Ancient love poetry, which specialized in celebrating and exploring the seamier aspects of society, regularly talks about women drinking, lovers gazing longingly at each other over the banquet table as the husband talks to other guests, or someone stumbling home drunk after a dinner party. Famously, the statesman Cicero accused Mark Antony, his enemy and later the lover of the Egyptian queen Cleopatra, of showing up to hear cases in the forum while still drunk from last night's revel, and in a state so bad that he vomited in his own lap before the assembled crowd of petitioners and fellow senators. Whether Cicero's accusation was real or made up is difficult to know, but what even these instances show was that while the ideology of moderate consumption was certainly prevalent, young men and women, especially of the aristocratic classes, enjoyed flouting societal conventions, as indeed they do to this day.

The foreigner, whether man or woman, monstrous or human, was a quintessential figure in antiquity for the unruly drunk – presided over by the god of wine, Dionysus, who comes to Greece from Asia and promptly leads respectable ladies into orgiastic frenzies. The reason, curiously, is not only a moral looseness shown through a lack of moderation, but also their inability to hold their liquor, being unaccustomed to good vintage, lower dilution ratios, or civilized drinking altogether. For example, the Cyclops, the one-eyed monster who terrorizes Odysseus and his men, including penning them up like sheep and picking four off each day for a cannibalistic meal, can only be brought down because he's sleeping off his very first night of heavy drinking of unmixed wine. In a very different sphere of thought, the Romans allowed husbands and fathers to punish their womenfolk for drunkenness, on the principle that a drunk woman was more likely to lose control of her morals and to commit adultery – indeed, that she drank in order to commit adultery.[2] Although these two examples are very different, they occupy two positions in a spectrum of ideas about drunkenness, wherein female drinking was immoderate because drunk women were deliberately morally loose, whereas men drank for pleasure, and thereby showed their moderation. Middle positions were occupied by a range of other characters, including (barely) functional alcoholics like Antony, by foreign women like Cleopatra (also notorious for conspicuously luxurious consumption) or later on the women of the Roman imperial family, who occupied powerful positions in their own right, or by young men sowing their wild oats. Moderate consumption of wine was a symbol of privilege: the ability to be drunk without remorse was in the main afforded to aristocratic men in sympotic scenarios. In moderation, wine was a symbol of status, taste, and relaxed leisure. In excess, wine was a marker of the threatening other: those who didn't know enough to keep themselves from drinking too much or too hard.

The world of *Game of Thrones* has several groups that anthropologists might term as the 'other', on the assumption that the 'we' or 'same' effectively refer to the Seven Kingdoms. There are, of course, some obvious problems: the Seven Kingdoms are not the same as each other, and while the central southern kingdoms bear distinct similarities to each other, both the North and Dorne in the South are markedly 'othered' from the center around King's Landing. The North, for example, follows the Old Gods, while Dorne practices non-gendered primogeniture. But the Seven Kingdoms at least have in common a language (usefully called the Common Tongue), a shared system of feudal rule, a currency, and a throne. Outside Westeros, however, is a whole world whose people behave in – to Westerosi eyes – exotic and bewildering ways, which can be lumped together under the rubric 'not us.' So it can already be seen that the 'Other' is a flat and reductive label, and it doesn't do much to tell us anything about the people thus labeled.

A quick example to clarify before we come back to wine. The Tyrells of Highgarden are the most agricultural of the Great Houses, who live in a sort of earthly paradise characterized by beauty and abundance. Their motto, appropriately, is *Growing Strong*. The Tyrells also have two hereditary enemies: the Martells of Dorne and the Greyjoys of the Iron Islands. The two are not of the same kind, however. The Martells, arguably, are merely competition for resources, and an example of a different and competing type of luxurious abundance. Both Tyrells and Martells enjoy good food, good wine, and good weather, and the Martel motto, *Unbent, Unbowed, Unbroken*, speaks to the same ideology of growth and resilience as *Growing Strong*. They are, in a sense, merely variations on a theme. The Greyjoys, however, are a different story altogether. They hail from the other side of the map, the stony North, and inhabit inhospitable and barren islands. Their economy is based on ships and piracy, in contrast to the Tyrell agricultural plow. And the Greyjoy motto cements the opposition: *We Do Not Sow* proclaims to the world a very specific rivalry, not with House Stark, who stand in the same relation to them as Dorne does to Highgarden, but with the emblematic House of growing things. To a Tyrell, Dorne is competition, but the Greyjoys are the definitive other.

In the same way, the civilized cities of the East are variations on a Westerosi theme, which is important since they will provide the school in which Daenerys, among others, will learn rulership. The Other, in this sense, is the uncivilized, whether the wildlings beyond the Wall or the horselords east of the Free Cities. The Dothraki are a nomadic people living in the continent of Essos, and are famed for their fierceness and savagery in battle as well as their superstitious fear of the sea, which appears to be the only thing keeping them off the Westerosi shore. But this is about to change as Daenerys Targaryen marries one of their chieftains, Khal Drogo, in exchange for his help in a campaign to put Dany's brother, Viserys, back on the Iron Throne. The Dothraki, while clearly modeled on Eurasian nomadic people like the Huns or Mongols, also tap into a standard ancient fascination with the taming of horses. Because horses were only used in battle and for racing, and were expensive to rear, maintain, and train, owning or taming a horse was a mark of wealth and status. In Rome, for instance, the mercantile class of the knights (the *equites*) was distinguished by keeping a horse at public expense, and thereby made up the traditional cavalry for the Roman army (they were later replaced by better mounted and trained foreigners, especially Gauls and Numidians). In the *Iliad*, the Trojan prince Hector is called 'tamer of horses,' and his funeral, like Khal Drogo's at the end of *A Game of Thrones*, provides closure for that part of the war's story.

We are properly introduced to the Dothraki at Daenerys' wedding, and through her point of view, which means we see them through the eyes of a frightened Westerosi girl rather than through their own. Like the feasts at Westeros, this wedding too demarcates social hierarchies: the *khal* and his bride sit on a big earthen ramp, with their important guests beneath them, and the 'sea of Dothraki' below them again. Viserys is galled at the insult offered him by being seated below his sister, even though Dany knows that this is considered a place of honor. As in Westerosi feasts and weddings, food is a focal point: Drogo and Daenerys are served first, which Viserys also takes as a mortal insult. Dany herself is too nervous to eat, and waves away the lavish offerings: 'steaming joints of meat and thick black sausages and Dothraki blood pies, and later fruits and sweetgrass stews and delicate pastries from the kitchens of Pentos...' (*GT* 102). Occasion notwithstanding, this festive meal sounds very much like a slightly more exotic version of typical pub fare, and the specification that at least some of it was made in Pentos' kitchens underscores the fact that this food is not only lavish but familiar. As such, it reminds the reader that Dany is both Western and noble, in sharp contrast to the people she is marrying into, who are having quite a different experience of the same festivities: 'They gorged themselves on horseflesh roasted with honey and peppers, drank themselves blind on fermented mare's milk and Illyrio's fine wines, and spat jests at each other across the fires' (*GT* 101).

Here are the Dothraki in a nutshell: eating horseflesh and drinking mare's milk, gorging themselves on someone else's fine wine, and spitting insults at each other, clearly without either understanding or appreciating the high cuisine served on the high dais. They are, straightaway, utterly foreign: they speak another language, they don't course out their meat, and they are given to drink-induced rowdiness. The pinnacle of this rowdiness, Daenerys discovers, is their lack of sexual shame and celebration of violence. They mate openly and under the sky, and they fight each other to the death at the slightest provocation. In fact, they appear to her like 'beasts in human skins and not true men at all' (*GT* 103).

Daenerys soon finds out her mistake and comes to love her new people, but her primal fear of these rough and ready men and women, whose main characteristic is their deep oneness with nature and especially the horse, resonates with one of antiquity's most celebrated myths: the Centauromachy, or 'war with the centaurs.'

8. Centaur and Lapith

The story begins with the wedding of the Lapith hero Pirithous and his bride Hippodameia (a name that means 'mistress of horses'). The centaurs, a mythical people who were half-man and half-horse, were invited to the wedding, and quickly became drunk and began to misbehave. Some versions of the story explain that the centaurs, normally creatures of the wild, were unused to wine, and therefore unable to moderate its influence. Whatever the reason, the centaurs disrupted the wedding and attempted to kidnap and rape the bride. A battle ensued in which Theseus, the legendary king of Athens, helps defeat the centaurs and rescue Hippodameia. Theseus' involvement meant that the Athenians thought of the myth as one of their own local stories, even though the Lapiths lived, according to the myth, in northwestern Greece, and it was one of a series of battles depicted on the great temple of Athena, the Parthenon. Each of the four battles depicted – against the Titans, Amazons, Centaurs, and the Trojan War – symbolized the victory of civilized Greece, marked by an ideology of aesthetic, political, and personal restraint, over an exotic, dangerous, excessive 'other.' For the Greeks, as for the Romans and for the people of Westeros, that Other always lay across the water, and to the east.

Feasts and Tyranny

Opposed to restraint on the ancient political and ideological spectrum stood tyranny, a concept which doesn't precisely map onto our modern idea of tyranny. The two main features defining tyranny in antiquity were illegitimacy and autocracy, and the two didn't always coexist. Nor was it always the case that tyrants were necessarily evil or bad rulers, even if they came into power through a coup or acted autocratically. The emperor Augustus, for example, one of the most competent rulers in antiquity, was technically speaking a tyrant, having come into power after a civil war and ruling the Roman state more or less autocratically. His long and successful reign, however, as well as his iron-fist-in-the-silken-glove style of rule, meant that very few labeled him a tyrant after his death, and fewer did so to his face (though some writers noted that it was only after the deaths of numerous opponents that Augustus exhibited the restraint associated with his rule). Others were less lucky, and tyranny, at least in Rome, became a byword for someone who aspired to kingship, that is, to depriving the Roman citizenry of its sovereign freedoms. This vague definition meant that almost any political leader could be labeled a tyrant, and both the Greeks and the Romans developed a rich vocabulary – none of it complimentary – to talk about the excesses and failings of tyranny. To a reader or viewer of *Game of Thrones*, these should all sound familiar: the tyrant was, primarily, unable to practice self-restraint – he whored; he was an adulterer, as well as incestuous with both his mother and his sister; he was given to harassing young boys of good breeding; he was cruel and impious, without regard for justice, order, or compassion; and lastly, he was capricious, murderous, and traitorous even toward his own family. This character was manifested through a lifelong penchant for petty cruelty – the emperor Domitian as a child allegedly liked to capture flies and pluck their legs off one by one – and through gluttony and, especially, drunkenness, with all the connotations of barbarity and lack of control discussed above. These traits were bad enough in men, and all the more so in women. The Egyptian queen Cleopatra, for example, the wife and lover of both Julius Caesar and Mark Antony, was loathed by the average Roman and especially by the young Augustus, who saw her as a direct threat to his claim to the throne and the stability of the empire. In due course, he declared war on her and her co-ruler, Caesar's bastard child. The resulting propaganda depicted her as mad, scheming, surrounded by eunuchs, worshipping monstrous gods, and above all drenched in wine – all, except for the monstrous gods, qualities she shares with Cersei Lannister, whose dependence on wine increases as she sinks deeper and deeper into her role as queen regent (and makes her more like the husband, and former king, she hated so much).

Feasts made a particularly good site for describing tyranny for two main reasons. The first is that food makes for something easily graspable and understood. It is regarded as morally dubious to eat too much, or to waste food while other people go without, and anyone who fails to recognize this immediately is marked as somewhat inhuman. Perhaps the most lavish feast in *Game of Thrones* is the wedding of Joffrey Baratheon and Margaery Tyrell, an event that came to be dubbed by fans as the Purple Wedding (by analogy with the Red Wedding, to which we'll come back later). The Purple Wedding is distinguished by its massive scale of excess. At a time when King's Landing is starving, the feast serves up 77 courses, including mushrooms, pastries, trout, spiced crabs, chopped mutton, fish tarts, partridges, swans, and blood sausage, and culminating in the wedding pie which the bride and groom break together, releasing the host of live pigeons that was hidden inside it – a dish straight from a fantastically satirical Roman menu.[3] And these are only the dishes we actually get to hear about, the rest being lost in Joffrey's amusements, fight with his uncle, and subsequent poisoning.

Tyrion Lannister, who is unfortunate enough to be saddled with planning the wedding, spends much of his time negotiating down the cost of the festivities, but his efforts obviously have limited success. He is keenly aware of this, and also of the gap between what the people see outside and what happens within the royal halls, from which the populace at large is barred. When the king and his new queen leave the sept, the people cheer for them, and especially for Margaery, on whose account the city is now fed: 'And the bounty of Highgarden had come with her, flowing up the roseroad from the south' (*SS* 812). By the time the tenth – or was it more? – course rolls along, Tyrion is keenly aware that the excesses of the feast are in stark opposition to the situation in the city outside: 'Seventy-seven dishes, while there are still starving children in this city, and men who would kill for a radish. They might not love the Tyrells half so well if they could see us now' (*SS* 818). The Tyrells may well be behind the lavishness of the wedding and the loveliness of the bride, but the reason the people might rise in rebellion is the unpopularity of Joffrey, who makes for the quintessential tyrant: the product of incest, spoiled and cruel, vain and capricious. And indeed, the Purple Wedding is a curious mix of lavish food, too much wine, and Joffrey's escalating series of petty but public humiliations, mostly directed at his uncle Tyrion: a joust of dwarves, after which Joffrey demands his uncle participate in the show by riding a pig; when that fails, Joffrey makes Tyrion his cupbearer, a role which in Greek mythology was reserved for beautiful boys, and in historical symposia to young slave boys and girls. The wedding thus becomes a perverted form of an ancient symposium, marked by tyrannical excess and ugliness where the symposium was marked by equality, moderation, and beauty.

9. Zeus and Ganymede

The Roman satirist Juvenal, who lived in the first century AD and wrote what today would be called trenchant (though heavily xenophobic and misogynistic) stand-up comedy, used the same combination of food and the culture of the court to criticize tyranny. His fourth satire tells how in the days of the emperor Domitian, whom later propaganda made notorious for cruelty and autocracy, a massive Adriatic turbot 'torpid with sloth, [and] fat from long hibernation' is found in an Italian lake.[4] Nobody is going to buy the fish, of course, because the emperor's spies are everywhere, and it is obvious that anything this big or this fine should belong to the emperor. The fisherman dutifully goes off to Rome, where the enormous fish is greeted with astonishment by those who see it carried through the streets. Finally, the fish is presented to the emperor with all due flattery ('the fish wanted to be caught!' says the fisherman), and the emperor is delighted. But trouble strikes fast. Despite Rome's fabulous wealth, there is no dish big enough to cook this fish. And so the senate, a once august body, is sent for, and the senators duly come to council, wondering what sort of catastrophe could have caused this rare summons – a war with a foreign enemy, perhaps? But all the emperor wishes to consult them on is simply how best to cook the fish ('they don't want it to be cut, do they?' intones the dread tyrant, and the senators, who have grown accustomed to having no opinions, the better to make it to safe old age, quake in their boots). Eventually, one of them, a noted gourmand who can tell at a lick where any oyster is from, steps forward: a deep-dish bake would be best, and a potter can provide just such an object. And so the meeting ends, and 'oh,' says Juvenal, 'if only he'd [that is, Domitian] chosen to devote the whole of that time to such trivia,' rather than his more favored pursuit of 'mangling a dying world.' Also implied is the idea that if Domitian insists on spending his time on serious matters, the senate ought to be consulted on those issues as well, instead of just the insultingly trivial.

This satire exposes another way in which food is symbolic of the organization of society. Inasmuch as the emperor is the head of the state, what the emperor consumes also represents the resources he requires from his state.[5] What the emperor consumes in this satire is an enormous fish, and both the fishiness and the size of the offering matters. In Rome fish were both a luxury item (they were kept as pets in special ponds and became a marker of an especially dissolute lifestyle) and a fairly common thing to eat; we have evidence of a number of poems from ancient Rome that focus on listing the variety of seafood and fish available for the table. (Homeric heroes, incidentally, never ate fish, and lived more or less entirely on roasted beef and lamb.[6]) The emperor Vitellius, who was notorious for his gluttony, liked eating a dish called 'The Shield of Minerva,' which included various types of fish and meat from across the empire, thus physically representing how powerful Rome was – the Roman empire was literally Rome's oyster.[7]

But in Juvenal's satire, Domitian doesn't eat a variety of fish, he just eats one enormous turbot – and actually, he doesn't eat it, he just consults with his advisors on how to cook it. His only contribution is to ask whether or not he should cut it. What kind of emperor is Domitian, then? One that hoards the finest things the empire has to offer, but without offering anything productive in return. His councillors tell him that making a dish for his fish would revivify the art of pottery, but Domitian doesn't really agree for economic reasons – he just doesn't want to cut up his new acquisition, and he certainly doesn't share it with anyone. The fish is both wasted and a waste of the senate's time, an example of excess even when the emperor tries to share out the 'burdens' of rulership. Robert Baratheon does exactly this to Ned Stark when they finally arrive in King's Landing, charging the Small Council, all of whom have better things to do, with organizing the Tournament of the Hand in Ned's honor, a lavish expenditure which the Crown cannot afford and which Ned himself explicitly does not want. And that, of course, is the positive reading; the emperor might be not so secretly hopeful that he'll get to chop up the giant fish, seeing as this is the same man who plucked off flies' legs as a child. And if so, Domitian's love of

cruelty is quite Joffrey-esque: Joffrey, who gleefully cuts up one of
the only four surviving copies of *Lives of Four Kings*, the book given
to him on the morning of the wedding by his uncle, and who took
such delight in seeing Ned Stark's head cut clean off his shoulders.

FOOD AS METAPHOR: STAGS AT THE FEAST

Food and foodstuffs appear regularly in the world of *Game of
Thrones*, and in all sorts of ways. Skin is regularly compared to milk
or cream, while the ranger Will, in *Game of Thrones*' cinematic
prologue, feels fear filling his gut 'like a meal he could not digest,'
and finds comfort in the taste of cold iron (*GT* 8). And before the
onset of winter Westeros is otherwise replete with foodstuffs: apples
and mushrooms, bacon, eggs, milk and cheese, onions, and honey
cakes are all mentioned regularly throughout the books and the
series. In a modern world saturated with food imagery, advertising,
blogs, and restaurants, the constant appearance of food is perhaps
unremarkable. In a literary or cinematic world, however, where
space on the page or the screen is limited, the constant mention of
food is worth remarking on (this is all the more true since most of
our more intimate bodily acts, like some sex acts and the expung-
ing of waste, remain a taboo). Especially with the specter of war
and famine looming, a threat that becomes more and more serious
as the War of the Five Kings progresses, any food more elaborate
than subsistence becomes conspicuous, an advertisement of class
and wealth.

Even so, some food items have more symbolic weight than
others, and none more so than venison. Deer carcasses have their
own tradition of heroic appearances (think Errol Flynn as Robin
Hood entering the Sheriff of Nottingham's great hall with a stag
across his shoulders), but in Westeros of all places they have more
significance. The symbol of House Baratheon, after all, is the prancing stag, and one of the very first things to happen in the books

is the discovery of an antler lodged in the throat of the first dire-wolf – the symbol of House Stark – to be seen south of the Wall in many years. The discovery is swiftly followed by the arrival of a human stag at Winterfell, as King Robert Baratheon arrives to visit the Starks and is appropriately feasted in the castle. Venison makes a symbolic appearance in the show as well; in 'You Win or You Die,' we meet the formidable Tywin Lannister for the first time. And what is he doing? Preparing for battle, telling off his son, and skinning a deer carcass.

Tywin's willingness to get his hands dirty is indicative of his toughness and cold-blooded ruthlessness, but skinning a dead stag and turning it into a feast was a commonplace of ancient epic. Here, for instance, the comrades of Aeneas, the hero of the Roman epic *Aeneid*, feast on the carcasses of seven stags:

> They skinned the deer, bared ribs and viscera,
> Then one lot sliced the flesh and skewered it
> On spits, all quivering, while others filled
> Bronze cooking pots and tended the beach fires.
> All got their strength back from the meal, reclining
> On the wild grass, gorging on venison
> And mellowed wine. When hunger had been banished,
> And tables put away, they talked at length
> In hope and fear about their missing friends:
> Could one believe they might still be alive,
> Or had they suffered their last hour,
> Never again to hear a voice that called them?[8]

The situation of the men here is tragic. Already refugees from their home, these men of Troy have just survived a storm at sea, and seen a large proportion of their fleet drown. Their leader, Aeneas, feels this loss particularly keenly. He climbs a cliff to look out to sea, and it is from there that he sees a herd of deer and a line of stags. In fact, he sees only three, and only in following them does he hunt down seven, one for each of his seven surviving ships. Having dragged back the carcasses (Vergil doesn't tell us quite how one man managed this feat), he tells the men that they have all survived greater troubles, but his heart is clearly not in it, since the poet tells us Aeneas has to fake a look of hope and optimism. Still, it works: the men believe him, the food is prepared, they stretch themselves out on the grass, and the feast is followed by cathartic fireside conversations.

Against the air of doom and gloom, it's worth noting both the elaborate detail and the practiced ease with which Aeneas' men prepare their food. They strip and prepare the quivering meat, cut it to pieces and fix it on spits, while elsewhere cauldrons and fires are made ready and someone taps into the wine barrels. Food in this scene is a communal act not only in the sense that it is food eaten together, but also in that it draws a ragtag fleet of fugitives together again, heals their wounds, and revives their spirits. More importantly, it illustrates the process of community-building, as Aeneas' people partake for the first time in the poem (although not in their voyage) in the activities that define an epic community of warriors. I use the word 'warriors' advisedly, for, even though we know that Aeneas' fleet contains women and at least one child, Aeneas' own son Iulus, the life they are about to lead is defined by epic wanderings and questing. That will be the topic of the next chapter, but for now it suffices to note that these people, regardless of gender, fulfill the part of companions, the equivalent of banner-men in the Westerosi world. Aeneas provides for them, and they in turn divide his largesse equally among themselves, thus confirming that they are, in fact, Aeneas' to lead.

The readiness and ease with which they execute the meal suggests that they have done this before – and this is true. By this point, Aeneas and his people have been wandering the Mediterranean Sea for some years, looking for a place to settle. The storm that drives them to the African coast – and Aeneas' torrid affair with the local queen, Dido – is but the last great obstacle before they set out to

Italy, where they are destined to build a new home for themselves. But Aeneas' people are all well practiced at preparing feasts because in the epic world in which they live feasts are a regular part of life, and are precisely what groups of warriors do throughout the *Iliad*, the Greek epic which recounts the Trojan War, and from which all Greco-Roman literature descends. In the *Iliad*, we see exactly what we see Aeneas here doing, and what we see countless lords do up and down Westeros. At the end of the day, the heroes gather around their leaders – say Agamemnon or Achilles – and there enjoy abundant meat, which is distributed to them according to their success in battle. The greater the warrior, the greater his share of the feast. This is a way of redistributing war booty among the troops, and a way also to establish social groups and hierarchies. Even young Bran is taught to do this when he serves as the Lord of Winterfell in his brother's stead:

> The serving men brought every dish to Bran first, that he might take the lord's portion if he chose. By the time they reached the ducks, he could eat no more. After that he nodded approval at each course in turn, and waved it away. If the dish smelled especially choice, he would send it to one of the lords on the dais, a gesture of friendship and favor that Maester Luwin told him he must make. (*CK* 325)

But Aeneas' people are engaged in the specific act of wandering, for which the template is not the *Iliad* but the other Homeric epic, the *Odyssey*. The feast of the stags, in fact, is modeled on a hunt performed by Odysseus when he arrives at the island of Ogygia. Like Aeneas, Odysseus climbs a cliff to survey the land, sees the majestic stag, and kills it to feed his men. As is the case with Aeneas, the language in which the hunt is described humanizes the stag, depicting it as engaged in a battle with Odysseus, as if the stag was an enemy soldier. Like Aeneas, Odysseus revives the spirit of his men with the offer of food, and like Aeneas,

Odysseus too will meet and have an affair with a beautiful queen: Circe, the daughter of the Sun. Circe is also a sorceress, capable of turning Odysseus' men into pigs, while other versions of the myth depict her as a princess suffering from unrequited love for a young man named Picus, whom she turns into a statuette. Unlike her Westerosi namesake, Cersei Lannister, she is not incestuous, but both women are strong, plotting, and spell danger for any men that come into their orbit. Epic leadership, as expressed on the field of battle and through the provision of food and security, comes up against feminine wiles, and, as frequently in Westeros, is found wanting.

The stag imagery gives structure to another pervasive theme in both the epic world and that of Westeros, which is the key issue of genealogy and inheritance. In a nutshell, one's ability to hunt and handle a stag is inextricably connected with concepts of rulership and dynasty. This is why the scene of Tywin skinning the deer forms the backdrop to a dialogue on Jaime's qualities to succeed his father as head of House Lannister, and perhaps one day the Lannister dynasty. Over the course of the scene, father and son discuss the idea of reputation, with Tywin disdainfully spitting out the word 'clean' even as he is elbow-deep in blood and entrails. The message is abundantly clear: rulership unavoidably involves blood and mess, and Tywin worries his son is too vain – too 'clean' – to do the work that must be done.

Game of Thrones, in a crucial and fundamental way, is a story of inheritances and the bloody battles undertaken to ensure that inheritance is 'done right' and allocated to the true heir. Unlike the castle economy of Westeros, the ancient Greeks and Romans did not practice primogeniture (where the eldest-born son inherits everything), instead dividing their estates between surviving sons. However, both cultures had strong ideas about how the relationship between generations ought to function. Primarily, fathers and ancestors offered models of imitation through which sons and grandsons were socialized into the ruling or warrior classes. Roman

10. Sarcophagus of Scipio Barbatus

culture went one step further and developed a veritable cult of the ancestors, wherein young members of the family actively strove to imitate the deeds of their fathers, and indeed to surpass them in glory and accomplishments.

This did not always work, and many young men in antiquity were a grave disappointment to their fathers, as Tyrion is to Tywin. That sense of failure echoed a cultural narrative of decline: the feeling that men were stronger and better in the old days and become worse with each new generation. There were numerous ways of expressing that idea in mythology. One such story was the myth of the Golden Age, a paradisiacal time when the land gave fruit spontaneously and all men lived harmoniously with each other. The Golden Age was followed by four ages, each deteriorating in quality: the Silver Age, the Bronze Age, the Heroic Age, and finally the Iron Age, which was the historical time of antiquity, when men fell far short of their heroic predecessors.

Antiquity also had a pronounced idea that sons should somehow resemble their fathers, whether in looks or behavior. Sons were thus expected to rise to societal standards in order to prove that they deserved the status of their father's son, and in the mythical Golden Age, so the stories went, all sons looked like their fathers, so there was no need to worry about adultery. Both these threads, of resemblance to and of deterioration from paternal standards, are endemic in *Game of Thrones*. The mystery of Jon Arryn's death revolves around a collective failure to take note of the fact that Joffrey does not look like Robert Baratheon, while Robert's bastards look exactly like him. Joffrey's blond looks, in fact, make him the spitting image of his real father, Jaime, and raise the important issue of bastardy and legitimacy. Jon Snow, too, looks most like Ned of all his siblings, while Robb, the heir to the North, takes after his Southern mother.

Stag hunting, as it happens, provides an epic language to talk about the same set of issues. We've already seen that Aeneas manfully hunts down seven stags for his men when they arrive on the shore of Africa after the great storm. The next step of their voyage, which begins exactly halfway through the poem, brings Aeneas and his men to Italy at long last, where they expect to find a new home and some peace and quiet. Instead, however, they encounter armed resistance, which flares into life when Aeneas' son Iulus goes off hunting. Not quite living up to his father's feats, he barely manages one stag, and that one a domestic animal, adopted by a peasant family and tamed by them as the pet of Silvia, the family's only daughter: 'Their sister, / Silvia, had trained the beast with love / to do her bidding. She would wreathe his horns / with garlands, groom him, bathe him in a spring' (*Aeneid* 7.669–72). Not only does Iulus not take on a whole line of wild animals, he also fails to kill this one, and the animal escapes back home, crying out its pain 'as though imploring mercy' (*Aeneid* 7.690). When the family and the farmers who live around them hear the animal's cries, they rally to help, and with some divine assistance from the fury Allecto, war breaks out, growing from a peasant dispute to a cosmic event, where even the sea swells participate.

As the heir and lord of Winterfell in his father's absence, Robb too gets a chance to try his hand at lordship, and he, too, has a harrowing experience on the hunt. The occasion is Bran's first outing with his new riding equipment, made for him on the advice of Tyrion Lannister. And although the outing isn't a hunt per se, it becomes one very quickly as the two brothers set off to 'hunt the hunters,' that is, find the direwolves, who have run ahead and eventually make a kill. For Bran, hunting is ill-omened; his father and brother, as well as the king's party, had been away hunting on the day of his fall. This smaller outing is designed to assure him of his horsemanship skills and allow him some outlet for exercise, but instead he finds himself again alone, helpless, and at risk of his life. As Robb rides off to find the direwolves, Bran is left on his own in a clearing, and is ambushed by a group of wildlings who have come south of the Wall. They threaten Bran, and even injure him by the time Robb rides into the clearing: 'He was mounted, the bloody carcass of an elk slung across the back of his horse, his sword in a gloved hand' (*GT* 404). This is a very heroic entrance, in keeping with the conventions of battle description observed by, for example, Julius Caesar, who liked describing himself heroically riding to the rescue at the crucial moment, his general's cloak marking him out. For Robb, however, the scene deteriorates: unlike Caesar, he stands out only in the company of outlaws and children. When among the elder folk of Winterfell, he is still very much treated as young and inexperienced, in need of many advisors. Even in the wood, Robb is unable to rescue his brother. The wildlings hold Bran as hostage and force Robb to drop his weapon so that both Starks are, for a minute at least, at the hands of the outlaws. It is the attack of the direwolves that drives off the wildlings, and Theon's lucky arrow shot that frees Bran from his captor. Robb himself, however bedecked by markers of authority, can do very little for himself or his brother.

The scene in the woods is a microcosm of Robb's patterns of influence and behavior. Despite a successful campaign in the South later in the story, when Robb captures Jaime Lannister and is crowned King in the North, he is in the end betrayed by his own poor judgment, by feminine wiles, and ultimately by the betrayal of his allies, both the Freys and later by Theon himself. We'll come back to the issue of betrayal at the end of this chapter, but for now it's worth noting that the scene in the wood is symbolic of the relationship between Robb and Theon as well. It is Theon's shot that turns the situation in the Starks' favor, since with Bran freed, Robb can unleash the direwolves. Rather than thanking his foster brother, Robb turns on him angrily: "'Jon always said you were an ass, Greyjoy,' Robb said loudly. "I ought to chain you up in the yard and let Bran take a few practice shots at *you*"' (*GT* 407).

The rebuke, which goes on a while, is calculated to hurt, and Robb speaks loudly, the better to be heard by everyone else present. The emphatic use of Theon's surname, 'Greyjoy,' in contrast to the familiar 'Jon,' and the mild expletives likewise isolate Theon from his foster family; the image of Theon chained up in the yard, used as target practice by an eight-year-old Bran, is further humiliation, and emphasizes that Robb not only has, but can abuse, his power over his father's ward. It transpires later that the guards' falling behind the two Starks was partially the fault of Theon, who took time to hunt a turkey. Theon is flustered when this is pointed out, but rallies: 'How was I to know that you'd leave the boy alone?' (*GT* 408). And he has a point – it is Robb's doing that Bran was left alone, and his responsibility to ensure that he wasn't. When a subordinate made possible what Robb alone could not, good lordship dictated gratitude, not anger, and certainly not petty public bullying. Robb's leadership, therefore, is problematic and immature, and like Vergil's Iulus, he cannot yet control the gifts of leadership that are his birthright. Where Ned Stark led a rebellion and won Robert the Crown, his son, named after the Baratheon king, cannot even reach further south than Oxcross, considerably short of the Lannister heartlands. And why? Because, like Theon, he was distracted on his way.

The stag symbolism in the *Aeneid* and the *Odyssey* are in their own ways feasts of welcome, or at least mark an arrival in a new land. It is also a fact of epic convention that heroes always arrive for a visit in the middle of a feast, or at least in time for dessert. *Game of Thrones* too begins with such a feast, one that for the first time in the series mixes together Stark and Lannister, glaring at each other over the unsuspecting head of the Baratheon king. As in ancient epic, a stag feast welcomes the Lannisters to Winterfell, and we the readers to the scheming politics of Westeros and the basic rules of the game of thrones: you win or you die.

EATING ONE'S OWN

If feasts are metaphorical, which is to say they are not always what they seem, they also play the important role of revealing duplicities. Being a formal court function, they require guests to be on their best behavior, but their true selves nevertheless shine through. This is a staple of ancient myth, and feasts were a favorite place where various people tested their guests to see if they were really the humble wanderers they pretended to be, or perhaps more lofty guests. This is a problem because such tests contravened the sacred laws of hospitality – *xenia* – which afforded a guest some security under his hosts' roof, but also because these tests tended to include something taboo, like the serving of human flesh in order to assess whether the presumed god would catch on. There are various versions of the myth, some more subtle than others. The stag Odysseus hunts on Ogygia, for example, gives some signs of being a man turned into a beast by Circe, as Odysseus will only later find out. Most of these occurrences, however, are deliberate. A mythical king named Lycaon, for instance, wonders whether a newly arrived guest in his kingdom is in fact none other than the

god Zeus, a proposition he tests by trying to murder the guest in his
sleep, and by serving him the boiled and roasted flesh of a prisoner.
As punishment, Zeus turns Lycaon into a wolf, thereby ironically
proving Lycaon's point for him.[9]

But the worst such transgression against the gods and the laws
of hospitality is committed by Tantalus, himself a son of Zeus,
who serves the Olympian gods the flesh of his own son Pelops.
All the gods immediately recognize the scent of human flesh and
refuse to eat, except for the goddess Demeter, whose grief for
her abducted daughter Persephone distracts her, and she takes a
bite from what turns out to be Pelops' shoulder. When the gods
later revive Pelops, they cannot replace the part of the shoulder
Demeter had consumed, and so she fashions an ivory shoulder
for him, with which he goes on to live a long life. Tantalus himself
is famously punished in the afterworld with constant longing for
something just out of reach, and gives us the English word 'tantalizing': he is doomed to stand forever in a shallow pool, with a
fruit tree hanging just over his head. Whenever he is hungry, he

11. Lycaon turning into a wolf, from a sixteenth-century manuscript of Ovid

reaches for the branches, only to have the tree yank them out of his reach. When he is thirsty, he bends to drink, only to see the water drain away. As often in Greek mythology, the punishment fits the crime: someone who serves the gods food they should not eat is himself doomed to eternal hunger and thirst.

Tantalus' own punishment was not enough. This double crime of kin-murder and cannibalism was so abhorrent to the Greeks that they imagined the family of Tantalus to be cursed ever after: generation after generation is doomed to unhappiness, betrayal, and in particular the turning of the family on each other – sons against their mothers, wives against their husbands, brothers against each other. Tantalus' example is so compelling that only two generations later the situation recurs. Pelops has two sons, Thyestes and Atreus, who are embroiled in the usual peccadillos of a Greek mythical family. In this case, Thyestes both sleeps with his brother's wife, and attempts to trick his brother out of the throne. As revenge, Atreus cooks his brother's children and serves them to him, except for the heads and hands, which he keeps back to taunt his brother with what he has done. Nor is this the only example of such revenge: after the mythical king Tereus rapes and mutilates Philomela, the sister of his wife Procne, the two women subsequently conspire to kill Tereus' sons and serve them to their unwitting father. Both these myths of revenge went on to inspire Shakespeare, whose play *Titus Andronicus* features the protagonist, Titus, feeding the unknowing queen a pie made from her sons, who had raped and mutilated Titus' daughter after the fashion of Tereus.

These stories are the clear ancestors of the scene in 'The Winds of Winter,' the final episode of the sixth season of the show, in which Arya Stark feeds Walder Frey a pie made from his sons before she slits his throat. The act is also inspired by an Atreid-like myth of Westeros called 'The Rat Cook,' where the eponymous character works at the Nightfort, kills the king's son, and feeds him to his father, for which he is cursed to be a rat who can eat only his own offspring. Bran even says: 'It wasn't for murder the gods cursed

the Rat Cook, or for serving the king's son in a pie... he killed a
guest beneath his roof... that's something the gods can't forgive'
(S3, E10, 'Mhysa'). In all these cases, not knowing what one eats is
a sign of ignorance and excess, but it's also emblematic of human
vulnerability: even the most everyday actions can be full of threats,
and we maximize the risk to us by the wrongs that we commit
and the enmities we earn.

In the legend of Atreus and Thyestes, the taboo of cannibalism
intersects with the betrayal of the bonds of brotherhood, another
mythical streak that ran strong in Greek mythology and even
stronger in Roman reinterpretations of it. The bond of brotherhood
was considered if not sacred then at least deeply binding. Brothers
were expected to help and care for one another, and twin brothers
in particular were considered alternate versions of each other. The
prime examples of proper brotherly love were the Dioscuri, sons
of Zeus and brothers of Helen of Troy, who are so attached to each
other that they prefer to share immortality between them, which
essentially means they will spend half the year dead and the other
in Olympus.[10] The family was close-knit, because when Helen is in
Troy during the war, a very poignant scene has her looking from
the city walls across to the host of Greek warriors who have come
to get her. She points them out to Priam, her new father-in-law,
and notes that she does not see her brothers, ignorant that by that
time they are already dead. This note of tragic irony – when the
reader knows something that a character does not – emphasizes the
closeness of the kinship relationship: even after having abandoned
the equally sacred institution of marriage and caused a deadly war
between two great nations, Helen still harks back to the memory
of her brothers, and wishes to see them, even if ranged against
her new city and family. It's against that background, that positive
example of what familial relations ought to be, that the escalating
rivalry between Atreus and Thyestes should be understood as a
corrupt distortion, and likewise Tereus' betrayal of his wife and
sister-in-law. At the level of motif, the image of the cannibal feast

is an inevitably fascinating and popular one, as the choice of Arya Stark's revenge illustrates. But beyond the motif itself runs the larger current of a betrayal of familial or social bonds: it is Walder Frey who plans the Red Wedding, to which we shall return at the end of this chapter, and it's that murderous deceit that 'earns' him his bitter feast.

BANDS OF BROTHERS

The first feast of the series is hosted by the Lord and Lady Stark in honor of the king and queen when they arrive in Winterfell. In the books, the feast is described from the point of view of Jon Snow, Eddard's bastard son, who both feels keenly his outsider status and enjoys the freedoms it accords him. Seated on a bench along with the other young squires, Jon is excluded from the family circle, and relegated to sitting in the hall among the commoners. This demotion, however, also allows him to get drunk freely, while his brothers and sisters are sat 'with the royal children, beneath the raised platform where Lord and Lady Stark hosted the king and queen' (*GT* 49). Here again are the same social divisions at work: the lord and lady are at the highest table, with their children below them, and the rest of Winterfell filling the hall. Jon's perspective is particularly important, as is the fact that he has had too much to drink, as both emphasize his status as not quite one of them. On the royal dais, Jon's brothers and sisters are under their father's watchful eye, and can only have a strict one cup – in this, Jon sees himself as freer and as having more access to the privileges of adulthood. On the other hand, his perspective, first from out in the hall, and then outside the feast altogether, underscores the fact that he is an outsider even in his own home. This is finally confirmed by the only two people who speak to him: his uncle Benjen, and the dwarf Tyrion. Benjen is a Ranger of the Night's Watch, attending the feast as a brother to the Lord of Winterfell but by law a Brother of the Watch who has sworn to have no family and no allegiances. Tyrion, meanwhile, tells Jon that 'all dwarfs are bastards in their father's eyes' (*GT* 57), and even when Jon grows angry at the comparison, Tyrion's point remains: they are both in the unique position of being at once part of and excluded from the deepest bonds of family.

But what Jon also gets from bastardy, besides the freedom to drink, is a special insight into the behind-the-scenes workings of the lordly families. This he gets both from having a good seat – the procession into the hall passes very near his place in the lower tables – and from having a bastard's skill at reading people: 'A bastard had to learn to notice things, to read the truth that people hid behind their eyes' (*GT* 53). And indeed Jon's perceptions of the feast are very much double-visioned, due, one suspects, as much to the wine he's consumed as to his special insight. Like feasts, processions are symbolic because they are a clear and visible demonstration of hierarchy and social bonds: who I walk with into a room is equally as revealing about me and my place in the world as who I sit down to eat and drink with. In this case, however, the procession has another function: to introduce formally – or, perhaps better, to concretize our impressions of – the principal characters and themes of the saga to come. What we've had so far by way of introduction has been a bit chaotic. For example, when Eddard Stark greets the royal party, his impressions are guided by his own lived experience: he of course remembers Cersei and her brothers, but the children are new to him, and their names aren't mentioned, even though they are all introduced to each other ('Then the children had been brought forward, introduced, and approved of by both sides' (*GT* 40)). Instead, Eddard's attention is entirely taken up with Robert, whose current appearance, fat and perfumed, he cannot help but compare to the young and strong usurper with whom he rode out of Storm's End. Like his father, Jon sees beneath the facade people show the world, but unlike his father, who is too caught up with memories of the heroic past, Jon represents a new and younger generation, and his attention is on the deceits of the present. So when the Starks walk into their feasting hall with the royal family, we are meant to learn not only the proper order of things in Westeros, but also Jon's instinctive understanding that all isn't as it seems. As later events will prove, and as Eddard will learn to his cost, Jon's bastard, displaced perspective is more accurate and sensitive than the skewed impressions created by distant memory and empty traditions.

First into the hall are Lord Stark and the queen, followed by Lady Stark and the king. This arrangement has some obvious sense to it – Eddard Stark is the Lord of Winterfell, and as such enters the hall first. But Robert is the king, and as such has precedent, and his relegation to second place tells us a great deal about what is about to happen: the story of *Game of Thrones*, after all, isn't really about Robert, but about what happens around and because of him. Robert himself, his Rebellion, and his mysterious love for Lyanna Stark remain ghostly and in the background – the real protagonists in this story, or at least this part of it, are Ned and Cersei. Robert and Catelyn, each in their own way, are doomed to being second best and left behind. In fact, Jon's reaction to Robert is exactly the same as his father's: he sees a 'fat man, red-faced under his beard, sweating through his silks' (*GT* 50). Without fond memories of the past, Jon sees the king simply as he is, yesterday's man.

Next come the children, led by little Rickon, who, with three-year-old dignity, stops to visit with Jon and has to be prodded back into place. As the book series now stands, Rickon's fate is still shrouded in mystery, but his prominent place here does suggest that the youngest Stark may still come to play an important part – though this is emphatically not the case in the TV adaptation, where Rickon dies near the end of the sixth season. Following him are three pairs: Robb and Myrcella, Arya and Tommen, and finally Sansa and Joffrey. Jon has no love lost here either. He dislikes all three of the royal children, and even Robb, with whom his relationship can only have been complicated at best, does not escape criticism: Myrcella, who appears shy, seems to Jon insipid, and

Robb, without sense enough to notice, basks dumbly in her adora-tion. Tommen's hair is longer than Arya's, and he is described as plump, while Joffrey has pouty eyes and looks at Winterfell's Great Hall with a bored, disdainful expression that Jon does not like, but Sansa nevertheless seems infatuated with him. This miniature procession reveals things that will be of consequence later on, not least – in addition to the obvious fact that Joffrey is haughty and cruel – about the Starks themselves: that Robb enjoys the atten-tion of women, that Arya is more boyish than some boys, and that Sansa's judgment cannot be trusted. These are all small but crucial character traits, which will come to determine the way events unfold for each of the siblings.

THE RED WEDDING

And so we come to the Red Wedding, perhaps the most quintessen-tial act of betrayal in a series packed to the brim with backstabbing. In fact, the Red Wedding is a double-cross: Robb Stark had betrayed the Freys when he wed Jeyne Westerling instead of one of the Frey daughters as he had promised, and the Freys exact their revenge, with Lannister connivance, when Robb comes to ask forgiveness. But the Starks do not come to the Twins simply to make amends. They require the Frey allegiance for tactical and strategic reasons, for while Robb was fighting in the West, Winterfell had fallen to the treachery of Theon Greyjoy and the ironborn. But the Starks cannot make genuine amends, since Robb is already married and has no intention of forsaking his new wife for one of the Freys. Instead, he offers his uncle, Edmure Tully, as a substitute. In this sense, at least, the Red Wedding is a not a single act of betrayal, but rather the last in a series of deceits and ill-faith on the side of all parties. Because everyone enters the Red Wedding aware of the fraught background, Catelyn Stark is conscious of the dangers potentially awaiting them at the Twins, but she cannot quite suspect their scope. She is therefore concerned that Lord Frey should offer them his bread and salt, thus accepting them as guests into his house, and feels safer when they finally drink Lord Frey's wine and eat his bread ('Catelyn tasted the wine and nibbled at some bread, and felt much the better for it. *Now we should be safe*, she thought' (*SS* 679)). I mentioned in passing already that such relationships of hospitality were called *xenia* in ancient Greek, and generally across the ancient world they were presumed to be sacred trusts, and the kind of social capital that was passed down the generations. The betrayal of *xenia* was thus sacrilegious, and the Freys, too, find that they stand accused on religious as well as moral grounds. The violation of such a powerful religious obligation centered on food and hospitality makes it especially appropriate that Walder Frey should ultimately himself violate a taboo in unintentionally feasting on his own sons, the ultimate act of trickery and vengeance to round off an escalating series of deceit.

But while communal feasting – in this case the ceremonial sharing of bread and wine – should spell safety, here the wedding feast already gives a sense that something is awry. Unlike the elaborate courses of the Purple Wedding to come, or even of Daenerys' Dothraki menu, this wedding is particularly paltry in its offering: 'thin leek soup, salad of green beans, onions, and beets, river pike poached in almond milk, mounds of mashed turnips [...] jellied calves' brains, and a leche of stringy beef.'[11] Catelyn immediately thinks of it as 'poor fare to set before a king' (*SS* 694), and indeed the menu resembles more Domitian's enormous trout than the feast of venison Odysseus and Aeneas share with their men. The food at the Red Wedding, on the other hand, is bland, cold, and anemic in color and texture.

But while Lord Frey serves up meager food, he does not stint on his wine – and here is another clue of how this wedding will turn out: excessive wine leads to excessive violence. 'The ale, wine, and mead were flowing as fast as the river outside,' Catelyn thinks, and as she surveys the scene, she notes that all the key Stark bannermen,

from the Greatjon on down, are already drunk during the feast, with
the exception of Robb's two bodyguards. Of this, she approves: 'A
wedding feast was not a battle, but there were always dangers when
men were in their cups, and a king should never be unguarded'
(*SS* 695). She is not entirely wrong, but as we have seen with the
Centauromachy and at Daenerys' wedding in Pentos, weddings
can and do devolve into battles.[12] Catelyn herself has a sense that
the analogy is not entirely misplaced: she thinks it's a relief that by
the next day Robb will be off to fight another battle, and notes that
it's odd to think he would be safer there than he is at the present
moment at the Twins. In this, as the ensuing carnage shows, she
is entirely right.

The Red Wedding stands at the intersection of feasting as a
symbolic action and another ancient pattern, that of the returning
hero. These stories, called *nostoi* in Greek, are a sort of sequel to
the story of the Trojan War. After Troy is destroyed, the victorious
Greeks scatter and begin to make their way each to his own home.
A very small number of them manage to do so safely, including
Menelaus, the original husband of Helen, for whom the war was
fought. Most of the others, however, must go through numerous
adventures and tribulations before they make it back home, and
even then most of them encounter a much cooler reception than
they had hoped for. The quintessential return story is the *Odyssey*,
the story of the hero Odysseus, but many others existed, including
the *Aeneid* (which is a variation of the same theme but from a Trojan
perspective) and versions wherein the heroes of Troy settle instead
in various corners of the Mediterranean, thus explaining in the
language of myth the extent of the Greek diaspora and colonization
across the Mediterranean basin. What's important for our purposes
here is that these stories share a number of common themes, and in
particular treachery lurking at home. Odysseus is again the classic
story. He is married to the most chaste and loyal of wives, Penelope,
and she faithfully waits for his return for 20 years. She does this
despite the fact that her house is soon full of obnoxious suitors. The

suitors presume Odysseus dead and demand that Penelope marry one of them instead. She puts them off, famously, by claiming that she must first finish a burial shroud for her elderly father-in-law, which she weaves during the day, and unweaves during the night. As they wait, the suitors make themselves at home in the household, gorging themselves constantly and literally eating Odysseus out of house and home. This rapacious, never-ending feast underscores the economies of war in the ancient world: in Odysseus' absence, there is no one to mind the estate, and while Penelope can keep things ticking over, she cannot keep the suitors from making a serious dent in her own wealth and that of her husband. Upon Odysseus' return, one of his first tasks is to get rid of the suitors, which he does by taking them by surprise at a feast and killing them all in a scene of bloody carnage, with cups spilled and wine mixed with blood.

The unveiling of Odysseus' identity does not take place at a wedding, though the suitors dine in anticipation that Penelope will choose one of them as husband. The central difference between Robb Stark and Odysseus, however, is that the young and headstrong Robb, though showing signs of tactical nous on the battlefield, is caught in a trap designed by the elderly Walder Frey. By contrast, the veteran Odysseus, famous for his cunning, stays hidden until he can assess the situation and exact vengeance from a position of strength. But while the killing of the suitors, sitting helpless at the banquet, may be the basis for the action at the Red Wedding, Odysseus' vengeance is part of a simpler moral picture than the one we find in *Game of Thrones*. To find a better analogue, then, we should look to another mythical episode referred to in the *Odyssey* and taken up at greater length in other classical works.

At various points in the *Odyssey*, the hero's return is contrasted with the reception and evil fate of Agamemnon, king of Mycenae and the brother of Menelaus. Agamemnon doesn't take a further ten years to return home after the decade-long campaign in Troy, but his wife, Clytemnestra, is of much less faithful stock than Penelope. In the king's absence, Clytemnestra takes a lover, Agamemnon's cousin Aegisthus, and together they plot to kill Agamemnon upon his return. There are several versions of the death of Agamemnon: in some he is killed in his bath, with a robe thrown over his head to hamper his movement; in others he is killed during a feast in Aegisthus' house. Twenty of the best recruits are dressed up for a banquet and packed into the hall while Aegisthus goes to receive the returning hero:

> …went with a team and chariot, and a mind aswarm with evil.
> Up from the shore he led the king, he ushered him in –
> suspecting nothing of all his doom – he feasted him well
> then cut him down as a man cuts down some ox at the trough![13]

The reference to killing an ox alludes to sacrifice and thereby highlights the sacrilegious nature of the crime, an extreme violation of *xenia*.

And yet the moral picture is cloudy. For his part, Agamemnon is no saint either, since he brings back a captive he has taken at Troy and has made his mistress (selling the population of captive cities and tribes into slavery was fairly common in antiquity, and seemed to have been one of the rallying cries for armies fighting for the defense of hearth and home). Clytemnestra is motivated in part by the affront she feels at her husband's bold infidelity, but it is Aegisthus' motivation that is more relevant for our concerns: he is the (third) son of Thyestes, who (as we've seen) had been tricked by Atreus into eating his elder sons at a feast, and Aegisthus thus pledges to avenge his father on Atreus' own son, Agamemnon. That cycle of deceit and vengeance in the course of seeking power is characteristic of *Game of Thrones* and the events leading up to the Red Wedding in particular. Viewed in isolation, the Red Wedding may seem to illustrate a morally simple world in which the Freys are the caricatured villains and the Starks innocent victims through whose eyes we see events and, therefore, with whom our sympathies lie. Set against the larger backdrop of *Game of Thrones*, however, we can better appreciate the episode as a microcosm of a morally complex world, in which the actions of one generation have consequences for the next.

12. Renly Baratheon

CHAPTER 2

THE KNIGHTS
OF SUMMER

Catelyn Stark: 'They are the knights of summer,
and winter is coming.' (CK 350)

Is *Game of Thrones* an epic? Most people, I think, would answer this question with a definitive 'yes.' Whether as book or TV adaptation, *Game of Thrones* checks off two of the boxes we intuitively look for when we think of something as an 'epic': size (epic things are large in scale) and register (epic things are grand and serious). These two criteria are, as a rule, widely applicable. For example, *Game of Thrones* is large in size in the sense that it is a long series of books (currently at approximately 1.75 million words),[1] or a long series of TV episodes (currently at 60 episodes), which tends to mean also that we invest in and attach ourselves to the characters and events of the story. But *Game of Thrones* is also large geographically. It encompasses a whole world, the Known World, as fans have started referring to it. Not only is the Known World large, but it is also not fully explored. There are whole areas – beyond the Wall or in the faraway Asshai, for instance – to which readers, and most of the characters as well, have never been exposed. In that sense, *Game of Thrones* is not only vast, it is also expanding: we meet new worlds (Westeros, The Free Cities, Slaver's Bay) as we read along, and of course George R. R. Martin himself is still writing, so the ending is not yet in sight. Register, or more specifically 'grandeur,' is more complicated still. *Game of Thrones* is the story of kings and queens, lords and ladies, castles and conquest. But it is also the story of sellswords and exiles, slaves, bastards, and other people who struggle to make themselves of importance in a world dominated by aristocrats. And yet the seriousness of tone that describes that struggle, the suffering of so many characters, and the violent conflicts between individuals and nations – that narrative mood also plays a role in forming the epic register of the series. Size and register, therefore, are two ways of conveying one of the most important aspects of epic: its totalizing tendency, which essentially means that epic, however focused on a single story, is also the story of the whole world and of everybody in it. It is as much about the past as it is about the present or the future, and it brings all the moving parts of human existence toward a single purpose. In *Game of Thrones*, at least so far, that purpose is seemingly political: winning control of the Iron Throne and of the Seven Kingdoms.

Epic fundamentally asks one question, though the answer is always far more complicated, interesting, and difficult to pin down: who is the best? The first author to ask it in classical epic form is traditionally regarded as Homer, whose *Iliad* asks who is the best of the Achaeans, and answers resoundingly: Achilles, the hero of the Trojan War. Finding out the identity of the best of all heroes, however, is merely the superficial pretext of most epic: although the *Iliad* repeatedly poses the question of who is the best of the Achaeans, no one is under any illusions about who fits the bill. The question of the central epic hero is a rather more fraught one in *Game of Thrones*, which by contrast with the *Iliad* or *Aeneid* deliberately exploits a little more ambiguity. Who really is the best knight? Arthur Dayne, slayer of the Smiling Knight and supposedly the best of his generation of Kingsguard? And yet he's bested by Rhaegar Targaryen at the tourneys at Storm's End and Harrenhal, and later killed by Eddard Stark's band at the Tower of Joy. How about Rhaegar himself? Well, he is killed by Robert Baratheon at the Battle of the Trident. And Robert was once defeated in a tourney by Barristan Selmy. The vast and terrifying Gregor Clegane, perhaps? Though Oberyn Martell might well have killed him. And of the younger generation, what of Jaime Lannister or Brienne of Tarth? The list goes on and on, rapidly becoming a source of contention for those fans inclined to hypothetical duels – with no definitive or even satisfactory conclusion possible. And what, in any case, does 'best' mean? Is it just a matter of martial skill, or is there some implied notion of chivalry, of morality? We'll be returning to the question of epic heroism in Chapter 3, and the ways in which we might understand who's the main hero (even if not the best knight), but for now I'd like to turn to a more basic question about epic: not who, but how. By this I mean the question of how epic tells its story of heroism and, even more fundamentally, how epic functions as a storytelling mechanism.

Classical epic (and indeed much later epic too, like John Milton's *Paradise Lost* or Henry Longfellow's *The Song of Hiawatha*) is always composed in poetry. Greek and Roman epic used the same verse form, called the hexameter, which repeats the basic rhythmic pattern *dum-dee-dee* six times, though with numerous variations. The meter served various purposes, including ease of memorization and structured improvisation, since epic began life as a purely oral art form before the advent of writing. There is still considerable debate about the origins of Greek epic poetry, at the center of which are the *Iliad* and the *Odyssey* and their supposed author, Homer, but also a number of other epics that remain to us in scanty fragments or not at all.[2] The standard view is that these epics were written down several centuries after they began life as a cluster of stories about the Trojan War and the Greeks' return home afterwards, besides other myths. Wandering bards – predecessors of the medieval troubadours – carried with them the central ideas of the poems – the war in Troy, the wrath of Achilles, Odysseus and Penelope, and so on – but they extended and elaborated them depending on what the audience wanted to hear, what they were adept at performing, and whatever new influences they were exposed to. As a result, no two versions of an epic were exactly alike, though contact between the bards and the various communities kept all of them more or less recognizable. And when the works were eventually written down, of course, some stability set in, which was further increased by generations of editing until the versions which come down to us today.[3]

This might all sound very much removed from the experience of *Game of Thrones*, which after all is not only composed in prose rather than epic verse, but is also not improvised or made up on the spot, and is instead the final product of an author's revision process. *Game of Thrones*, or at least each of its individual books or episodes, comes to be complete and non-negotiable in the form that is published or televised. That situation, however, is only the tip of the iceberg, since in fact we have not one authoritative version of *Game of Thrones* in circulation but at least three or four. There are the books, which have the authority and imprimatur of George R. R. Martin's sole author credit. There is then the HBO TV series, which began as an adaptation and has since departed from the original books in a number of interesting ways, which include not only altering the names of characters, but also removing some characters altogether, writing new plotlines, and changing the emphasis of the books. Some of these changes are made to cater to the medium's strength: TV can do certain things better than print, and vice versa. Some are almost a new draft: Cersei, for instance, has a scene in Season 1 (E7, 'You Win or You Die') of the show, in which she confesses that she did, once, love her husband. The scene adds depth to her character and interest to her story, and indeed makes her more relatable to some members of the audience, but it is not in the books, where Cersei's initial feelings for Robert are more opaque. So we have already two versions of *Game of Thrones*, each catering to slightly different sensibilities and audiences, and both with the imprimatur of Martin, though for the show he of course shares credit with other screenwriters, producers, and actors, all of whom are not really separable from the final product in any one viewer's awareness.

The boundaries are even more blurry if you've both watched the show and read the books, if you have an intimate knowledge of the production process of either format and the changes made from draft to final version, or if you've just been exposed to any of the public chatter. So, books and show are at a minimum versions one and two, and we might term them 'official' versions. Another 'official' category is any licensed merchandise and offshoot stories, like *A Knight of the Seven Kingdoms*, which adds temporal depth and texture to Westerosi history as we know it. There are also comic books, maps, and other tie-ins. Then we come to the vast category of 'unofficial' versions: from books about *Game of Thrones* (like this very book you're holding), to fan-based interactive material like games, forums, fan fiction and wiki entries, all of which are ways to experience *Game of Thrones* without, or in addition to, actually reading or watching it. None of these might sound very epic, but it is quite comparable to the way epic initially circulated: multiple versions, audience engagement, and a loose cluster of stories about a common theme, which develop and change in accordance with supply and demand. These very stories would go on to circulate in different genres and media, with epic material realized on the stage of tragic drama, sung to the accompaniment of the lyre, painted on vases, and embodied in statuary. Granted, the specific mechanisms may have changed since the archaic age of Greece, but the overall effect, of a work of literature growing and taking shape before our eyes and proliferating in its manifestations, is strikingly similar to what we encounter today.

I've so far been using *Game of Thrones* as a sobriquet for the entire series, and I'll keep on doing that in the rest of the book.

When thinking about the series' epic connections, however, that's misleading in an important way. The series' proper name is *A Song of Ice and Fire*, and both song and song culture are an important part of Westeros and of ancient epic. It was regular practice to name epics after their main character or main location, and 'A Song of…' is a good way to translate many of them: the *Iliad* is a song of Ilium, another name for Troy; the *Odyssey* is a song of Odysseus; the *Aeneid* a song of Aeneas; and the *Thebaid* a song of Thebes. This pattern raises some interesting questions, because *A Song of Ice and Fire*, at least by ancient naming conventions, avoids telling us precisely the two features we can see are regular in the ancient traditions: the name of the hero and the location of the action.

Now the question of the 'hero' of *Game of Thrones* is a big one, and the subject of the next chapter, but *Ice and Fire* is still quite revealing as a stand-in for what we'd like to know. As a replacement for names, *Ice* evokes most clearly the sword of Ned Stark, and indeed the whole Stark family, many of whom launch claims to be the protagonist of the story. But *Ice* can also invoke the frozen landscapes of the North or indeed the massive Wall, made entirely of ice and guarded by the Night's Watch, an order which casts off any family affiliation and which includes Ned Stark's own bastard son, Jon Snow. Since many of these characters die in dubious circumstances, it's difficult to pin down any one of them as the hero, but collectively they make one pole in the tension between North and South that drives the politics of the Seven Kingdoms. *Fire* does much the same work, but in the other direction. It naturally evokes the Targaryens, whose power is based on their mythical control of the dragons and their obsession with fire. It may also invoke the hot desert of Dorne, a sometime Targaryen stronghold and, for the moment, bitter rivals of the Baratheon settlement. But above all the title signals a fundamental – literally elemental – conflict, a war between forces that are naturally and eternally opposed. This sense of timelessness, universality, and a struggle of significance, in which the medium of mere words is almost magically transmuted into song, gets at precisely the core of the epic tradition. So even though *A Song of Ice and Fire* doesn't quite fit ancient conventions – a *Westerosiad* might have been more recognizable to the Greeks and Romans – it has a similar kind of effect: it traces out the contours of what's important, the edges of the canvas on which the drama of the game of thrones can play out.

PERFORMING EPIC IN WESTEROS

What about song? Ancient Greek epics were sung, or recited in verse. *Game of Thrones* is not, but it's still called a song. Why? One hint is to look for the songs mentioned in *Game of Thrones* itself, all of which have an important function, and in fact usually point out when something important is about to occur or be said. Not all songs are epic, of course: 'The Bear and the Maiden Fair,' which recurs quite a few times, is clearly the kind of song one sings around the fire with friends and several pints of ale. 'The Rains of Castamere,' however, which likewise recurs at crucial moments, is rather different.[4] Although there's not quite enough of it to piece together the full lyrics, it's clearly a story of how House Lannister outmaneuvered, thoroughly destroyed, and finally came to own the possessions of House Reyne of Castamere. It is, therefore, a song about history, and also a song about the characteristic qualities of the Lannisters. It's meant to teach one a lesson, and warn others against repeating the foolish mistake of messing with House Lannister. As such, it isn't quite epic, but it begins to come closer to what epic does: celebrate great men, pass down the legacy of their glorious deeds, and memorialize their foundations of cities and dynasties. 'The Rains of Castamere' does exactly that: it celebrates and commemorates, and so is a nice small-scale variant of the *Iliad* or the *Aeneid*.

The song economy of Westeros – or at least of the aristocracy of Westeros – is in fact a mix of epic song culture and sympotic song culture; in other words, it is a mix of poems about the deeds of great men and kings, and ribald drinking-party poetry about (usually) sex. Take, for instance, the wedding of Joffrey Baratheon and Margaery Tyrell. As the guests work their way through the 70-odd courses, they are also treated to a parade of singers, each of whom performs their own versions of famous songs as well as some new creations. So, poor Tyrion has to sit through Collio's version of 'The Dance of the Dragons,' a doomed love story set against the ruin of Valyria, which, Tyrion thinks to himself, the audience might have enjoyed more had Collio not sung it in High Valyrian, a language most of the guests did not speak (*SS* 821). Never mind, though, as 'Bessa the Barmaid' with its ribald lyrics wins the audience back, and of course the performance concludes with the obligatory 'Rains of Castamere' to celebrate the might of the Lannisters. Tyrion, who *can* read and understand Old Valyrian, is being a bit snooty about the performance, but Collio is clearly reaching here for either crowd favorites ('Bessa'), or the sort of grand poetry appropriate to the occasion ('The Dance of Dragons'). 'The Dance of Dragons,' however, is perhaps more lyric than epic – it tells a small-scale story set against grand events, rather than the grand events themselves.

It's a different kind of poem that comes closer to ancient epic: Hamish the Gray's newly composed song, 'Lord Renly's Ride.' This ballad tells how Lord Renly after death repents of his treachery against the rightful king, defies the Lord of Death, and returns to the world of the living to defend the realm against his own brother. The poem itself is obviously fantastic, but equally it fits within the parameters of Martin's plot. Renly hasn't come back to life – though, at least as far the HBO show goes, there's no reason to think he wouldn't, since the dead coming back to life is a big theme of the story. The White Walkers recall the industry standard in ghastly resurrection (zombies), but there's a long list of other candidates too: Beric Dondarrion, Catelyn Stark, and Gregor Clegane all return to life in some form or other, as does Jon Snow in the HBO version, and, if one were inclined to view the concept more metaphorically, dragons return to the world, and characters thought deceased turn out to have been alive all along. There's also another way in which Renly comes back to life, and that's through the simulation of him by either Garlan or Loras (depending on whether we go by book- or show-verse, respectively) at the Battle of the Blackwater Rush. Here too, Renly's resurrection fits in with broader themes: Reek, the young Aegon Targaryen, Arya, and Sansa all live a life of playacting and pretense, surviving in the world by becoming someone else. And the idea of impersonation fits well, because the song, too, imitates something else: it mimics, or pretends to be, a history, a version of something that truly happened. Of course, a song that starts 'From his throne of bones the Lord of Death looked down on the murdered lord' (*SS* 820) isn't likely to be very historical, in the sense that it cannot recount what really happened and how. Instead, the song occupies a halfway house: it takes what really happened – the Battle of the Blackwater Rush, the arrival of Renly's forces and the alliance with the Lannisters, and the final victory – and embellishes it, renders it more exciting and literary by virtue of making it less credible, putting fantastic flesh on historical bones. That's an important aspect of epic poetry and what it does: it's poetry about grand events and, more specifically, about grand events that form part of a national mythology or national history, or, better still, national mythical history. This can happen on a smaller or larger scale: so the *Aeneid* is about the origins of Rome, but the *Iliad* and *Odyssey* are about the prehistory of almost the entire Mediterranean, while Statius' *Thebaid* is ostensibly about Greece, but also about Rome, and most especially about civil war, wherever it might occur.

At the end of 'Lord Renly's Ride,' the shade of Renly flies back to Highgarden to look one last time at his true love's face, and Queen Margaery herself is seen to be teary-eyed at this point in the story. Margaery is not alone in having epic poetry rouse such emotion. The poet Vergil gave a recitation of a new section of his new poem, the *Aeneid*, an epic which told the story of Aeneas, who escaped the ruins of Troy to lead his people to a new home in Italy and to found the Roman empire. The *Aeneid* would go on to become an instant classic, and one of the cornerstones of the Western literary tradition, but at the time it was fresh, ambitious, and hotly anticipated. One of the features of the *Aeneid* that makes it so vibrant, today and when it was first written, is that the mythical action reverberates right down to the present age. This is particularly so in the section Vergil happened to be reciting that day.

In the middle of his voyage, Aeneas goes to the underworld, where he meets the ghost of his recently deceased father, and receives from him a great prophecy about the future glory of Aeneas' people. In a verdant corner of the underworld (not all gloom and doom, according to Vergil) gather the spirits of future Romans as they await birth and destiny. Aeneas' father points each one out to his son, identifying them and giving Aeneas potted histories of who they will become, just as if the two were strolling through a portrait gallery or exhibition. At the end, with Rome's empire proclaimed and all the great Romans recognized and introduced, there remains one shadow – a boy who might have been the greatest of them all, had he but lived to adulthood. 'You,' Anchises announces, 'you will be Marcellus,' in one of the poet's most poignant moments. Now the *Aeneid* as a rule is deeply interested in the premature deaths of bright young men, and in the human cost of glorious wars, but Marcellus to us remains a historical footnote.[5] The audience that day, however, was not made up of modern-day historians, but rather the Emperor Augustus himself and his sister Octavia, the boy Marcellus' bereaved mother. Upon hearing Vergil's lines, she fell in a faint, and the emperor was in such tears that the recitation came to an end.[6] It's true that while Octavia's pain was genuine, Margaery's may be a show put on for political purposes, but the experience of strong emotion while listening to epic poetry was seen in antiquity as a desirable part of the experience. You felt the pain and suffering of the epic heroes, but while they suffered and died, the patrons would also enjoy their dinner and the absence of their own woes.

This idea is so entrenched that we see it narrated in epic poetry itself, which very much likes to dwell on moments where epic is being performed for the heroes and kings. Achilles in the *Iliad* receives an important delegation while playing the lute and singing about 'the glories of men.' In the *Odyssey*, Penelope, Odysseus' wife, begs the bard Phemius to stop singing about the return of the Greeks from Troy, and instead choose something more charming from his vast repertoire. This particular song, which we might call 'The Greeks' Return,' is too painful for her to hear, since her own husband is still stranded at sea, finding his way back home from Troy (and having many adventures in the meantime, all of which are recounted in the following books of the *Odyssey*). Penelope too sees her personal anguish performed for other people's entertainment. The list goes on: Aeneas, shipwrecked in Africa, is asked by Dido, the queen of Carthage, to recount his own story of return from Troy. 'You ask me to revive an awful, unspeakable pain,' he tells her, but tells the story anyway, which only makes the queen fall more fatefully and disastrously in love with him. Epic, therefore, is a way of making people feel things acutely, but it is also a way to make people connect their own personal experience with something larger than themselves, to show how the personal is representative of the human experience.

Epic has another important function, and that's as a training ground for young people learning how to live according to their status. While not exactly a manual in the arts of jousting or war, epic poetry is meant to inspire young people (and the old as well, though they're usually the ones doing the telling) to be just like epic heroes, indeed to live epic lives. This training comes in many forms, and one of the main ones, at least in Westeros, is by offering a framework of how life ought to be, in a perfect world where the sun always shines, the knights are all chivalrous, and the ladies are all lovely. In this world, young people go about having romantic love affairs, perform deeds of great glory, and achieve either everlasting fame or earthly power, or both. This fantastic world, of course, never quite materializes for anyone – in fact, one of the most important points of the *Game of Thrones* series is exactly the disappointment and disillusionment when faced with cruel and harsh realities – but there is a group of characters for which this motif is the most pronounced: Renly Baratheon and Loras Tyrell, and, of course, Sansa Stark. Because Renly and Loras are men, they get the privilege of actually playing out their make-believe epic, and we'll spend the rest of this chapter looking at how that works relative to the ancient poems. Sansa, on the other hand, trapped as she is by the conventions of female courtesy and helplessness, is perhaps the most avid consumer of chivalric epic song, and sets much store by them as a template for life. She expects all knights to be chivalrous and courteous, because that's what knights are in the songs. She expects the king to be majestic and the queen gracious, because that's what kings and queens are in the songs. And she dislikes her sister Arya's rebellious streak because it disrupts what she thinks to be right: for women to sew, and for boys to run around with swords.

This acculturation doesn't come only from songs; Sansa's mother and septa both reinforce it with their expectations, behaviors, and aphorisms like 'Courtesy is a lady's shield.' But songs complement their teaching, and it's in relation to songs that Sansa appears at her most foolishly naive. Perhaps the most glaring mistake she makes under the influence of mythic song is becoming senselessly infatuated with a series of pretty young boys, from Loras Tyrell to Beric Dondarrion to Prince Joffrey, all of whom she imagines to be good and kind simply because they are beautiful and have the trappings of glamorous chivalry. This idea that external beauty matches or indicates internal goodness is an important one for Sansa, who learns more about the world the more she comes into contact with uglier men: the Hound, Tyrion Lannister, and finally Ser Dontos and Petyr Baelish, none of whom quite conforms to the heroic type. In ancient epic, physical beauty is paramount, as is youth. All the great epic heroes are attractive men, while those who are ugly or deformed are mocked and ridiculed. For example, in the second book of the *Iliad*, the Greek forces hold a council before resuming hostilities with the Trojans. A man named Thersites gets up to speak. He is

> the ugliest man who ever came to Troy.
> Bandy-legged he was, with one foot clubbed,
> both shoulders humped together, curving over
> his caved-in chest, and bobbing above them
> his skull warped to a point,
> sprouting clumps of scraggly, wooly hair.[7]

To make matters worse, Thersites is also very unpopular with the leaders of the expedition, because he is one of the few people to bait the leaders 'all for no good reason, insubordinate […] anything to provoke some laughter from the troops.'[8] In this, Thersites is a precursor for Tyrion Lannister, who likewise compensates for his outward appearance with wit and humor (more on this in the next chapter). In the Greek camp, however, Thersites does not even have this option. As soon as he is done speaking, Odysseus stands up to threaten Thersites with physical attack and humiliation if he continues mocking men like Agamemnon. Not only that, but Odysseus also strikes Thersites to put him back in his place. Homer, who is known for his sensitivity to emotional response and situation, here gives us a heart-wrenching image of collective bullying:

> The rascal doubled over, tears streaking his face
> and a bloody welt bulged up between his blades,
> under the stroke of the golden scepter's studs.
> He squatted low, cringing, stunned with pain,
> blinking like some idiot […]
> rubbing his tears dumbly with a fist.
> Their morale was low but the men laughed now,
> good hearty laughter breaking over Thersites' head…[9]

Here is a lesson taught in the epic mode: public humiliation will keep Thersites from interfering with his betters, and anyone else who reads the *Iliad* will likewise learn the same lesson.

Elsewhere, songs have a more direct influence on what Sansa and others do and say. One of Sansa's favorite songs is the one about Florian (who was homely, as she notes) and Jonquil. When she must reassure Cersei of her loyalty in King's Landing, she promises that she loved Joffrey like Jonquil loved Florian, and when the drunken Hound demands a song from her, the song of Jonquil and Florian is the one she offers and he refuses. The Hound, of course, knows better than anybody that songs have little value in the politics of the realm, but Sansa's whole story is a slow discovery of the same sad truth. As she begins to associate with men who disappoint her, she continues to play the role of Jonquil, but instead of her gallant prince the fool Dontos comes to play the role of Florian, as he plots with Littlefinger to steal her

13. Actaeon attacked by hounds

away from the city. The story of Jonquil and Florian is not fully sketched out: Florian is both a great fool and a great knight, and he sees Jonquil bathing in a pool and falls in love with her. The motif itself is frequent in classical mythology, but the young man usually comes to a sorry end as he spies a bathing goddess in a forest. Perhaps the most famous instance is the story of Actaeon, a young hunter who stumbles upon the goddess Diana bathing in a pool. Embarrassed, the famously chaste goddess turns Actaeon into a deer, and his own hunting dogs chase and tear him limb from limb.

In the classical myth, the power lies very much with the divine woman, who has the capacity to punish any invasion of her privacy. Sansa, on the other hand, is marked significantly as a plaything of others, increasingly so as she approaches puberty. Likewise, her Florian isn't stumblingly innocent, but rather a series of men (and women) manipulating her for their own purposes. Dontos, who actually becomes a jester, is manifestly unable to live up to Florian's example otherwise. When he comes to tell her the news of the Battle of the Blackwater Rush, he proclaims 'O, to be a knight' – because he isn't really one anymore, and in fact has never been worthy of the title.

Sansa, therefore, clings to song and myth as a way of being, as a source of empowerment, and as a guide to behavior and judgment. It's not always her fault that it fails, but in consequence her main role is to be passive and stoic in the face of adversity. She is, at least until she leaves King's Landing, the paradigmatic damsel in distress, a figure who attempts to participate in epic but never quite finds a way. It falls to others to actually live the adventure. Whether her character in the books will take on some of the increasing authority of her television counterpart remains to be seen, and – since the books make more of her connection with song – we also wait to see whether her maturity will be reflected in a shift in her attitude toward song.

Living Epic

When I teach the *Game of Thrones* books, I often start by asking the
class to share their favorite characters. Some answers are predictable,
like Tyrion or Arya; others, like Catelyn or Hodor, are less so. But two
answers I've never received have been Renly Baratheon and Loras
Tyrell, and I always get raised eyebrows and confused looks when
I suggest that these two are my personal favorites. It's not hard to
work out why Renly and Loras are unpopular – they're far from main
characters, spending most of their screen time on the periphery of
the central events. In fact, when Renly does decide to force his way
onto the main stage, his campaign is mostly dismissed by those in
King's Landing, and is taken seriously only by the Starks. Stannis,
of course, loathes the very idea of a Renly usurpation, while Loras
is merely an aside – a pretty boy without much political sense. The
campaign itself is short-lived and doomed, and while it ends in
mysterious circumstances, events move at such a rapid pace that
there's never any sense that Renly's death was a great loss, except for
the people who loved him best, Loras himself and Brienne of Tarth.
But something else I always tell my students is that literature, or
any other art, including TV, doesn't have the time or the budget for
gratuitous characters or plotlines (even if both text and the screen
arts will often find time for gratuitous sex and nudity – but more
on that later!). The inherent economy of literary representation
means that an author has only so much time and so much space to
describe his world to the reader; wasting those resources on something unnecessary makes no sense. So rather than Renly's story being
merely a distracting digression, we should strive to understand what
importance it really holds within the context of the whole series.
Paying attention to the little things and the apparent sideshows is in
fact one of the best ways to grasp a work of literature, to figure out
how it functions, and how the different parts interrelate.

   In the rest of the chapter, I want to focus on the single story of
Renly and Loras, break it down into its constituent parts, and put

it back together again in a way that makes sense of its existence in the plot of *Game of Thrones* as something other than comic relief. In fact, the story of Renly and Loras is a variation on a very old theme: young men who go off to a war they are too young to understand, and the loss of innocence they undergo as a consequence. This story sounds very modern to our ears, partly because of the vast literature produced in the time of the World Wars, but it goes back to ancient culture, and finds expression in the earliest of epic themes. In fact, the hero who loses a close comrade predates classical antiquity – the Greeks are likely to have received it from the near east (where we find a parallel in *The Epic of Gilgamesh*), and it is equally attested in other cultures as well. While the motif is universal, this book can cover only the Greeks and Romans, and so I will focus in particular on one Roman parallel for Renly and Loras, the story of Nisus and Euryalus in Vergil's *Aeneid*, as a way of digging deeper into the various parts of this story. Each of those parts, in turn, branches out to other parts of both *Game of Thrones* and ancient literature, culture, and thought. What are those parts, you ask? They are as follows: duels and athletic games, homoeroticism, and trauma. Overlaying all that is one more important question: how to manage the transition between imitation and reality, or, in other terms, the question of growing up and coming into one's own as an adult participant in adult society. Neither Renly nor Loras ever really grows up, but if *Game of Thrones* is about anything, it is about growing up, growing old, and the disillusionments of both. And that's the real reason – spoiler alert! – that Renly and Loras get any screen time at all: their story is about love, and trying to grow up quickly in difficult conditions.

The tragedy of Renly and Loras is therefore both universal and very personal. It is universal because Westeros is a war-torn kingdom, and the needless loss of loved ones repeats from one family to another, across both the highborn and the low. It is personal because every tragedy is distinct and different from every other human story. But Renly's camp and Loras' devotion also sit at the intersection of personal and universal, since they represent a fantasy of a world which is not only impossible but never actually existed. Young and beautiful, they treat the war – or are imagined by old men like Maester Cressen ('one-and-twenty, and still he played his games' (*CK* 11)) and jaded women like Catelyn Stark ('it is all a game to them still...' (*CK* 349)) to treat the war – as a game, a matter of play and chivalric song. This is typical of Renly, who as a child liked to play at make-believe: 'look at me, I'm a dragon,' or 'look at me, I'm a wizard,' recollects Cressen, while Barristan the Bold introduces him to us for the first time as a 'prancing jackanapes,' which is an elaborate way of calling someone a monkey, an animal famous for imitating what it sees other people do. Renly's penchant for playing a part is matched neatly by Loras, who, admittedly, only plays one part – the beautiful young knight of legend, the one whom all the girls want to seduce, and whom all the boys wish to be. Given that we know that at least part of that is a facade, Loras' pretense is important in all sorts of ways.

But it's the female leads that, as ever, capture the truth most bluntly. Caught up in melancholy, Catelyn pities the young men who have declared for Renly. Their youth and joy and strength will not last, she says, 'because they are the knights of summer, and winter is coming' (*CK* 350). *Winter is Coming*, of course, are the famous words of House Stark, an emblem of their constant vigilance – or perhaps better to say jadedness – against the pleasures of summer. And in some sense, Catelyn herself is a bad omen, bringing the frost of winter among this host of bright happy people; as she herself recognizes, she is the specter at the feast. For the young people themselves, however, this particular campaign is about hope and glory: 'Winter will never come for the likes of us. Should we die in battle, they will surely sing of us, and it's always summer in the songs' (*CK* 350). Of course, the harsh realities of Westeros are anything but a song, and Catelyn turns out to have been right all along. Winter does come, at least for Brienne and Loras, both of whom fail to die and thus fail to make it into song. Renly, who does die, becomes the stuff of song, performed with due melodrama at Margaery's wedding to Joffrey, with the queen suitably teary at the thought of her former love. But we know better, of course. That song is a lie, and one obviously made to flatter the Lannisters. However, there is another song, the *Song of Ice and Fire*, and that song does indeed contain Loras and Renly and Brienne and all the others too – and here too, winter comes. Thus, Loras and Renly's story is about the coming of winter and the dying of hopes, and as such it is a microcosm of the whole series: from Sansa's love of heroic song to Ned's standards of honor to Dany's experiences in the Red Waste and in the East. Some people grow up by wandering; others grow up by passing through the crucible of war. *Game of Thrones*, like many epics of antiquity, is the story of both, and Renly and Loras offer an acute case: the whole world of Westeros in a grain of Stormlands sand.

Nisus and Euryalus

Before we start, I want to sketch out the story of Nisus and Euryalus, which Vergil tells us in the ninth book of his *Aeneid*, and point out the basic similarities and differences between Vergil's heroes and Renly and Loras.

Nisus and Euryalus (pronounced Nee-sus and You-ree-lus) are two of the companions Aeneas brings with him from the ruins of Troy. Of the two, Nisus is the elder, while Euryalus is the most handsome of all the Trojans that come to Italy. The two are close friends, and we first encounter them in Book 5 of the *Aeneid*, when they both participate in funeral games held in honor of Aeneas' father. Funeral games are an ancient institution for which the nearest modern equivalent is the wake. When someone of sufficiently lofty status died, his family (usually his sons) would stage athletic and gladiatorial games in the deceased's honor. These games are a staple of epic poetry, but they continue into historical time: Julius Caesar, for instance, put on funeral games for his father, with 320

pairs scheduled to fight in
the Roman forum.

The games offer the
first opportunity to see
the friends' devotion to
each other. Both enter
the footrace together, and
both are competitive for
first place, but toward the
end Nisus slips on a patch
of dried blood and loses
his footing. Trying to help
Euryalus win instead, he
uses the opportunity to
trip up one of the other
contestants, who then
complains to Aeneas
about flagrant cheating
before peace is restored.

14. Gladiatorial combat

We next encounter our intrepid heroes in Book 9 of the *Aeneid*,
when they are about to go on a daring raid of the enemy camp.
Aeneas, the Trojan leader, has left his forces to go and recruit some
allies among the local people, and the Trojan camp is feeling his
absence. Earlier in that book, the Rutulian prince Turnus (the
Rutulians were an Italian people who were fighting against the
newly arrived Trojans) has managed to breach the Trojan defenses
and burn the Trojan fleet. The Trojans at this point are smarting;
they've been explicitly ordered by Aeneas to stay behind the camp
fortifications, and not emerge for any reason. They obey, but they're
unhappy both about the slight to their honor and the loss of the
ships. At night, posted on sentry duty, Nisus tells Euryalus of his
plan to go out after Aeneas and bring him back to his people;
Euryalus, for his part, is offended because Nisus does not pro-
pose to take him along, which Euryalus feels is a slight both to

his honor and to the affection they have for each other (the Latin word is *studium*, which can mean 'fondness' or 'devotion' and in this case seems to shade into erotic desire, but more on that later). Nisus explains that it was not down to neglect at all, but in fact out of concern both for Euryalus' safety and his responsibility as an only child of an aged mother. After some discussion, the two agree to undertake the mission, and because Aeneas is away they ask permission to do so from Iulus, Aeneas' son, who is now in command, and from the council of more senior men who were left behind. Iulus, who is both a bit taken aback by Turnus' attack and has a taste for impulsive adventure, gives his blessing, as do the other councillors, and they even promise the pair elaborate gifts if they should be successful. In return, Euryalus asks that Iulus looks after his old mother, should Euryalus fail to return – a first hint of the tragedy to come.

Having gone through the niceties, the intrepid duo sets off under cover of night. The immediate challenge they have to overcome is simple: the Trojan camp is besieged by Rutulian forces, but they know that once they clear the siege, their path should be easier. They also know that the Rutulians, having feasted well during the night to celebrate Turnus' achievement, would be 'buried with sleep,' so conditions would be ideal for sneaking through their lines. But being young and excitable, Nisus and Euryalus get carried away with the excitement of the mission, and when they come up to the sleeping and helpless Rutulian heroes, they cannot help but indulge themselves in slaughtering a path through their enemies. Even this they might have gotten away with, but they also help themselves to the spoils of the dead – a traditional right of the victor in ancient warfare but a rather foolish thing to carry along in what is supposed to be a stealth mission. Euryalus in particular has to be pulled away from his rampage, and even so he still makes away with a heavy golden helmet, a helmet that spells his destruction.

As Nisus and Euryalus stumble away from the Trojan camp, they are discovered by a returning Rutulian patrol, and a chase ensues. What happens next is almost predictable, but certainly not less pathetic for being so. Stumbling through the woods, unaware that he has already passed into safety, Nisus realizes that Euryalus is no longer by his side. Horrified, he retraces his steps through the woods, and finds that Euryalus, whose shiny new helmet reflected the rays of the moon and betrayed him to the enemy, has been captured and dragged away by the Rutulian patrol. Crouching in the shadows, Nisus debates what to do, and decides to cause some confusion in the patrol by throwing his spear into their ranks. This he does, successfully hitting and killing one of the Rutulians. He does it again, and kills another man. At this point, a lot of things happen at once. The Rutulian leader, Volcens, draws his sword and goes at Euryalus. Nisus leaps out of hiding and begs Volcens to spare Euryalus' life, but it's too late, and he can only watch, in the epic equivalent of slow motion, his friend run through with the sword, dropping to the ground like a poppy that's been cut down by the plow. At the sight of the dead Euryalus, Nisus loses his mind and leaps at the Rutulians, killing Volcens and dying in the process of trying to avenge his companion's death. The next morning, the Trojan camp, including Euryalus' old mother, are treated to the sight of Nisus' and Euryalus' heads mounted on spikes and paraded before the walls. The old mother raises a lament, and the Rutulians prepare for another wave of attacks against the shell-shocked Trojans. Aeneas eventually returns, but not before Turnus enters the camp and savages the Trojans.

As a piece of epic yarn, both these stories – the race and the raid – are good ones, but for all that they are hardly consequential. Nisus and Euryalus and their daring raid is really nothing more than a digression, a flare of youthful overexcitement that ends without making any real change to the way the plot unfolds. The same, it might be argued, is true of Renly's campaign: it's a burst of energy and color, a fleeting prospect of the possibility of a new order, one where the most charismatic brother is preferred to the random order of birth – but in the end it goes nowhere, with Renly dead and his men going over to the Lannisters in King's Landing. Both pairs also operate in a somewhat fantastical environment, where the responsible adults have all vanished and the younger generation is allowed free sway for a disastrous moment. The sense of futility is important for the way this story works within the larger context of the two respective plots, and in fact is something that the story retains whenever it is retold in the tradition: the end result of the quest must be beyond the realistic ability of the characters to achieve, even if it's not in itself impossible or against the odds. And that is in turn important because it engages our emotions as readers and activates what literary critics call *pathos* – a sympathy with the terrible mistakes of others that could have been our own, a sense of tragedy that might have been averted.

Perhaps the most pathetic image in the story of Nisus and Euryalus is the lament raised by Euryalus' mother when she sees her son's head on an enemy pike. Renly, of course, has no parents to mourn him, and that very orphanhood generates its own sense of pathos, for the estranged Baratheon brothers and the impossibility of any reconciliation. Even earlier, old Maester Cressen, in the prologue for *Clash of Kings*, thinks about the laughing young boy he had helped raise, and wonders if Renly has anyone advising him now that he has set off on his folly. Renly does, as it happens, but his closest advisor seems to be the Knight of Flowers, who is too young and too impulsive for the job. A host of others are either equally young or owe him allegiance but not affection. This situation is in turn analogous for the state of the whole of Westeros, a land sunk into civil war and being pulled apart by men eager for power but without a clear sense of what to do with it once they've got it. This is the first sense in which Renly and Loras' story is paradigmatic of the entire plot of the *Game of Thrones* saga, and it is an important quality they share with the Nisus and Euryalus story. Stripped down to its skeleton, Nisus and Euryalus' raid is merely an escape from a besieged town. But such an escape already occurred in the *Aeneid*, when its eponymous hero escapes

the burning city of Troy. Like Nisus, Aeneas loses his beloved in
the case – though it's his wife – and retraces his steps to try and
find her. Nisus finds his Euryalus, but with tragic consequences;
Euryalus might have survived, and Nisus would have done but
for his attempted rescue. Aeneas, however, finds not his wife but
her ghost, who tells him not to waste time but forge on away from
Troy. Aeneas does, thus giving his people hope of redemption.
Nisus, therefore, is a failed Aeneas, a vindication of the decision
Aeneas has made. Aeneas gave up his wife in order to fulfill his
destined role in the foundation of Rome, but Nisus refuses to
give up Euryalus, and his turning back means he is lost and his
fellow Trojans, already under the cosh, are further debilitated by
the loss of two able warriors. Loras operates under slightly different conditions, but much of his story vacillates between looking
back toward vengeance for Renly and ahead toward the future of
his house and of Westeros (again the books are bleaker than the
show, not least because Loras is too established a character in the
show to let waste away, while the books can more easily afford to
let characters diminish or be killed off).

The overall pattern of events, therefore, is only part of what
makes Renly and Loras' story similar to Nisus and Euryalus': the
pathos, the quality of the relationship between the two young men,
the events themselves in which they participate, as well as a number
of smaller tropes and commonplaces, all give this particular story a
strong epic flavor. In the next few sections, I want to dig a bit deeper
into a few particular instances of similarity, cases where Renly and
Loras' story takes up or participates in epic commonplaces, and
explore further how these epic commonplaces work in the world
of *Game of Thrones*. That these instances are relegated to a somewhat marginal storyline does not detract from their importance
or interest: indeed, minor characters are often the most intriguing
to fans, precisely because their stories aren't as fleshed out as the
main characters and are hence ripe for the imagination. As it happens, however, this particular story is itself a very old one, and it

tends to get used in the same way throughout most of its literary history – to pass commentary on the human costs of war. Since epic is the story of war, the two boys who love each other enough to die together also tell us a story about epic itself, or in our case the sprawling world of *Game of Thrones*.

It's All Fun and Games...

I hope that even at this basic retelling you can already start seeing some parallels in theme between Nisus and Euryalus and Renly and Loras: both pairs are young, with more enthusiasm than discipline, fond of the exciting aspects of warfare, and in possession of quite a lot of the confidence of youth. There are structural similarities as well: both pairs participate in stylized games (in this case the Tournament of the Hand), and those games turn out to be preparation for the more serious business of war.

Athletic games have always been – and still are – a way to express human achievement at the limits of human ability and endurance. This is also precisely what epic warriors demonstrate on the field of battle, and the connection between sports and warfare is familiar enough to be almost clichéd. In their epic form, at least, athletic games closely reflect the skills required of a warrior in battle: the spear-throw, for instance, reflects exactly many epic scenes, including the climactic duels of both the *Iliad* and the *Aeneid*. Chariot-racing, too, mimics behavior on the battlefield, as does running, and to a lesser degree wrestling. Further, like feasts, games reflect a social order. They are usually convened as part of the death rituals of a great hero, and the person sponsoring them provides gifts and keeps the participants from cheating, fighting, or in other ways subverting normal procedures. And although we tend to think of sport as a great leveler, this does not always hold true in the epic world. Sometimes, as in the *Iliad*, minor heroes who win an event are given a smaller prize than someone older or more famous who did less well; the unequal distribution reflects the hierarchical position of both men, and acquiescing in that supposed unfairness can benefit the wronged party, who might get a bigger reward for respecting what society considers due decorum.

It's important to distinguish between the athletic games in Greek and Latin epic and the historical phenomenon of games in Greece and Rome. The former is a stylized set of descriptions of athletic endeavors in which the heroes of the epic take part as a substitute for real warfare. This relationship between war and sports was certainly behind historical spectacles like the Olympic Games, though epic games are not exact literary depictions of the ancient Olympics (which postdated the origins of the *Iliad* and *Odyssey*). In the Greek world, exercising in the gymnasium or the training fields was part of the training required for citizen life, and good preparation for enduring the heavy armor and discipline required of a citizen-soldier. Competing in the Olympics (or in the three other great Games: the Pythian, Nemean, and Isthmian Games) brought glory to the city, and victors were feted and celebrated in song and ritual. Romans sometimes competed in the Greek games, and had their own games, called *ludi*, which began with dramatic performances and chariot races, and later also included gymnastic competitions. The athletes in Rome, however, were usually paid professionals rather than citizens showing off their prowess, while the idea of the gentleman-athlete is at the heart of the epic program of games.

Almost every epic has the obligatory set piece of funeral games, and they are all, in their own ways, modeled on the games for Patroclus' funeral in the *Iliad*. The games there are lavish and emotional, both because the *Iliad* is a poem that is very concerned with proper burial honors for the dead, and because of the special relationship between Achilles and Patroclus. But whatever poem they are situated in, epic games offer both a relief from the fighting and a microcosm of it, and therefore they, too, are a way for the epic to speak 'about itself', to give us a snapshot of things as they stand in the poem and in the realm. Vergil's Nisus and Euryalus both enter the footrace in the funeral games held for Aeneas' father, Anchises. This change in circumstance is very Roman (the Romans felt very strongly about piety toward one's parents, and Aeneas' devotion to *his* father was thought to be characteristic of Roman values), but it also means that the young couple enter the work before the real martial action begins, a difference important for understanding what's going on with Renly and Loras – as we'll see.[10]

The event in the *Aeneid* is the running, an event which had pride of place in the Olympic Games as well as in the epic tradition, and which was generally held to be a young man's game. In epic memory, running was particularly associated with Achilles, nicknamed 'Swift-footed,' and for him, at least, speed was a double-edged sword. On the one hand, it was a quality that helped distinguish him in battle above all others, and which was celebrated especially in his duel with the Trojan prince Hector, whom he chases around the city three times. Achilles' swiftness, however, also symbolizes his short life: in returning to battle before Troy, Achilles chooses a short but glorious life over the peaceful retirement in his homeland he might have had. The choice between long life and glory is exactly what Brienne picks up on when she tells Catelyn that they would be sung of, should they die in battle – 'and it's always summer in the songs.'

Swiftness, *celeritas*, was also a quality of another Achillean figure, the great Roman commander Julius Caesar, who was famous for pushing his legions to march so quickly he was able to surprise his enemies by arriving at a battle scene long before anyone expected him. Caesar's swiftness was clearly a military asset, yet it was also described as destructive and compared to a lightning bolt bringing destruction from the heavens – but destruction that eventually turned on his fellow countrymen rather than on Rome's enemies. Such meteorological and cosmological images aren't uncommon metaphors for speed: Achilles is compared to a storm and to an evil star bringing sorrows to mankind as he moves across the battlefield. Running fast, in other words, suggests youth and vigor, as well as a great but ultimately self-destructive success. An over-reliance on raw speed alone suggests also a little bit of naivety, or at least a youthful preference for brawn over brain. In the games for Patroclus in the *Iliad*, it is Odysseus who wins the race, despite being older than all the other contestants. Odysseus achieves his victory with the aid of the goddess Athena, to whom he prays mid-race; she in turn sees to it that Ajax, the main competition, slips and falls in some dung. Even from the beginning, then, epic races were about more than just physical attributes – they were also about the numerous other factors, including intelligence, luck, and the gods, that could separate winners from losers, factors equally crucial in determining outcomes outside the sporting arena.

Nisus and Euryalus – neither, as events demonstrate, the sharpest arrow in the Trojan quiver – both enter the running, and the prizes offered by Aeneas are both impressive and suitable for the events. Everyone will get two Cretan arrows, weapons that are associated with speed and flight, as a token of participation. The first-place winner will get a stallion (another gift associated with swiftness) and all of the necessary trappings. The animal might put us in mind of the joust, where the winner often won the loser's horse and trappings, and of the horse the Mountain kills as the cause of his defeat, thereby making it impossible for Loras notionally to obtain it. In Vergil's footrace, the second place would get a quiver full of arrows (swiftness yet again), while the third place would get an Argive helmet. This last award is an odd one, because helmets have little to do with swiftness. They do, however, have everything to do with Euryalus, who will meet his end because of a golden helmet he loots from one of the Rutulian soldiers. This, too, is appropriate: Euryalus looks set to come in third place, and would have duly won the helmet. But he comes first instead, and therefore does not win the one item that might have prevented his death: the helmet that might have foreclosed his desire to take one. Now, helmets also have a special place in the Tournament of the Hand and in the Loras/Renly story for another reason – Renly too competes in the

Tournament, but he loses in the early round, and breaks his helmet when falling off his horse. We'll come back to the importance of that later, but for now it's enough to note that Euryalus and Renly both have a connection to the same physical item, and in both cases that item foreshadows a tragic end.

Despite the foreboding (after all, the young heroes themselves – and indeed we as readers – have no way of knowing what the future might bring), Euryalus wins the race, with the assistance of none other than his beloved Nisus. At the final turn, Nisus is leading, while the other runners, exhausted, are falling back. Sniffing victory, however, Nisus loses his footing on ground wet with blood from an earlier sacrifice conducted on that spot. Down he goes, face-first into the sludge. Even at this point, however, Nisus thinks of Euryalus, and positions himself such that he trips over Salius, who's left sprawling on the ground. From third place, Euryalus surges to first. Naturally, much complaining ensues, chiefly from Salius, who feels quite rightly that he was robbed of his just deserts. The viewers, however, aren't very impressed with these complaints: Euryalus appeals to their sentiments. He weeps, and his beauty seems to them to enhance his virtue; he is aided also by Diores, who snuck into third, and hardly wants to let it go now. At this point, Aeneas steps in. He assures Euryalus and Diores that their rewards will stay fixed, but also offers Salius a prize in consolation for having tripped: the hide of a massive Libyan lion. This proves too much for Nisus. If everybody is getting prizes, even for falling down, he claims, then he too ought to get *something* – he, after all, was about to win the race on merit, and was as much the victim of bad luck as Salius was (a baldly disingenuous claim, to be sure, given that he had deliberately tripped Salius up!). All this while showing off his face and body covered in the bloody sand of the racecourse. And it works, too, since Aeneas laughs and gives him a shield stolen from a god's temple – a quietly appropriate gift for a cheat.[11] The thing to note about this scene, however, is how minor-key the whole thing is. The complaints of the contestants make Aeneas laugh, and he easily and generously dispenses gifts, performing one of the main functions of leadership and of such events: to redistribute surplus in the economy as rewards to heroes of both primary and secondary status. In the end, it is implied, everyone leaves happy: Euryalus with his victory, Salius with his greater spoils, and Nisus with his shield and his sacrifice.

With this, contrast the Tournament of Hand and its outcome. The tournament is put on by King Robert to celebrate Ned Stark's appointment as Hand of the King, and organizing it is Ned's first official task as Hand. It consists of at least three events: the jousting, the archery, and the melee (in which Robert nearly participates, though he is prevented from doing so by Ned). Robert's outsize enthusiasm for the melee offers a moment for him to reflect on what has happened to him since winning the throne: he admits that he was never more alive than when fighting for the throne, never more dead than since he won it. For Robert, even fake battle is better than none at all, and Ned and Barristan Selmy manage to convince him to stay away from the melee by persuading him that the fight would be genuinely fake, since none would dare strike the king. At this Robert deflates and crisis is averted, but the role of games as an outlet and as an exhibition of one's prowess and ability is clearly demonstrated. In addition to preserving the king's safety and pride, however, there is another reason why Robert must stay out of the melee: a fight with the king might have real consequences – a change in the identity of the king, or even a suggestion that the king might be weak and mortal. Even though it is a game, the tournament can turn real and deadly. Here too we have a hint of what is to come: just as the melee is a simulation of war, capable of getting out of control in the confusion of action and unknown motives, so too the hunt in which Robert will die substitutes for battle, yet on that occasion no one will be able to prevent his drunkenness or warn him about the Lannisters' intent.

The change in atmosphere from entertainment to deadly seriousness happens even without the king's participation. Ser Hugh of the Vale of Arryn dies on the first day, while the final joust of the day almost ends in bloodshed. Loras Tyrell manages to knock the terrifying Gregor Clegane clean off his horse, which prompts the Mountain that Rides to kill his horse and attack Loras, who is only saved by the intervention of the Hound, Clegane's brother. It requires the king's command and 20 swords to separate the brothers, and Loras then cedes the honors to the Hound. Even this vignette is telling of the upcoming future: the two fighting brothers suggest civil war and its tearing of the family unit; Robert's command, effective only with the backing of 20 swords, suggests the decline in his powers and charisma, and so on. Above all, this disruption of the proper order of the games suggests that the future is uncertain and dangerous – a foreboding Ned shares, and which will shortly be confirmed for him by the eunuch Varys. Just as a disastrous feast suggests a breakdown of society, so too disrupted games suggest a failure of morality and leadership.

At the root of this tournament failure is the plain fact that Loras Tyrell has cheated, riding a mare in heat to agitate the Mountain's stallion and distract its rider. The ploy succeeds beautifully, and even though it is clear to everyone what has happened, there is no suggestion that Loras has done anything illegal – only immoral. The question of how to deal with the ensuing problem is resolved by Loras himself, who gallantly cedes the victory to the man who had saved his life – but the practical resolution also suggests another bigger problem: the king and his Hand, the two men charged with ensuring the peace and prosperity of the realm, are usurped by young boys and lawless fighters.

But there still remains the question of why Loras – and why Nisus – cheats in the first place. Nisus, it's clear, cheats out of affection for Euryalus; if he can't win himself, he wants the glory and prize to go to his beloved. But although Renly participates in the tournament, he goes out of it so early that he is merely a viewer by the time Loras makes it to the final round. If we remember that in Vergil, the older viewers help validate Euryalus' claim to victory because they correlate his beauty and his sportsmanship, we can get a sense of the erotic dynamic of spectatorship, both with Renly, who is, after all, involved with Loras, and with Sansa and the myriad other spectators who gush and fawn over the Knight of Flowers.

Loras, however, cheats out of simpler motivations: he wants to win (another characteristic of epic heroes, who are competitive in every aspect of their life), and he wants the prize money, or at least Renly suggests he does ('Small honor and twenty thousand golds' (*GT* 316)), though the Tyrells are certainly wealthy enough not to have to rely on tourney victories for their income. If he knows Renly has bet on his victory, that is yet another motivation. Still, the money, like the prizes Aeneas hands out, is a way of keeping score, of making public and conspicuous both one's prowess and the appreciation for that prowess by others (usually one's superiors, whether by birth or by office). This might well look like greed to a modern audience, who manage both to accept the massive remuneration paid to elite athletes and resent those same sums as 'spoiling' the innocent spirit of sport – and there's more than a hint in both *Game of Thrones* and the *Aeneid* that greed comes at the expense of honor, and in some cases of life. Nisus and Euryalus, for instance, are offered gifts again before they leave on their raid, this time by Aeneas' son Iulus, but even those gifts and the promise of honors upon their return don't keep Euryalus from looting in his battle fever, an act of despoiling that is both the appropriate thing for a warrior to do and at the same time a sign of misplaced priorities and excessive desire.

Fundamentally, however, Loras' cheating, unlike Nisus', is grounded in necessity: Loras is slight, while the Mountain is huge and had already demonstrated the potential danger to Loras by killing Ser Hugh. At a joust, where physics gives the advantage to the heavier of the contestants, Loras' size puts him at a disadvantage, which he can compensate for only by creating ideal conditions for him to use his own strengths: accuracy and speed. The combination of physical attributes and trickery makes Loras into a composite figure, at once both Nisus and Euryalus. But the joust also inter-sects with another commonplace tradition, which begins with epic poetry, but ramifies to historical writings and gladiatorial combat. This tradition is that of the uneven duel, where a hulking giant is faced with a nimble smaller warrior. In epic and Olympic terms, the event thus shifts from the running to the boxing, another event which showcased an idealized form of the citizen-warrior. Epic boxing derives its potency from the fact that the contestants are aware of the gap between boxing and war and, further, they seem to acknowledge that they are better at one thing (the boxing) than the other (war). Epeius, one of the two boxing contestants in the *Iliad*, declares:

> This mule is mine, I tell you. No Achaean in sight
> will knock me out and take her – I am the greatest!
> So what if I'm not a world-class man of war?
> How can a man be first in all events?
> I warn you, soldiers – so help me it's the truth –
> I'll crush you with body-blows, I'll crack your ribs to splinters![12]

And indeed, Epeius quickly knocks out his opponent, Euryalus (not the same as our Euryalus, but the similarity in the names is intriguing nevertheless). Epeius is further gentleman enough to lift Euryalus back to his feet and help his comrades carry him from the ring and fetch the prize. In another example closer to Martin's, taken from Statius' epic *Thebaid*, the gigantic Capaneus is losing his boxing match to the small and dexterous Alcidamas when he finally grows furious and threatens to kill his opponent, before being forcibly held back by his comrades. In this way, the violent boasts of Homer's Epeius come closer to being realized and Statius' games seem about to descend into real war – just as Gregor threatens Loras' life before the Hound intervenes. Perhaps Loras was only being shrewd in using whatever trickery he could to mitigate Gregor's potentially lethal threat?

Our fun and games are almost disrupted by Capaneus' or The Mountain's excesses, but perhaps we can recover from the mere threat of violence, a forestalled murder, the death of a minor character such as Ser Hugh, or a slain horse. The bouts and duels give a taste of something sinister, but we're made to feel certain that much worse is to come beyond the context of games and tournaments. And that taste also makes us reflect on how we feel about this violence, potential or actualized – perhaps, like the spectators of gladiatorial shows, we're more bloodthirsty than we would like to think of ourselves? Epic may have its noble side, but it also provides a cheap thrill, a vicarious enjoyment of illicit imaginings.

But before we get too deeply into the dark side of events, I should emphasize the point that by and large the games and tournaments step back from the worst kinds of violence. Loras' joust nearly turns into a close-range sword fight, and, much later on, he'll be involved in another close combat in the melee in Bitterbridge, but what matters in both cases is that they are showpieces without real consequences other than for Loras' pride. As much as the events may be full of foreboding and intriguing details for us to interpret, the action itself is fundamentally trivial and futile, a placeholder for more meaningful conflicts. And this notion of non-fulfillment is crucial for understanding Loras and Renly's narrative.

Part of the impetus for that narrative is that the pair become arrested in time and place not only in the games but in their every action; Renly by virtue of dying before accomplishing anything, Loras by virtue of constantly seeking revenge against Stannis or Brienne (both of whom he considers Renly's killers), but without any satisfaction or even the slightest progress. As such, it matters that we never see Renly actually lead forces. Instead, he spends most of his screen time performing the ceremonial and symbolic roles of a king: presiding over feasts, councils, and games. In these, he shows himself to be a potentially good king – the HBO show is particularly emphatic about developing these images into a contrast between Renly's fairness and affability and Stannis' blind justice, or the Lannisters' equally blind greed and cruelty. Until Renly's death, Loras too is only a tourney knight, and while we know he is a successful one, we also see him fail to win on his own merits, and he is even beaten by a woman. The fact that Loras in the end loses or doesn't collect the winnings in both duels may also foreshadow Loras as a failure – a knight of more flash than substance. Whenever the fighting gets real, Loras seems to be either incapacitated or out of the picture; it is only after Renly's death that Loras actually participates in winning a battle, when Tywin Lannister's forces swoop down on King's Landing after the Blackwater Rush.

A brief digression is in order here. Loras' joust isn't the only instance of uneven duels in the *Game of Thrones* saga, and power asymmetries in general are very common in Westeros, where strong knights take what they want from those unable to defend themselves. The uneven duel, however, pits two types of fighter against each other, usually with one warrior heavy and powerful, and the other light and dexterous. The best example of this in *Game of Thrones* is undoubtedly the duel between Oberyn Martell and Gregor Clegane, the former championing Tyrion Lannister's claim to be innocent of Joffrey's death, and the latter championing Queen Cersei. Here, the two contestants exemplify two different approaches to fighting, and each one is typical, in some sense, of the culture they represent. Oberyn Martell is nimble and quick, and fights with a poisoned spear, suggestive of the snakes of the Dornish desert. Clegane, who is an extreme version of the heavy-armored knights of the central part of the Seven Kingdoms, is in contrast more lumbering but also more powerful, and is likewise typical of a world view that prefers might to cunning.

In this sense, Oberyn and Gregor's duel resembles a series of encounters between nimble Romans and heavy hulking Gauls, the classic example of which comes from the Roman historian Livy. The story was either passed down the family or otherwise invented to explain the family's last name *Torquatus*, which means a torque or twisted collar traditionally worn by Gauls. A few years after the Sack of Rome by the Gauls, a new Gallic army invaded Italy, and met the Roman army at the River Anio, just north of Rome. The two armies were encamped on either side of the river, waiting for a good opportunity to attack. Every day, a huge Gaul would come out of the camp to insult the Romans, calling them cowards who refused to fight. Now, this kind of insult-exchange seems to have been a fairly common prelude to battle, from the ritualized exchange of two heroes in epic poetry to the earthier exchanges of two armies waiting for the signal to advance. Trained soldiers were expected to ignore the abuse and give as good as they got, and it seems that fraying of tempers in such exchanges was often what started the battle proper. In this case, however, the Romans did not take the bait, until one day the Gaul challenged the Romans to send someone to come out and fight him. A young man named Manlius immediately took up the challenge, but not before correctly checking with his general and asking for permission. He then stepped out to meet the giant near the bridge over the Anio, and although he was dwarfed by the huge Gaul, he could dance circles around him. After a short while of huffing and puffing, Manlius managed to dart below the Gaul's shield and strike him dead with his sword. As reward for his courage, Manlius took the Gaul's heavy golden torque from his neck, thus earning himself and his family the name *Torquatus*.

The story was told in Rome as a way of teaching young men how to behave: Manlius is incensed at the insult to Roman honor, but does not get carried away with his anger. He asks for permission to fight, following proper protocol and showing respect for rank and hierarchy. When he does fight, he does so with the blessing of the commander and thereby also of the Roman state and its gods. And when he wins, he does so by showing skilled use of the quintessential Roman weapon, the sword, and by ducking below the shield – in other words, by finding a way around even a seemingly impenetrable opposition. All this was crucial for Roman military ideology: the Romans valued obedience above all, and prided themselves on being able to outthink the enemy as well as outfight it. The Gauls, by contrast, seemed to the Romans to rely on brawn and brute force, without much thought or attention to discipline, which made their physical resources, however impressive, vulnerable.

What does Oberyn and Gregor's duel teach anyone, if anything? The duel is predicated on the assumption that as a dwarf, Tyrion is powerless in his own right: the point is to expose both his social vulnerability (nobody will fight for him), as well as his physical vulnerability (he cannot fight for himself). But the duel also exposes the frailty of the Crown: as a woman, Cersei is in the same situation as Tyrion, while Tommen is a boy, and even worse off than the dwarf. Oberyn Martell's sudden entry into the fray revives the old grievance of the Martells against Gregor Clegane, the murderer of Elia Martell, wife to Prince Rhaegar. As such, it also recalls another famous duel, that between Robert himself and Prince Rhaegar on the river Trident, a duel that is evenly matched in both ability and brawn, though not in enthusiasm – Robert Baratheon was rather more keen for blood than his Targaryen rival, or so the story goes, and certainly carried the grudge for much longer ('In my dreams, I kill him every night […] A thousand deaths will still be less than he deserves' (GT 44)). By contrast with the Trident, here the duel is staged and ritualized as part of a trial (trial by champions was part of medieval law, but not that of the Romans, who organized their duels, if any occurred, based on the situation at hand). As a legal instrument, then, it is important that there is no trickery, and indeed there is none of the type Loras engages in. And yet the outcome is complicated by Oberyn's getting carried away with his success and his use of poison. Poised to defeat The Mountain, against all expectation, Oberyn's determination to extract a confession of Elia's murder allows Gregor the opportunity to catch him off guard and kill him. Oberyn's skill and cunning give way to premature triumphalism and momentary heedlessness. The audience is left disappointed; our sympathies naturally lie with the more exciting, better-looking, and – crucially – smaller and more lithe underdog rather than the

inhuman giant, rapist, and murderer. As Vergil's viewers note about
Euryalus, virtue goes better with a beautiful form.

But Oberyn is no angel, as his mastery of poisons attests. And the
aftereffects of his spear-venom are extraordinarily grotesque, with
Gregor suffering what can only seem like an appropriately extreme
and drawn-out punishment.[13] As so often, then, Martin's duel builds
on and complicates a Greco-Roman tradition: the contestants may
look like so many pairs in classical and Renaissance epic, as well as
historical duels, but the way in which we are to evaluate the result
and the two men themselves is a many-layered puzzle. And just as
with Nisus and Euryalus or Loras Tyrell's scenes, that puzzle is as
much a key to understanding *Game of Thrones* as a whole as it is to
understanding the microcosm of the race or duel. Complex values,
motivations, and characteristics are brought into conflict, and we the
audience must interpret what counts as a win, what brings victory
or defeat, and what consequences follow from the result. From this
perspective, games, jousts, and duels aren't simply serious because
people might die – they're also serious because they provoke the
choices and assessments that define our view of the world.

...UNTIL SOMEBODY GETS HURT

What really cues us to see the similarity between the two pairs
(Nisus and Euryalus, and Renly and Loras) are two things. The
first is the fact that both pairs are potentially romantically involved,
and the second is that the younger half of both pairs – that is,
Loras and Euryalus – are youthful, beautiful, and characterized by
floral imagery. Loras, famously, is known as the Knight of Flowers,
whose armor and other chivalric equipment display all manner
of flowers, and whose sigil is the rose. When Sansa first sees him
(which is also when we first see him), she states emphatically that
she had 'never seen anyone so beautiful.' His plate is intricate and,
most importantly, 'enameled as a bouquet of a *thousand different*

flowers, and his snow-white stallion was draped in a blanket of *red and white roses*' (GT 297, emphasis mine). Loras even hands out red and white roses to the crowd of admiring young ladies, and it's the highlight of Sansa's day when he hands her the prized red rose. Euryalus, meanwhile, doesn't quite match the Tyrell flair, but he is nevertheless introduced to us as the loveliest of the young Trojans, vibrant in his youth. More famously for readers of Vergil, he is compared to a drooping flower at the point of death:

> Euryalus
> In death went reeling down,
> And blood streamed on his handsome length, his neck
> Collapsing let his head fall on his shoulder –
> As a bright flower cut by a passing plow
> Will droop and wither slowly, or a poppy
> Bow its head upon its tired stalk
> When overborne by a passing rain.[14]

Here we also run into an important difference: Loras is like Euryalus because they are both connected to floral imagery, and because they are both young and beautiful, but it is not Loras who dies, but rather Renly, while Loras is the one who goes mad like Nisus. Further, Renly's death is a lot like the poppy simile: having had his throat cut, Renly chokes on his own blood, with his neck bent and his head drooping. Nisus starts out like Renly and ends up like Loras, while Euryalus does the opposite. There are a few ways to think about this crossover, but the most compelling one harks back to Vergil's own epic, in which heightened moments of drama often make two rivals look an awful lot like each other. Madness – or in other words, trauma – changes the characteristics of a person. If that's the case, then the trauma of Renly's death makes Loras change his behavior from that of a Tyrell, whose motto is *Growing Strong*, to something else, something less fruitful; and indeed, Loras takes on the mantle of the Kingsguard, thus disavowing his family ties. In the show, which is more invested in the Tyrells' political machinations, Loras remains part of his father's and sister's plans, and is offered up as a husband to Cersei before being arrested by the Faith. But his main role, long before all that, is to bring Renly's troops over to the Lannister side, which he does by donning Renly's own armor – in effect becoming Renly himself. For that purpose, his madness is the best possible tool: the Baratheon family words, after all, are *Ours is the Fury*. Thus, at the moment of Renly's death, Loras stops being a beautiful young boy, and takes on the mantle of becoming a more seasoned (and indeed more political) participant, and one that is invested above all in avenging his dead lover, as does Nisus for the last moments of his life.

The other thing that cues us to think that Loras and Renly are the *Game of Thrones* equivalents of Nisus and Euryalus – or to give them a more famous pedigree, Achilles and Patroclus from the *Iliad* – is that they are, or seem to be, lovers as well as comrades. I say 'seem to be' because for all these couples, from Achilles to Renly and through a number of other instantiations in between, there is a prevailing uncertainty over whether or not these couples are lovers, or whether they are simply comrades with intense but purely platonic feelings for each other. For *Game of Thrones*, at least, we are aided by the fact that George Martin has announced that he did 'intend those characters to be gay,' and that the TV show is quite explicit, so that there is really no question over their erotic relationship.[15] Nevertheless, it's worth noting that the HBO decision has caused some controversy, with many fans of the books claiming that it is either impossible for Renly and Loras to be gay, or that they never noticed or considered the possibility. Curiously, antiquity too had much the same discussion about both the *Iliad* and the *Aeneid*, with scholars and commentators going back and forth over whether heroic pairs were couples or simply the best of friends. To be fair, the *Iliad* offers no conclusive evidence – hardly any evidence at all – for an erotic relationship between Achilles and Patroclus. They are, it is true, very close, share a tent, act as each other's 'second-self,' and generally behave as if they are entirely content in their own little bubble, but the poem also depicts them as going to bed with women (though admittedly even that they do in parallel with each other).[16] It's not until Aeschylus' *Myrmidons*, a tragedy on the Trojan War which no longer survives, that we start seeing explicit treatment of the two as lovers, including Achilles bewailing his lover's death with lines like 'venerating the intimacy of your thighs.'

From Aeschylus onwards, we get two separate strands: one that insisted that Achilles and Patroclus were lovers, and the other that insisted the opposite. And any epic couple that came after them was subject to the same speculation, complicated by a semantic gulf. Nisus, for instance, feels an *amor pius* for Euryalus; the term translates most plainly as a 'loyal' or 'dutiful' love. But what does that mean, exactly? Does Nisus love Euryalus as a friend? As a lover? Is *pius* supposed to sanitize a relationship that might otherwise come into question, or does it assert the propriety of homoeroticism? Is Vergil following a particular Greek tradition in the manner of Aeschylus or Plato, or is he emphasizing by contrast a tradition of non-sexual heroic friendship? On the one hand, elements of Greek and Roman society – especially aristocratic culture – were tolerant of, even naturalized to, homoeroticism. On the other hand, our texts record numerous insults against men who played the submissive or passive role in homoerotic relationships, or who were promiscuous with other men.[17] We can amass all the historical and scholarly information we like, but nothing will resolve what Vergil leaves delicately inexplicit – in many ways that lightness of touch and suggestiveness represents one of Vergil's famed gifts. But at the same time we should make sure to register the force of the ancient context and the diverse views of homosocial and homoerotic relationships: namely, that we shouldn't read Nisus and Euryalus' bond with all the baggage of our contemporary views of sexuality; the ancient world is both like and unlike our own and we must be careful not to assume too much similarity to or difference from today's customs and ideas.

But one thing that the debate around the relationship status of Achilles and Patroclus does resemble is the tremendous interest created by such pairings; not only does the theme recur in literature (so much so that it becomes a commonplace) but it also appears in more popular and contemporary forms, such as fan fiction, fan forums, wiki pages, and so on. And part of the reason for this fascination is the added pathos and heightened register that an erotic relationship adds (remember 'The Dance of the Dragons'?). This is all the more true for Nisus and Euryalus, who are reasonably unimportant in the greater scheme of the *Aeneid*: while Achilles' grief for Patroclus drives the plot of the *Iliad* and determines its outcome (once Hector kills Patroclus, he's a dead man walking), Nisus' love for Euryalus matters very little for what happens next. When we do get Aeneas taking vengeance for the death of a beloved comrade, Pallas, right at the end of the epic, the relationship is far more unclear; Aeneas and Pallas are not the doomed lovers of the *Aeneid*, at least not in any obvious sense, but Nisus and Euryalus may well be. Likewise, Renly and Loras are fairly inconsequential; certainly Renly's death has more impact on the progression of the war than anything he did in life. But Renly's death does define how Loras behaves for the rest of the books and show, and it's his involvement with Loras that makes those consequences all the more tragic.

Epic isn't all games and battles, kings and monsters: it's also the story of individual human relationships placed under the strain of extreme circumstances and subjected to the interpretation of a broad swathe of societal views. In this way, we can see how something as seemingly superficial to the plot as a fleeting homoeroticism can carry the weight of a serious component of the epic tradition. Sexual or nonsexual, the ties of loyalty and affection between Nisus and Euryalus are the principal source of their fame in epic, as Vergil himself states explicitly. Yet it is also the case that their romanticism – especially with its notes of immaturity, rashness, and desire – may be a necessary casualty of the foundation of Rome;

a moment of admiration and pathos to be sure, but one that must be subordinated to the pragmatic and imperial values of survival, security, and growth.

The Real Deal

Renly's death makes Loras into a changed person; he becomes catatonic with grief, and emerges from that state profoundly altered ('The Knight of Flowers had been so mad with grief for Renly that he had cut down two of his sworn brothers' (*SS* 925)). But what is it that Loras becomes? In an important sense, he becomes a cipher, a shadow of his former self – or at least the former self we as reading and viewing audience have come to know. But in this, too, he is like Renly, who is more or less a cipher for his elder brother Robert – a fake that cannot measure up to the reality. Renly, in fact, who is emphatically seen by Catelyn Stark as the living image of his elder brother, the late King Robert:

> In their midst, watching and laughing with his young queen by his side, sat a ghost in a golden crown.
> *Small wonder the lords gather around him with such fervor,* she thought, *he is Robert come again.* Renly was handsome as Robert had been handsome; long of limb and broad of shoulder, with the same coal-black hair, fine and straight, the same deep blue eyes, the same easy smile. (*CK* 341; italics in original)

The ghost metaphor, compounded by the repetition of 'same,' immediately establishes Renly as an imitation, a shade of the real thing – the brother whom he seeks to replace. The ghost image then finds full realization in Renly's own death, when he becomes more literally a ghost in the morning mist, 'gone like his brother' (*CK* 504). When Renly's ghost appears to win the Battle of the Blackwater Rush, this too is a moment of substitution, but the show here flattens some of the nuances. For Loras to don Renly's armor (as he does in the show) works well with the Vergilian template, because it emphasizes that Loras becomes Renly, just as he had become the maddened Nisus. But in the books, it is not Loras but his brother Garlan who wears Renly's armor, because the armor is too broad and tall to fit Loras' slimmer figure. This too is a replication: Renly attempts to fill out Robert's shoes, Loras tries to fill Renly's, but really also his own brother's. Both of them, however charming and debonair, cannot quite (and this despite the Knight of Flowers' celebrity) live up to their elder and more accomplished brothers.

Being dressed in another man's armor has good epic pedigree: Patroclus dresses in Achilles' armor to fight the Trojans, and dies in the fighting. But Patroclus is marked in the *Iliad* as a lesser version of Achilles, a warm-up for the main act that will be Achilles' triumph. One of Achilles' main characteristics is anger – it is the quality that drives the entire poem and is its very first word – and epic anger often means epic madness, when a man is inspired by fury to go berserk and unleash destruction.[18] Further, Achilles' anger changes at a critical juncture: he is first angry at a petty slight against his honor, which makes him retire from the fighting and sulk at the camp behind the lines. But after his beloved Patroclus falls in battle, Achilles' anger becomes a godlike fury focused on revenge. Dressed in Renly's armor, and inspired by the hope of vengeance against his supposed murderer, is the Loras of the show an Achilles figure, or a Patroclus figure? Is he the real deal, or a mere fake? Compare Jaime Lannister's arrogant 'there are no men like me, there's only me', a statement redolent not only of self-confidence, but of being utterly sure of your own singular irreplaceability – more than a little ironic when the speaker is himself a twin, but nevertheless a stark contrast to Loras' search for identity.

Even before Renly's death, Loras is already a bit of a fake himself. For one thing, his gift for and interest in showmanship means that he cannot but be seen as a superficial image rather than someone with any personal depth. 'Seen' is the imperative word here, because in the books, at least, we hear very little from Loras himself. Because he's not a point-of-view character, his interior world remains blocked to the reader. The show, of course, changes this drastically, and we have glimpses of Renly and Loras' relationship when they are in private. These in turn paint Loras as much more the force behind Renly's attempt at the throne, and portray him as a more audacious and outside-the-box thinker than Renly, who turns out the less heroic member of the two (he is, for instance, scared of blood and of violence – we get a moment of strong cinematic foreshadowing when Loras cuts him playfully to make his point).

In the books, however, there remains a gap between what we see of Loras and what we know about him, and this gap allows Martin to manipulate his appearances so as to ask some pointed questions. So, for instance, when Loras officially enters the plot at the Tournament, he is introduced as the Knight of Flowers. Sansa, who is the episode's point-of-view character, fetishizes Loras' armor, just as the poet's gaze lingers on Euryalus' beauty in death. This one moment lies at the intersection of a number of thematic concerns. At the tournament, Loras' riding of a mare in heat and the subsequent effect on Gregor's stallion mirrors the effect he has on Sansa, who gazes at him with somewhat mindless adoration. Indeed, the metaphorical overlap between knights' treatment of horses and their success with women is a commonplace of the chivalric epic. But Martin has of course changed the signification, with Sansa envisaging one romance stereotype while the reality of Loras' sexuality is quite the opposite.

The eroticism of the tournament also intersects with a systematic Vergilian concern, as Euryalus is only one of a sequence of young virgins whose deaths evoke the blood of virginal defloration (on both the tournament and the beautiful death, see below). Flowers thereby become a loaded symbol in this allusive economy, and as we already noted, both youths are attended by floral imagery. The opening description of Loras informs the reader that his armor is worked into a 'bouquet of a thousand different flowers, and his snow-white stallion was draped in a blanket of red and white roses'

(*GT* 297). The detail of the roses is meant to catch the eye, and advertise Loras' house, whose sigil is the golden rose. It's also an allusion to the Tudor rose, or the red and white roses of Lancaster and York, and the English 'Wars of the Roses,' and in that sense it also foreshadows the civil war that comes next – death lurks behind the flowers of youth.

But when Loras appears next, his floral armament changes, and he's wearing not roses but forget-me-nots:

> When the Knight of Flowers made his entrance, a murmur ran through the crowd, and he heard Sansa's fervent whisper, 'Oh, he's so *beautiful*.' Ser Loras Tyrell was slender as a reed, dressed in a suit of fabulous silver armor polished to a blinding sheen and filigreed with twining black vines and tiny blue forget-me-nots […] Across the boy's shoulders his cloak hung heavy. It was woven of forget-me-nots, real ones, hundreds of fresh blooms sewn to a heavy woolen cape. (*GT* 314)

The point-of-view character this time is Sansa's father, Lord Eddard Stark, and despite the differences in gender and age, Lord Eddard responds to Loras in much the same terms as his daughter: a fascination with the details of the armor, and of Loras' physique; though where Sansa finds Loras beautiful, Eddard thinks of him as a 'boy' (which emphasizes his youth) and as 'slender as a reed' (which emphasizes his slight frame), assessing him as a warrior would. Unlike the previous joust, where cape and arms bore different flowers, now the flowers on Loras' cape and suit of armor are identical, a similarity to which the text draws explicit attention ('forget-me-nots, real ones…'). We can explain the difference between the two appearances as the vanity of a young knight seeking to be seen and remembered (hence 'forget-me-nots') because of an ostentatious wardrobe change as much as his feats in the lists, and both occasions are clearly meant as a spectacle of wealth and excess, a token of Loras' *nom de guerre*. But the attention to whether the flowers are

15. 'forget-me-nots, real ones'

real or embroidered suggests also that the sober Eddard is think-ing – and inviting us to think – not only about the extravagance of using so many fresh flowers but also about what is real and what is an imitation. Loras himself, a storybook knight whose prowess, at least so far, is all in the tournament rather than on the field of battle, hovers between the two realms. His identity for the time being is bound up in being 'Renly's little rose', but even when he outgrows that phase, he remains trapped in an identity, and in an armor, not really his own.

ARMING SCENES

The idea that weapons and armor say something meaningful about their owner or wearer is especially familiar to us today from medieval

heraldic traditions, and this is something *Game of Thrones* uses ubiq-
uitously and extensively. But the significance of arms to the identity
of the warrior goes back to ancient epic poetry, which itself drew on
an ethical code that made losing one's armor shameful and unmanly.
Spartan mothers were famous for demanding that their sons come
back from war either 'with their shields or on them,' meaning that
they expected their sons to return victorious (with the shields) or
dead (carried on them). In epic poetry, warriors often negotiate the
terms of duels in advance, stipulating that should one of them die, his
opponent would keep his arms as a token of his victory, in exchange
for sending his body home to receive proper burial. In the *Iliad*,
Patroclus wears Achilles' armor to go into battle, in effect trying to
playact as a doppelganger for Achilles. This almost works, but when
Patroclus gets carried away in the heat of battle, the gods intervene
to allow Hector to kill him and take his armor away as the spoils of
war. Hector not only strips the body, but goes on to wear Achilles'
armor and weapons, with the result that when Hector and Achilles
finally meet for their duel, the event toward which the entire poem
has been building, Achilles is fighting a Hector who is dressed in
Achilles' own armor. Is he fighting himself? Of course not, but he
is fighting an image of himself, and has to triumph over a part of
himself that is no longer his. On the other hand, one of the ways we
know Achilles must win the duel is that he is the son of a goddess,
and that this goddess, a good and loving mother, has commissioned
him shining new armor made by the god Hephaestus. Achilles' new
and superior armor signals his development over the poem, as well
as his impending victory over Hector: in modern terms, he has the
technological edge over his opponent.

Armor is also symbolic by its very appearance. It is meant to
distinguish you from the other warriors or the enemy, or protect
you against their charges and weapons. It is not, however, something that one would typically wear outside a martial context;
putting on one's armor means that one is going into battle. Here,
for instance, is the great warrior Achilles about to enter into battle,

and putting on for the first time the new armor prepared for him by the gods:

> And in their midst
> the brilliant Achilles began to arm for battle [...]
> A sound of grinding came from the fighter's teeth,
> his eyes blazed forth in searing points of fire,
> unbearable grief came surging through his heart
> and now, bursting with rage against the men of Troy,
> he donned Hephaestus' gifts – magnificent armor
> the god of fire forged with all his labor.
> First he wrapped his legs with well-made greaves,
> fastened behind his heels with silver ankle-clasps,
> next he strapped the breastplate round his chest
> then over his shoulder Achilles slung his sword,
> the fine bronze blade with its silver-studded hilt,
> then hoisted the massive shield flashing far and wide
> like a full round moon – and gleaming bright as the light
> that reaches sailors out at sea, the flare of a watchfire
> burning strong in a lonely sheepfold up some mountain slope
> when the gale-winds hurl the crew that fights against them
> far over the fish-swarming sea, far from loved ones –
> so the gleam from Achilles' well-wrought blazoned shield
> shot up and hit the skies. Then lifting his rugged helmet
> he set it down on his brows, and the horsehair crest
> shone like a star and the waving golden plumes shook
> that Hephaestus drove in bristling thick along its ridge.
> And brilliant Achilles tested himself in all his gear,
> Achilles spun on his heels to see if it fitted tightly,
> see if his shining limbs ran free within it, yes,
> and it felt like buoyant wings lifting the great captain.[19]

Arming scenes are therefore characteristic of epic, and not only of epic. The ancient city of Rome had a sacred boundary, the *pomerium*.

Within that boundary – that is, within Rome's city limits – everyone was a citizen together, and notionally at peace. Outside that boundary, all Romans were in a state of military service, that is, notionally at war. A change of clothes was symbolic for the change in the function, and so Roman generals took off the toga (the clothes of home and peace) and changed them into the *paludamentum* (the cloak of the general) when they left Rome to assume their command of an army. When they came back, they changed again, from the general's mantle to the citizen's toga, and nobody was allowed to carry a sword within the city limits of Rome. Epic arming scenes have some of that formal distinction between types of space and function: one moment I have my citizen's hat on, the other my warrior's helmet. But arming scenes are also cinematic, which accounts for just how many we find in modern cinema, from King Théoden in *Lord of the Rings* to Sigourney Weaver in *Aliens*. Such scenes have a logic of their own: they build up the tension, they prepare the transition from one phase of events to the next, and they have an important aesthetic appeal as well, since they celebrate both the beautiful warrior and his equipment, often, as we have seen in Loras' case, just as lovely.

Loras doesn't get an arming scene – we only see him once he is dressed in his armor. In the show (S2, E3, 'What is Dead May Never Die') we see rather more, as Renly and Loras are given a scene written entirely for the show, in which they almost have sex before Renly manages to offend Loras, who stomps off in a sulk. Now, Loras' mood in the scene has to do with many things: the stresses of Renly's campaign, the presence of Loras' sister Margaery and her role as Renly's wife, and his recent public defeat at the hands of Brienne of Tarth. But what immediately triggers his sulk is Renly's discovery of bruises on his chest, which appear in the slow process of *undressing* – or trying to undress – his lover. This action is just as symbolic: nakedness is intimate because it removes both the barriers between lovers and the apparatus of daily life, which marks the moment as special, as outside the normal routines of life

THE KNIGHTS OF SUMMER

(contrast Margaery simply taking off her shirt when it's her turn with Renly: the functionality of her action signifies how political and utilitarian the relationship is). Loras' nakedness – or near nakedness – in the show is also a marked contrast to how polished and buttoned-up he is in the books: we almost always encounter him in his fabulous armor, and when he takes up the vows of the Kingsguard he becomes notable by his pristine whites instead. Loras' image, therefore, is consistently externalized: he has no other way to show inner depth, which might in turn account for the extra story the show's writers give him.

But if Loras doesn't get an arming scene, Renly certainly does, though unfortunately it's the scene in which he dies. Catelyn Stark comes to Renly's tent in the early morning to make a final pitch for a unified front among the Baratheon brothers and the King in the North against the Lannisters. She finds Renly dressing for battle, with the aid of Brienne, and the scene interweaves the conversation and the details of the armor being put on, and those in turn contribute to the building suspense of the pre-battle preparations. When Catelyn comes in and asks to speak to Renly, Brienne fits the king's breastplate and backplate over his tunic, and we dwell on the color of the suit: 'a deep green, the green of leaves in the summer wood, so dark it drank the candlelight.' The natural metaphor, it's worth noting in passing, is emblematic of Catelyn's mood – everything is dark and deadly, even the idea of renewed life in the summer. This is part of the pathos of the scene: for Catelyn, summer and youth and innocence are all in her past. Renly and Brienne, gearing up for battle, hope those things are to remain. As the scene unfolds, so too is Renly dressed further for battle; the lords reminisce about the siege of Storm's End, and Brienne fastens his gorget in place, ties his hair back, and fits a cap on his head to cushion the weight of the helmet. Renly dismisses his lords, and Brienne sweeps his cloak over his shoulders. And when Catelyn asks him again to give up his crown, Brienne brings his gauntlets, and most importantly his greathelm, 'crowned with golden antlers that would add a foot

and a half to his height.' The timing of the crown/helmet juxtaposi-
tion is not coincidental, just the same as when a minute later Renly
announces that the time for words is done and Brienne happens to
kneel down to fasten his sword-belt, the last act of homage Renly
receives in life.

But it's the helmet that's particularly worth paying attention to,
not least because helmets have a unique epic pedigree. We have
seen already that it's the helmet Euryalus takes from the body of
Messapus, made of heavy gold and shining in the moonlight, that
betrays him to his pursuers. In the *Iliad*, the Trojan hero Hector
is known as 'Hector of the Flashing Helmet,' and his baby son
Astyanax takes fright at seeing his father armed for battle, so
that Hector has to take his helmet off to make the baby laugh.
Helmets, because they obscure the face and protect the head,
thus have a metonymic function: they stand in for the whole,
living man. Euryalus is thus betrayed by his enemy, chasing him
from beyond the grave; Hector is betrayed, ultimately, by his own
family feeling, which compels him to fight the doomed war in
defense of Troy. Now, Renly's helmet seems quite impressive when
Brienne brings it round, and we know it to be both tall and heavy,
as well as, crucially, decorated with the stag antlers that are the
symbol of Renly's house. Assiduous readers of *Game of Thrones*,
however, will have recognized in this helmet an echo, perhaps a
newer version of one Renly has worn before. It appears for the first
time at Renly's introduction (*GT* 144–7), where he is armored and
holding his helm, thus forming a ring composition with his last
appearance. It next appears, though briefly, during the Tournament
of the Hand:

> Renly was unhorsed so violently that he seemed to fly backward
> off his charger, legs in the air. His head hit the ground with
> an audible *crack* that made the crowd gasp, but it was just the
> golden antler on his helm. One of the tines had snapped off
> beneath him. (*GT* 296)

The moment dissolves quickly into humor, as the crowd fights over the golden antler until Renly walks among them to restore order, foreshadowing his attempt to claim the throne through popularity and alliance. The breaking of the tine, however, is ominous, and here it stands explicitly for the snapped neck the tournament audience fear, and also looks into the future at the severed neck that will mark Renly's death. As so often in epic, what is farcical in games becomes all too real in war.

16. Code of Chivalry

CHAPTER 3

EPIC HEROES

Jaime Lannister: 'There are no men like me.
There is only me.' (CK 791)

W e have so far dealt largely with a host of minor characters, but we can now turn to one of the big *Game*
of Thrones questions: who is the main character? It's
a question that inevitably arises from the organization of the
novels, with their chapters reflecting the perspectives of various
individuals competing for the reader's attention. The question is
equally raised by the plots of both the books and television show,
which pit various prominent characters against each other, many
of whom appear to have a role in the future development of the
narrative only to be killed off unexpectedly. For most works of
fiction, the question of who is the main character is a simple one.
In fact, their identity is often explicit in the very title itself: the
Odyssey, Antigone, Hamlet, Emma, Batman, and so on. Even if
the main character doesn't survive until the end of the work, they
do enough to emerge as the key player in the action, the focus of
our attention.

Game of Thrones, on the other hand, like other ensemble works
such as *The Wire*, doesn't suggest that one character is necessarily

more important than the others. That thought is cut off along with Eddard Stark's head toward the end of the first book and the first series. Unlike *The Wire*, however, *Game of Thrones* reflects almost obsessively on the idea that one individual will finally emerge victorious, one character will rise above the others and recast the prior narrative as leading to their eventual ascendancy. Will it be Daenerys? Will it be Jon Snow? Or Aegon? Or someone else? Meanwhile, the audience is left wondering what feature might define someone as the main character: is it the one who lasts the longest? The one who makes the most impact on the storyline? The one who has the most star quality, the most prominent billing, or the highest-ranked position? And is the main character at one point in time indicative of anything at all, given the remarkable fragility of life throughout the narrative? The lesson of Eddard Stark is never far away.

We often use another word to designate the main character, 'hero.' These days we tend to employ the term with a variety of meanings, ranging from merely a good person to something more like a superhero. And yet the idea of being the center of focus, someone worthy of attention, someone of whom we approve, applies to the full range of uses. As a result, we often assume that the main character is a broadly sympathetic or admirable figure; that is, he or she is not the villain of the piece, an assumption that has a bearing on how we might read *Game of Thrones*: is the main character, then, also the hero of the story, and if so what kind of hero are we talking about?

This is an area in which the ancient world can help us to shake off some assumptions created by our experience of much modern culture and get us to better appreciate *Game of Thrones*. For the Greeks and Romans, heroes were powerful individuals, typically superior fighters but also kings and prophets and singers, who after their deaths received a form of worship from communities; the heroes thus occupied an intermediate level between humans and gods.[1] But they weren't necessarily good or ultimately successful.

Almost all classical heroes are more ambivalent figures than we're used to: not just a flawed individual that we're fundamentally supposed to root for (for example, a Wolverine or a Gregory House), but someone who could be a hugely destructive or genuinely tragic figure. Achilles may be the best fighter in the Trojan War, but he both causes the deaths of countless comrades because of his pride and fails to sack Troy because he is killed by Paris. Oedipus may be smart enough to solve the riddle of the Sphinx, but he's practically the last one to work out that he has killed his father and married his mother. Whereas Hollywood asks us to look past a hero's flaws and fall for the loveable rogue, classical literature and myth treat those flaws on a par with – or perhaps even above – the hero's virtues. We're supposed to feel shock and awe when confronted by these figures in a story or on the dramatic stage; we're not supposed to like them, even if we should feel sympathy for their fate and learn lessons from their stories. It's in this tradition that we should view the characters (heroes?) of *Game of Thrones*: not only multiple instead of singular, but also ambivalent instead of basically good.

One important aspect of ancient heroism is the tension between the exceptional and the average, between the special and the everyday, and it's a tension that's often expressed in political terms: the rights of one man over many, of one favored nation over another. In this way the struggles between individuals, often boiling down to their personal characteristics, symbolize larger conflicts between groups, or values, or ways of viewing the world. Thinking about heroes in *Game of Thrones* as partly political symbols can thus help us to appreciate the features and risks of different regimes, as well as the overall system within which the characters operate, a system that shows the familiar tension between the exceptional and the average, the heroes and ordinary people. This system is evident in the *Iliad* too, as Agamemnon and Achilles contend over which of the two – the chief lord or chief warrior – is the best and the most valuable of the Greeks, a contest ultimately measured in the lives of rank-and-file soldiers and lesser heroes.

Politics doesn't always have to be grand and systemic; sometimes it bears on the psychology of the individual hero seeking to understand and define their leadership role in changing circumstances. While the battlefield setting of the *Iliad* isolates its heroes from ordinary society, the tradition that starts with the *Odyssey* is deeply interested in how these extraordinary people manage not only to return home but also reintegrate into civil society after the traumatic events they have lived through.[2] Most of the returnees from Troy, for instance, arrive back to find their wives unfaithful and their courts, livelihoods, and positions usurped. The unlucky ones are killed, like Agamemnon, the king of Mycenae, who is stabbed in his bath by his own wife, as we saw in Chapter 1; the luckier ones, like Diomedes or Odysseus, leave again to found new cities in the western Mediterranean. Very few find domestic bliss again. The exceptional and the everyday aren't natural bedfellows, and it's far from straightforward to make the transition from epic heroism to daily life, even if one's daily life is being king of Ithaca.

Yet sometimes one finds that the politics of war, with its competition and ruthlessness, has found its way into one's home, and the seemingly private act of bringing one's house to order becomes symbolic once again of attempts to rule a state gone awry. The heroes of *Game of Thrones*, whether Tyrion or Daenerys or many of the others, have their traumas to survive and voyages to endure, and at the end there is no guarantee that they will find peace either in victory or at home. But it's in seeing their struggles along the way, both public and private, that we the readers and viewers gain some greater understanding of the relationship between the hero and their kingdom or people.

In both Greece and Rome, the question of what to do with citizens who stood head and shoulders above the rest was a persistent problem, since both societies highly valued equality among

17. Ostrakon with the name of Pericles

citizens, whether across the whole city-state (as in Athens), or within a political class (as in Rome). Different places came up with different solutions, though exile was often a tried and true method of removing anyone who didn't quite fit in. In Athens, a procedure called ostracism was employed, where citizens chose the most prominent among them to be removed if they felt it was for the best; the person was exiled for ten years, the better to keep a lid on their growing influence.

In Rome, exile was achieved by trial, and was often accompanied by disenfranchisement and poverty. And who were these dangerous citizens? Aristocratic men who were either gifted demagogues, had large followings, or had the charisma and star quality the ancients accorded those who enjoyed great success in the service of the state. These people may not have been heroes in any strict sense, but we can see the clear overlap in the patterns of their lives: success followed by failure, leadership followed by separation from the community. In both cases the ancients were testing out the limits within which exceptional individuals could be accommodated and sustained by their society. In Rome, that process would culminate in repeated civil wars and the establishment of a monarchical system of government, thus enshrining an individual as the head of state, an individual who would come to be seen as a kind of god, just as heroes like Achilles and Oedipus once were.

There is, however, one problem with overfocusing on exceptionality as the distinctive marker of the epic hero: epic, and indeed politics, rarely accommodates only one genuine hero. In the *Iliad*, for example, Achilles is the most prominent of the Greek heroes, but he is far from alone: Agamemnon, Diomedes, Hector, Ajax, Odysseus, and a slew of others all have their part to play, and not merely as members of the supporting cast. Achilles is young – according to some versions only 15 when the fighting starts – and is only the prince of a minor principality. Agamemnon, by contrast, is his senior in age and position, and much of the *Iliad* tracks the power plays between them as they each attempt to assert their own pride of place within the Greek camp. The Trojan prince Hector, meanwhile, is usually seen as the poem's antagonist, the main counterpart to Achilles – and while it was universally accepted in the ancient world that Achilles was the superior warrior of the two, the *Iliad* is also the story of how that competition plays out. In fact, competition, and in particular the struggle for recognition and glory, is precisely what drives the epic: competition between the warring sides, but also, more importantly, competition between the various heroes, for whom the war in Troy is a means to establish who is 'the best of the Achaeans'.[3] Much the same tensions existed in Rome, where the aristocracy was engaged in constant efforts to bring glory to Rome, and by so doing to bring glory to themselves and their respective families. This they did by the same means as the epic heroes: by political and military performance, and by proving constantly how much better they were than anybody else. This tension between personal glory and the glory of Rome proved tremendously productive, catapulting Rome from a small village in the Tiber marshes to a world-spanning empire – and the same tension proved equally destructive, as the constant squabbles of the aristocracy brought down the Roman republic and replaced it with an autocratic empire.

Besides big abstract questions of morality and politics, ancient heroism was also a matter of more concrete personal characteristics and the creation of distinct archetypes. This process of delineation was already in evidence in the *Iliad* with its diverse characterizations of the heroes, but it comes through even more clearly in the first sequel to the *Iliad*, the *Odyssey*. Although Odysseus appears in both epics, the treatment of him in the *Odyssey* represents an important shift in how we view epic heroism: where Iliadic heroes tend to be evaluated and praised in terms of their martial ability, Odysseus is also distinguished by his almost proverbial cunning. Where many Iliadic heroes are youthful and tall, Odysseus is older and shorter – which does not stop him from either excelling in battle or from enticing the most attractive women everywhere he stops. The *Odyssey*, further, is not quite an ensemble piece in the same way that the *Iliad* is. In fact, beginning with its first word, 'man', the epic almost pointedly plays on the singularity of Odysseus, as his comrades constantly fall around him, whether lost at sea, turned into pigs, or eaten by the man-devouring Cyclops. Odysseus' journey is a lonely one, and this became characteristic of other return-stories (*nostos*, or *nostoi* in the plural). Thanks to the two Homeric epics, Odysseus and Achilles represent two of the most famous types of heroes in antiquity, and many subsequent epic characters partake of the qualities of one or the other to varying degrees. Heroic and literary characterization thus consists in part of a kind of modular experimentation, building combinations of personalities and attributes in various configurations that draw on the extensive epic genealogy that preceded.

This brief snapshot of what is a long and extremely rich tradition is meant to show that ancient epic already recognized multiple types of epic heroism. In fact, one could say that one of the main interests of the ancient epic poets, and of their premodern and modern predecessors, is to explore through the epic medium precisely what it means to be 'epic' or 'heroic' in a changing set of extreme circumstances. The Homeric epics provide two basic templates – the younger hero competing in war, and the older and wiser hero trying to survive against nature and the gods. The civil war in Westeros certainly accords with the extreme circumstances of epic, and its vast physical scope and multiple storylines mean that George R. R. Martin has the opportunity to explore various types of heroism side by side. We have a whole set of brooding young heroes keen to show off their prowess: Loras Tyrell, Robb Stark, and Theon Greyjoy all strive to show that they are the best among the masses of up-and-coming young men, some of whom even aspire to the throne (to-the-manor-born Joffrey, we might note, has no such compulsion. 'My dog will do for him,' he says (*GT* 274), with the hauteur of someone who never had to fend for himself). We likewise have a set of heroes struggling to return home to claim what's theirs, or even to find out what exactly it is they're claiming as birthright. We further have unlikely heroes, like Tyrion, whose physical appearance might have held him back in the Iliadic world but who has Odysseus' strength and cunning; and we finally have a large set of female heroes, who showcase various ways in which women participate in, claim, or enable the heroic code. *Game of Thrones* thus has the full gamut of epic heroism, adapted and expanded to fit the particular needs and norms of Westeros.

Some of *Game of Thrones*' epic conventions are drawn directly or indirectly from Homer, like the feasting already discussed in Chapter 1, or the heroic connection between personal and family glory, or the obsession with military prowess over other forms of achievement – these are all constant themes in any heroic litera- ture, and they have lasted to this day. Others, however, are largely owed to postclassical influences or are more distinctively Martin's: the lord and castle settings, the frequent prominence of women in

political positions, or the particular kinds of magic and the supernatural at play – all these, while each individually familiar from
prior literature, convey the medieval flavor of *Game of Thrones*
and contribute to its unique, many-sourced world. This constant
push and pull between the traditional and the new, the inherited
and the original, is itself part and parcel of the dynamic of the epic
tradition, where all poets strove to imitate Homer and Vergil. All
poets, sometimes on their own admission, fell short, and all poets
innovated to create something they hoped would be newer and
better. The change in epic heroism from Achilles to Odysseus is a
change on which the success of the *Odyssey* depends, just as Aeneas'
distinctive brand of heroism inspired by both Achilles and Odysseus
drives the success of the *Aeneid*. In thinking about Martin's heroes
in ancient terms, then, we're not just getting an insight into the
morality, politics, and character types of his fictional world, we're
also discovering the terms on which the success of *Game of Thrones*
as an epic should be judged.

TRADITIONAL HEROISM

If we were to go looking for the most traditionally heroic type in
Game of Thrones, we would not go far amiss with Jaime Lannister,
eldest of the Lannister siblings, brother to the queen and member of
the Kingsguard. Here we find many of the attributes we might look
for in a fully formed epic hero: Jaime is a nobleman, of proven prowess both on the field of battle and on the jousting field, incomparably
handsome, and in possession of a suitably heroic self-assurance:
'There are no men like me,' he informs Catelyn Stark. 'There is only
me' (*CK* 791; S1, E10). Nor does he merely toot his own horn: Jaime
is hyped, adored, and feared in equal measure, and is generally held
to be the gold standard when it comes to what a knight ought to
be (but for one crucial black mark, to which we shall return). The
only one to eclipse him is the fabled Arthur Dayne, the Sword of

the Morning, who was so heroic in both character and achievement that he has truly passed beyond imitability. And yet for all the hype, Jaime himself turns out, by the time *Game of Thrones'* plot begins, to be resting on past laurels. He is defeated in the joust by Loras Tyrell and on the battlefield by Robb Stark, loses his hand to a group of mercenaries, and becomes increasingly marginalized in court. And yet as things go from bad to worse in politics and battle, Jaime's character becomes all the more interesting, not least because his tremendous arrogance becomes tempered with a sense of decency and his character acquires previously absent nuance. Jaime is a hero if not heroic, heroic if not quite a hero: in short, a bundle of contradictions.

Perhaps the first place to start sorting out these contradictions is the distinctive epithet Jaime carries. 'Kingslayer,' they call him, though not always to his face, a title earned for killing the Mad King, Aerys Targaryen, in the most egregious betrayal of Jaime's knightly duty. Heroic epithets have a long pedigree, and almost all the ancient epics use them as tags to mark a distinguishing character trait. Aeneas, for instance, whose *raison d'être* is to fulfill his duty toward his father, his son, and his people, is most commonly referred to as *pius Aeneas* ('pious Aeneas'), piety for the Romans being the quality of doing your duty toward father, homeland, and the gods. In the *Iliad*, Achilles is called 'swift-footed' Achilles, and speed is one of his trademark qualities: he is quick to anger, as well as physically swift on the battlefield and on the running track. His crowning achievement in the *Iliad* is the killing of Hector, which he accomplishes after chasing the Trojan prince down, going three times around the walls of Troy. Finally, Achilles is also quick to die: doomed to choose between anonymous long life at home and a swift but glorious burst at Troy, he chooses the latter, and never comes home from war. Odysseus, conversely, is *polutropos*, a 'man of many turns'; he cannot find the straight path home, however much he searches, and each new twist and turn adduces in him new forms of cunning: his mind is as shifty as the road ahead of him, his words and identity subtle and ever-changing. Such epithets, then, describe not only the hero but something more deep and meaningful about him, some programmatic trait that will come to define him and determine what he does and how he does it.

What about 'Kingslayer'? An ancient reader might have been both horrified and impressed. Killing kings was nasty business: in the *Aeneid*, Achilles' son Pyrrhus kills the elderly king of Troy, Priam, as he seeks protection at a sacred altar. Pyrrhus himself is described as a snake coiling and rising before his victim, and the act itself is both pathetic and cruel. Priam is old, and offers little by way of a fair fight, while his executioner cares nothing for the violation of the altar. Pyrrhus himself is a more arrogant and less nuanced version of *his* father, Achilles, who was described in the full flowering of his wrath as the ill-omened star Sirius, bringing doom to the Trojans. But Achilles, despite his temper, learns how to show mercy even to his enemies, and allows the same Priam to ransom and bring home the body of his son Hector. Pyrrhus, on the other hand, murders another of Priam's sons before the eyes of his cowering parents, and kills the father in the son's blood. There is a moral lesson here: in doing what even the great Achilles didn't do, his son aims to surpass him, to make a greater name for himself. But the way he does it forever marks him as less than his father, who became a greater hero still by showing mercy. These dynamics – of sons and fathers, and of cruelty and mercy – run through the tradition, and Jaime Lannister is certainly no stranger to strong-willed fathers whose reputation one cannot (and perhaps ought not) surpass. Tywin Lannister remains more or less a two-dimensional character, but what we know of him is not sympathetic: unyielding, Machiavellian, and ruthless, he would stop at nothing to gain his aims. And yet it was his son, the Kingslayer, who did the deed and lived with the dubious glory.

What else do we learn from the name 'Kingslayer,' however? Certainly it stands for duplicity and treachery. Jaime Lannister

was, after all, a member of the Kingsguard when he did his king-
slaying, though he did so only after Robert's victory was all but
assured, so we also get a hint of calculated utility. Jaime himself has
many justifications for his action, not least that Aerys Targaryen
was a tyrant, and that his killing ended the war and put an end to
the bloodshed – but however he might try to explain his reasons,
'Kingslayer' has more than a tinge of irony to it. It was won not in a
heroic duel on the open battlefield, but through cloak-and-dagger
betrayal in the throne room. It is Robert Baratheon, perhaps, who
ought to have received such a vainglorious title as 'Princeslayer' in
reward for his killing of Rhaegar at the Trident, a duel that echoes
throughout the action of *Game of Thrones*, so much of which happens at the Trident itself. But Robert becomes king, and Jaime is
left only as the Kingslayer – a badge of his treachery, and almost an
invitation to repeat the deed. This, however, is something he is quite
unable to do. Unlike many ancient epithets, 'Kingslayer' connotes
a single, and so far non-repeatable action, and not, like 'pious' or
'swift-footed' or 'many-turning,' a state of being.

Nevertheless, Kingslayer also precisely codes what Jaime
Lannister has become: a has-been, a futility, a killing machine
without aim or cause. He is, in other words, a hero put to pasture,
past the heroics of the battlefield but without either the rewards
or the cathartic *nostos*: for what is a Kingslayer to do when there is
no king? The entire state of Westeros is predicated on one simple
question: whether or not Robert Baratheon has legitimate issue.
We know the answer to be no, and in consequence there are five
kings in Westeros, not only the one sitting on the Iron Throne. The
legitimacy of the Baratheons is itself further in doubt, and Jaime
had been the one to kill the last legitimate king, in an effort both
to win power and to bring the peace. Instead, the country is in
disarray, the inheritance in question, and the Kingslayer without
purpose – so much so, indeed, that he spends much of his time
away from King's Landing, wandering aimlessly with the formidable
Brienne of Tarth. In that quest, the closest he comes to a cathartic

nostos, he loses not only much of his previous arrogance and mystery, but also his fighting hand. Upon returning to King's Landing, he is no longer the golden knight of yore, but is left instead in the grey area of the early retiree, a symbol of the general deterioration of the entire land.

Epic heroes, and indeed men in any heavily militarized society in antiquity, waged battle not only against enemies on the battlefield for victory or against their peers for glory. They were also the subject of constant comparison between themselves and their fathers or predecessors, a comparison in which they rarely came out on top. Achilles' spear, for instance, weighs so much that no other hero in the *Iliad* can wield it, though his son Pyrrhus, however morally degenerate, will be an exception. For the heroes at Troy, the looming shadow they cannot escape is that of the great hero and demigod Hercules, who had once already captured the city of

18. Roman man with images of his ancestors

Troy and pulled down its walls. Most of the heroes present for the war are too young to remember, but they have in their midst the aged Nestor, who was there, and who takes pains to remind them of their failure to live up to the past.

The war at Troy was popularly taken to be the boundary between myth and history, so that the warriors at Troy were the very last of the heroic age of myth. Interestingly, the Roman aristocracy, nearly a millennium later, lived by the same dynamic: sons were expected to increase the fame of the family, but it was a rare son who managed to outdo his predecessors, all of whom had the benefit of having already passed into the family's mythical lore. The best an average Roman could hope for was making his ancestors proud, but the truly great Romans – a Scipio or a Julius Caesar – could well boast of doing what no Roman before them had done. This was their talent and blessing, but in the end proved their undoing as well.

The problem of paternal expectation and filial fulfillment is neatly encapsulated in Tywin Lannister's words to Jaime in 'You Win or You Die' (S1, E7): 'I need you to become the man you were always meant to be. Not next year, not tomorrow... now.' The Lannister family dynamics are indeed complicated, and Tywin Lannister has little warmth to show either of his sons. There can be no doubt, however, that it is Jaime who has the lion's share of it, while Tyrion's legitimacy is grudgingly acknowledged and any affection consistently withheld. By the same token, when Jaime shows some resistance to his father's wishes – for example that he remain as heir to the Rock, despite being part of the Kingsguard – Tywin is quick to hurt and criticize (SS 856). Jaime's physical handicap might seem to injure his father's dignity as much as his own, but in fact it merely sharpens a disappointment that was always present.

Indeed, in *Game of Thrones*, heroic failure usually brings about a physical disability, which reduces the hero back to, and perhaps lower than, the average man they used to excel. There is no more chilling example of this than Theon Greyjoy. Taken as a hostage and ward by the Starks at a young age, Theon grows up with the Stark children, and is as near to Robb as his half-brother Jon. No matter how settled he is in Winterfell, however, Theon can never quite become one of the Starks himself, as the people of Winterfell often remind him. But after he comes home to the Iron Islands, he finds that his sister Asha (Yara in the TV show) has usurped his place, and that his father deems all his achievements with the Starks as evidence that he has gone soft and is unfit to be an Iron Islander. Right down to his gold jewelry, his body already begins to broadcast his outsider status. Bad enough, perhaps, except that Martin then steps up the intensity: Theon insists on a doomed excursion to Winterfell to prove his merit (a perverse *nostos*, perhaps?), which although initially successful leads to his capture by Ramsay Bolton, the Bastard of the Dreadfort, who tortures him and breaks him down both physically ('I send you each a piece of prince,' he writes in letters attached to bits of Theon's flayed skin (*DD* 365)) and mentally. If the return to Winterfell is an attempt to assert his own mastery over his former masters, his torture inscribes his failure deep on his body, even to the extent of emasculating him – literally – in contrast to the masculine qualities of his more successful sister.

The processes Jaime undergoes are therefore not unique to him. Inasmuch as epic often involves an ensemble cast, Jaime is part of a group of heroes all dealing with the same issues, a cluster that is highly programmatic for *Game of Thrones*. The most prominent of these is the issue of paternity, or more specifically the relationship between fathers and sons. Across the famous families of Westeros, by far the most dominant model of the father–son relationship is imitative. Fathers aspire to have sons who are like them, of whom they can be proud. And nowhere is the issue of similarity and difference more pronounced than when it comes to the royal succession: Joffrey neither looks nor behaves like Robert, whereas Robert's bastards look just like him, as does his younger brother

Renly. Physical resemblance thus stands in as a token of kinship and affinity, but it can also be a very problematic index in some cases. Take, for example, the Starks: the Stark heir takes after his Southern mother in looks and complexion, while it is the bastard Jon Snow who takes after the Starks more than any of his siblings. Yet Jon Snow's paternity is one of the more vexed questions in the plot, and in any case his bastardy excludes him from any of the rewards of being a true Stark. Still, the half-brothers both come to positions of leadership (Jon at the Wall and Robb as King in the North), even if their ends diverge.

For every hero, there is a foil, a counterpart whose successes and failures set the hero's own doings in high relief. Jaime Lannister, however, has many, and each one draws out an aspect of his failure as a hero. Closest to home are his siblings, one of whom, Cersei, is as like to Jaime as like can be, but for the fact that she is a woman. The other, Tyrion, is a dwarf, unwarlike and a shame to his father. Both, however, seem more cut out for the business of heroism than their much-feted brother. Cersei recounts how she and Jaime used to swap clothes as young children, and nobody could spot the deception. In her mind, at least, she is the one with the daring and courtcraft, while Jaime merely plays at the joust or withers away in a Stark prison. Whether she is right or wrong, her positions as queen and then queen regent bring her much more power than Jaime ever enjoys, and certainly she has the temper and charisma required of a leader of men, at least until her drinking starts to resemble that of her deceased husband. Jaime, for his part, is content to follow – not the most heroic of qualities. While Jaime and Cersei between them would make one decent epic hero, Tyrion is an altogether different paradigm: as physically unsuited to heroism as Cersei is, but unfettered by the chains of gender – and indeed of dynastic obligation. Still, of the three Lannister siblings, it is Tyrion who acts most heroically, both on the battlefield before King's Landing, in his wanderings across the Narrow Sea, and in his compassion toward and use of natural, human, and financial resources all around him. Jaime, though he conforms more easily than either of his siblings to the heroic norms society expects of noble-born children, nevertheless ends up a heroic disappointment.

An important part of what makes the epic tradition dynamic is the replaceability of the heroes, even while each is unique unto him or herself. In a basic sense, the economy of the heroic world makes this absolutely necessary. In order to keep a fresh supply of heroic cannon fodder, each of the heroes must be to an extent replaceable by someone else, otherwise neither individual battles nor the epic tradition itself can be perpetuated. Aeneas takes over from Achilles, who took over from Hercules, while a Jason might take over from Odysseus to continue a different branch of the tradition, and so on and so forth. Each generation, as we've seen, usually falls a bit short of the previous one, but the overall sense of epic as a never-ending project continues through to today. The primary quality of the epic hero is success in battle, which in the ancient world is measured by the number of enemy dead and spoils taken. Since epic heroes are primarily interested in fighting against other heroes or monsters, against whom they can honorably measure their worth, the people they kill, even when they do so in great quantity, are typically named and described. The progression of a hero through a battlefield is called an *aristeia*, or 'show of valor,' and a lack of an *aristeia* in turn entails a lack of quality as a hero. It is telling that Jaime has none to his name, at least so far as we can see. In fact, the only battles we see him engage in are ones when he fails: against the Stark forces in the Whispering Wood, when he is taken captive, and then against the Bloody Mummers, when he is no more successful.

So, if Jaime isn't much of a hero, what is he? There are a few ways to answer that question, and the first is to acknowledge that being a less successful hero is itself a vaunted tradition. We already saw that the heroic tradition is a diminishing one, so being a disappointment to someone older than yourself is itself a recognized epic activity. Further, as epic heroes aged, as Jaime does here, they came to occupy an interesting position, where they were still revered for their wisdom and experience but also mocked for their dwindling battle prowess. The aged Nestor in the *Iliad* is a good example of this trope, as is Aeneas' father, Anchises, a man who gets every direction he gives his son wrong, but is still followed and respected until his death. There are also moments when a hero is incompetent or foolish. Odysseus, despite his reputation for cunning, manages to lose all his companions on the way back to Ithaca, while Jason (of the Argonauts) can't prevent his wife from murdering their sons, and Aeneas repeatedly displays reluctance or poor decision-making in the pursuit of his stated objective. Jaime Lannister, on this reading, combines reluctance ('the things we do for love'), a resulting failure to achieve goals or impress in battle, and a sense that he is already fading into a nostalgic past. Rather than being part of the vibrant present, the heroes of Robert's Rebellion fight a losing battle against being entombed too soon in the monument of history. And in that sense, *Game of Thrones* is the story of a fraught and bloody generational transition, with one generation just growing out of fame, and another doing its very best to fight its way into the newly emptied limelight.[4]

Finally, we might look at a different answer: that Jaime Lannister is not so much an epic hero but a cipher of one. That is to say, that he looks and talks and behaves like a hero, but is in fact not the great and glorious protagonist, the Achilles of the story, but just a placeholder for other people to try to jostle their way into fame. One indication of this is that Jaime is one half of a set of twins. This is not to suggest that twins in the real world are ciphers of each other, but in ancient literature in particular twins often share a complex relationship wherein one acts as the other's alter ego, whether willfully or not. One of the best examples of this dynamic is in the twin sons of Oedipus, Eteocles and Polyneices, whose story is narrated in the epic poem *Thebaid*, written by Statius about a century after the *Aeneid* and under the Roman emperor

Domitian. Eteocles and Polyneices are already the inheritors of a
closer than normal relationship to the self: since they are the sons
of Oedipus and his mother, Jocasta, they are part of an incestuous
family and more than usually obsessed with defining and assert-
ing who and what they are, even to the point of war and mutual
destruction.[5] When their father abdicates his position as the king
of Thebes, the brothers are caught in a dilemma: since they are
twins, there is no way to establish who deserves to inherit the
kingdom. Instead, they decide to alternate years: each year one
would rule, and the other go into exile, with places swapped the
following year, and so on. This cunning plan, however, goes to
pieces when Eteocles refuses to give up the throne at the end of
the first year, and his twin decides to claim his right by recruiting
a vast army against Thebes.

The war on Thebes (or 'the Seven Against Thebes,' as the ancients
called it, to mark the seven heroes who led the attack) was part of
the generation before the Trojan War, and according to the chronological matrix, members of this generation were meant to be greater
and more heroic still than the men who laid siege to Troy, though
their sons contest that characterization.[6] This idea underlies the way
Statius tells the story in his *Thebaid*, making both the heroes and
their various actions hyperbolic and extreme, including the brothers'
hatred for each other. It is also the case that the *Thebaid* aims to
assert its own superiority to epics that came before it in historical
time, like the *Aeneid*, its main model and interlocutor, and other
versions of the myth of Thebes, like the fifth-century BC Greek
play *Seven Against Thebes* by the Athenian playwright Aeschylus,
or the lost epic on the subject by Greek poet Antimachus. Finally,
the literary taste of Statius' contemporaries was precisely for the
grotesque and creative displays of masculinity and death – this is,
after all, the age of the Colosseum and its larger-than-life gladiatorial battles, as well as reenactments of mythical themes in which
criminals were punished by playing out the deaths of mythological characters. Further, the emperor at the time, Domitian, was

himself one of two brothers (both emperors), who, though not twins, nevertheless had a close if complicated relationship, with each other as well as with their father. All these considerations play into the way the poem presents the relationship of the twins Eteocles and Polyneices, and they are all concerned with identity, one's place in the world, and the relationship between art and life. Statius wants to be seen as an alter ego of Vergil, just as Vergil did of Homer, while at the same time both also want to be better than their predecessors and set a bar which future generations will not be able to surpass.

This dynamic, too, is a good indicator that Jaime functions partially as a pointer to the way heroic careers can decline, which is itself a major theme of the *Game of Thrones* series: Robert Baratheon begins gloriously and becomes a drunk; Ned Stark begins honorably and dies a traitor; his son Robb makes an audacious start on a campaign for the throne and for vengeance, and dies ignominiously, and so on. Even Joffrey, whose only claim to epic heroism is his tremendous self-regard, comes to a suitably heinous end. This laundry list of disappointed hopes is, on the one hand, an authorial habit (Martin likes killing off characters as a way of keeping things interesting), but it is also a way of playing up some of the inevitable consequences of epic heroic ideology: you either die in a blaze of glory, or you suffer the indignities of reintegration. Tywin Lannister, who was particularly averse to failure, would have put it differently, though the expression is that of his daughter Cersei: 'You win or you die.' Jaime, like all the other heroic characters of *Game of Thrones*, exists in the grey spaces in between.

The twinning relationship is a convenient and economical tool for characters, poets, politicians, and philosophers to think and talk about identity politics, literary and ideological inheritances and attachments, and one's place within a bigger hierarchy of roles, importance, or prominence. Twins in literature, in other words, are themselves already a cipher, a way for us to think about how we fit and how we might have fitted, if we were still ourselves but slightly different. This applies also to sibling relationships, like that between the violent Sandor and Gregor Clegane, whose interactions are likewise characterized by violence. Over time their kinship only emphasizes their divergent trajectories: Sandor is increasingly humanized while Gregor becomes ever more dehumanized. Because of this, it isn't always the twins themselves who struggle with their identities: Eteocles and Polyneices, for instance, are both convinced they are as different as can be from the other, and their hatred for each other is deep and heartfelt. We might interpret the fact that they kill each other at the end to be a sign of some self-loathing, but the real interest lies not in how they feel about each other, but in how other people think about themselves in relation to the brothers. The hero Tydeus, whom Eteocles recruits to help him reclaim his right, is thoroughly devoted to his dear friend, so much so that Eteocles decides to send him as ambassador to Thebes, to convince his brother to cede the throne before any bloodshed can happen. This turns out to be an odd choice, because Tydeus is temperamental, rude, and uninterested in a peaceable solution, so that the diplomatic meeting deteriorates quickly into a shouting match, at the end of which Eteocles attempts to have Tydeus ambushed and killed. But what is especially interesting here is that Tydeus is utterly devoted to his friend, so much so that he sees himself as the true alter ego of Eteocles, usurping the place of his real twin, whom Tydeus has no ability to see as his friend's kin, or indeed as his biological twin.

Some might point out, and rightly so, that Tydeus' ability to move beyond the superficial likeness of the twins into their motivations and sense of justice marks him out as more astute than he is usually given credit for. It remains the case, however, that visual likeness is important in epic twinning, and especially in *Game of Thrones*. In the *Iliad*, Achilles lends his armor to Patroclus, and the resulting likeness means that Patroclus also takes on Achilles' fate to die violently at Troy. Jaime Lannister, by contrast, is constantly replaced by similar-looking versions of himself. Cersei, the closest to him, remembers herself as a girl failing to understand why she and Jaime were taught different things when they could visually pass for each other. As a woman and a queen, she commits incest with him partially because they are so much alike, but when Jaime is gone she replaces him with their cousin Lancel, who looks a bit like Jaime and fancies himself a bit like his more famous cousin as well. Ironically, both Jaime and Lancel end up shadows of their former selves, Jaime because of the loss of his hand, Lancel because of his devotion to asceticism. Narcissism seems to drive the Lannisters, and like the famous mythological Narcissus it is self-love that leads to the inevitable wasting of the Lannisters' former good looks, trapped in their attempts to become closer to the object of their affections than is physically possible.

There is another member of this triad, who, like Lancel, is a younger version of Jaime: Loras Tyrell. Unlike Lancel, Loras seems destined to succeed in usurping Jaime's place as the court's golden boy, even to the point of defeating the Kingslayer in the joust. Like Lancel, he has illicit erotic ties to the royal family, and like Lancel he represents a physical type associated already in antiquity with youth: slim and light versus Jaime's greater bulk. More than Lancel, however, Loras has several more substantive attributes that make him a new Jaime. For one, they both have ambitious sisters, to whom they are remarkably similar, and who in effect boss them around. Margaery and Loras are not twins, but by description they are similar enough to be taken as twins. Like Jaime and Cersei, they operate in tandem, and in focus around the king's body. Cersei is married to the king, whereas Jaime guards him. Margaery is married first to a wannabe king, then to Tommen the boy king, while Loras guards both and does rather more with Renly, yet another brother-pretender. Margaery herself is involved in a parallel relationship with Cersei, who is convinced Margaery is fated to be her replacement. Jaime and Loras, meanwhile, both end up members of the Kingsguard because of their respective failures to gain the true object of their affection: Loras' is dead,

Jaime's is married. Loras' career also tracks Jaime's closely: a noble upbringing, courtly success, and an attempt to rise to power on the wings of a coup d'état. Pointedly, Jaime and the Lannisters rise by attaching themselves to the victorious Baratheons; Loras succeeds by detaching himself from genuine Baratheons and attaching himself instead to the victorious Lannisters, who parade themselves as Baratheons. This act of repetition, however unconscious or unintended, is telling. Identity becomes blurred and difficult to define in the context of civil war.

THE FEMALE HERO

As ever in times of political crisis, the whole world seems to participate in the death throes, with strange omens and stranger things emerging from the depths of myth and legend. It is no coincidence that *Game of Thrones* opens with a rare direwolf sighting, or that the red comet bleeds the sky as the War of the Five Kings begins, or that at the same time White Walkers rise in the North and dragons in the East. Epic heroism, for all that it follows fairly clear paradigms, likewise participates in this mentality: when heroes explore far and wide, or when a war reaches a particularly long duration or height of intensity, unusual heroes are often called for. In antiquity, these unlikely heroes were often warrior women, an exotic and strange sight in societies which kept their women strictly off the fighting fields. This was true in history as well as in myth, as the Roman (and modern!) fascination with Queen Boudicca attests: not only was Boudicca a leader of men, but she also participated in battle herself and suffered a heroic death on the battlefield. The Egyptian queen Cleopatra, lover first of Julius Caesar and then of Mark Antony, was a dab hand at political intrigue (she was 17 when she manipulated the Romans into helping her regain her throne), but also participated alongside her husband Antony in the decisive battle of Actium in 31 BC. Antony's ships went down to heavy and decisive defeat, and Cleopatra fled the battle shamefully, at least according to Roman sources. But she held out in Alexandria until the Romans came, and refused to submit to their captivity. Rather than being led in chains throughout the streets of Rome, the crowd jeering and booing while she and her kingdom's riches were paraded through the city for the enjoyment of the people, she chose to commit suicide – an act which even the Romans, who loathed her, could admire.[7]

Both Boudicca and Cleopatra, however, were foreign women, and as such already objects of fascination and fetishization. Proper Roman women – and Westerosi women – did not fight, with one notable exception. That one exception is Brienne of Tarth, who is both mannish in appearance and surpasses many men in war. Arya Stark too is in this mold, growing up jealous of her brothers' training in sword fighting, a tomboyish contrast to her more stereotypically feminine sister Sansa, and eventually travelling as a boy and taking up a life as an assassin across the Narrow Sea. Daenerys Targaryen leads her Unsullied into battle, but she herself is isolated from the fighting by her bloodriders. Whereas Arya and Daenerys are nevertheless pictured as physically small, dexterous, and attractive, and whereas both participate in battle somewhat indirectly, Brienne comes close to a carbon copy of the stereotypical male knight: imposing of stature, she fights in her own right, and even comes to own a sword of Valyrian steel, forged from Ned Stark's greatsword Ice. Oathkeeper, as the sword is called, has been given her by Jaime Lannister, and Brienne intends to use it in her search for the missing Sansa – a desire to fulfill her duty that contrasts with Jaime's past failure and represents Jaime's evolution of character through his relationship with Brienne.

Brienne herself is fundamentally modeled on the ancient Amazons, warrior women from the edge of civilization. The Amazons have a peculiar status in Greek myth: because of their exotic origin, and because of their countercultural existence without men and away from male dominance, they were seen as a threat to be vanquished in order for civilization to prevail. As such, they are usually depicted as enemies of the Greek heroes, and wars with the Amazons are depicted in temple friezes in parallel with wars with other mythical creatures like the centaurs or the monstrous Titans. Hercules and his companions fight the Amazons when they go to retrieve the belt of Hippolyta the Amazon queen as Hercules' ninth labor. Although Hippolyta promises to give him the belt, the goddess Hera goads the Amazons to drive away Hercules and his men, and in the ensuing battle Hercules kills Hippolyta and strips off her belt, much as a warrior in the field would take away the spoils of a fallen enemy.

Late in the Trojan War, after the death of Hector, the Trojans find themselves in need of allies to fill their depleted ranks. Aid comes from the east in the shape of troops of Amazons, the fabled ancient women warriors, who cut off their right breast (or simply did not cover their left breast), wore trousers, and had no need

19. Achilles and Penthesileia

for men. Leading them was their queen Penthesileia, who was so lovely that the great Achilles himself was said to fall in love with her at the very moment of killing her, and he is even driven to weep over her dead body. Tyrion does a similar thing to Shae, his former lover turned informer: after he chokes her with the gold chain he has given her, he apologizes to her dead body. For Jaime Lannister, however, there isn't even this measure of cold comfort: instead, as he journeys through the Riverlands with Brienne the Beauty, he finds that heroes and Amazons have rather a lot in common, both excluded from 'normal' society, and expected to conform to impossible standards.

Penthesileia's literary descendants conform to the same basic structure: they typically fight on the other side of the war (even if they're subsequently converted to the 'right' side), are never quite able to triumph over all the male heroes, and, crucially, are made to represent something different and exotic. It is no wonder, then, that the other prominent warrior woman in *Game of Thrones*, Theon Greyjoy's sister Asha/Yara, hails from the Iron Islands, a society worshipping the Drowned God and practicing a marauder's code that is alien to the rest of the Seven Kingdoms. Unlike her brother Theon, Asha/Yara is ironborn to her back teeth, right down to possession of her own warship, her father's approval, and considerable influence among her people. She is hampered only by her gender, by being the daughter rather than the son, a biological obstacle she can never quite overcome despite being more competent and less desperate than her brother. A pertinent comparison to Asha/Yara is Artemisia, queen of Halicarnassus, who appears briefly in Herodotus as she leads a contingent of ships in aid of the Persian invasion of Greece. She appears last in the list of Persian allies given in Herodotus, a prime spot, in large part by virtue of the novelty of a warrior woman ('It seems to me a marvel that she – a woman – should have taken part in the campaign against Greece,' says the historian).[8] Of all the commanders under the great king, she is the only one to warn him against engaging the Greeks in a sea battle at Salamis, though the king refuses to listen. During the battle itself, her main contribution is to ram one of her own allies' ships, for reasons not fully known to Herodotus. But even this action redounds to her favor. Disappointed with the showing of his other commanders, King Xerxes sees this as an act of bravery. 'My men have become women and my women men,' he says – and he does not mean this as a compliment.

What, then, does it mean to be female in Westeros? The very first time Cersei Lannister is mentioned in the *Game of Thrones* books, she is nothing much more than a piece of luggage, a part of the king's retinue. 'Cersei and the children travel with them,' Catelyn Stark informs her husband, on the eve of the royal visit to Winterfell, and adds, 'the queen's brothers are also in the party.' Ned, for his part, is less than pleased: 'an infestation of Lannisters,' he calls the visitors, and while Catelyn at least accords the queen the use of her proper name, to Ned she is 'the Lannister woman,' on whose teat Prince Tommen was suckling (*GT* 27). This dialogue tells us more about the Starks and their attitudes than it does about Cersei herself, for here already is a woman reduced to her essential functions. Despite the fact that she is queen, Cersei is here merely the king's accompaniment, the sister of her brothers, the mother of his children. Even in this role she is not accorded her own personality: she is merely her gender ('woman') and function ('teat'). As Ned finds out, however, to see Cersei as only a spare part in the paraphernalia of the Seven Kingdoms is not only to underestimate her, but also to place his own head in mortal danger.

For Cersei is a grande dame in the best tradition of the genre: a mother fiercely protective of her children, a wife scorned, and a woman consumed by ambition. One of the more successful women of Westeros, she is not always in full control of her power, and she is given both to wine and to incest, two qualities that ancient authors ascribe to men, and especially to tyrants. The ancients had a name for women like her: man-hearted, and the specific woman thus described is another woman immersed to her ears in court intrigue. When Agamemnon, the king of Mycenae, sails for Troy, he finds that the winds of the crossing will not cooperate. To appease them and ensure passage, he must sacrifice his youngest daughter, Iphigeneia. Child sacrifice is not unheard of in ancient mythology, but it always bodes ill for anyone who practices it, and so it does for Agamemnon.[9] What he thinks of as necessary sacrifice, his wife, Clytemnestra, sees as opportunistic murder, and rather than keep hearth and kingdom together, she falls instead into an affair with her husband's cousin, Aegisthus, who bears a familial grudge against Agamemnon. As it happens, Aegisthus is himself a product of incest, like Cersei's children, and as a rival for the throne of Mycenae and seeker of a long-standing vengeance, neither he nor Clytemnestra has any love for the king. And when Agamemnon finally returns after ten years away, Clytemnestra lures him into a bath, where she slaughters him and the beautiful young mistress he brought as a captive from Troy. She and Aegisthus go on to rule Mycenae for seven more years before they, too, are killed by her revenge-seeking son Orestes. The story might have resonated with Cersei, who arranges to kill her husband, hides the illegitimacy of his children, and broods long over the injustices Robert Baratheon has dealt her.

But despite the fact that the Agamemnon story is part of the Returns from Troy, and features in the *Odyssey*, it is not itself an epic story; it is, instead, best represented in a tragedy of fifth-century Athens, by a poet who described his plays as 'slices' from the banquets of Homer.[10] Tragedy, in fact, would suit Cersei much better than epic, a genre which, for all its capaciousness, leaves its women by and large secondary to men. Tragedy, however, focuses heavily on domestic intrigue and political infighting, and female voices often take the rebellious lead as they struggle against the authority of the male-dominated state. Such women were described with verve as living, breathing people with ambitions, plans, and emotional conflicts: witness Medea's determination to kill her own children, even as she is torn apart by her maternal love for them. Tragedy, further, took place in a confined personal space: usually the palace, or, as per the conventions of ancient tragedy, just outside the royal dwelling, where the audience could see events unfold. Epic, by contrast, was played out on battlefields and in council halls, where men performed feats of masculinity to be admired by other men and by women safely behind city walls.

If in tragedy certain transgressive women can appear to control the fate of the city or state, epic women – even impressive ones – tend to be either sidelined from power (as Telemachus begins to take over from his mother, Penelope, in the *Odyssey*) or derelict in their political duty (as Dido in the *Aeneid*). Women like Cersei, with a keen interest in wielding political power, tend to be left out of the epic world, except among the gods, where figures like Juno and Athena can play by different rules from mortal women. Still, a few glimpses suggest a richer world beneath the surface. Hector's wife, Andromache, gives him cogent advice on strategy, which he seems not to have found for himself.[11] Penelope, Odysseus' patient wife, manipulates the suitors for 20 long years, and manages to keep her husband's estate running well enough to sustain them all.

But perhaps the most Cersei-like of these epic women is the fabled Helen of Troy, whose beauty was legendary enough to incite an alliance of all of Greece against the rich and powerful Troy. Helen's guilt in the matter of the war was much contested in antiquity, with poets and scholars calling her both an adulteress and a hapless victim. There was even a story that Helen was never in Troy at all, but instead spent the war waiting patiently for her husband in Egypt, while in Troy men fought and died for a mere *eidolon*, a figment of the imagination.[12] Whatever people thought of her, she certainly aroused enough interest for two princes to risk all for her favors, and for generations thereafter to tell the story. In Troy she was hated by the other women, who saw her as the cause of their men's deaths. The conduct of her new husband, Paris, a pretty boy with not much to recommend him, shamed her at times, and when the horse appeared before the walls of Troy, she mumbled incantations around it to draw out its secrets, for all the good it did the Trojans.[13] Her failure perhaps secured her survival, since both victors and losers in the war wanted her dead in the aftermath. Her beauty played its part for certain, but it generally held that she, despite all the animosity of her exciting life, lived to rich old age as queen in Sparta – a fate that many a woman in the Red Keep, including its queen, can only hope to match. Cersei, too, knows how to use her body to her advantage, and to manipulate the men around her, but unlike Helen she is never the ultimate object of men's desire. In fact, part of Cersei's tragedy is that another woman, something of a cipher, more properly plays the part of Helen as the cause of war: Lyanna Stark, over whom Rhaegar and Robert had fought. In fact, it is Robert's uttering of Lyanna's name when consummating his wedding to Cersei that poisons their marriage and turns Cersei – at least in her view – from a beautiful and innocent pawn into a Machiavellian states-woman with a grudge.

Cersei is certainly a scheming queen, but one thing she is not, at least, is a witch or sorceress. In fact, she is terrified of a prophecy she received as a girl from a foreign *maegi*, who predicted that another queen will come, younger and more beautiful, who will steal her power and turn her greatest joy to ashes. The coincidence of timing focuses Cersei's attention on Margaery Tyrell, who Cersei believes (as it turns out, correctly) to have connived at Joffrey's death. What Cersei does not know is that another queen is rising in the east, likewise younger and more beautiful, who has her sights set on returning to Westeros and claiming her birthright. This triangulation of women parallels what is happening across the land on the male side: a question not only of who will come into power, but also of what kind of power they will bring with them to the throne. Like Cersei, Margaery's power is rooted in her beauty, upbringing, and family wealth, all of which allow her to marry her way into the centers of power. Daenerys Targaryen, on the other hand, has been robbed of all the advantages both Cersei and Margaery enjoy: she has no family left to rely on, her upbringing is erratic and leaves little room for training in courtly behavior, and she and her brother have been forced to sell off whatever Targaryen heirlooms they might have had in order to survive in exile. Still, the difference is ultimately not so great: Dany is in a position to rule her own destiny because she comes into her own not as an exile, but as *khaleesi*, and because she is in possession of dragons, the emblem and symbol of her house. She thus has both position and resources, both of which she has obtained by marriage to a powerful man. This, in fact, is where Cersei and Dany are most alike: both have been pawns in alliances made by their menfolk for the benefit of the whole house, and neither has had much say in the matter. When their husbands die, they finally begin to exercise power in their own right, and the difference between their styles is telling: Cersei is driven by the need to protect her children and a desire to be involved finally in affairs of state. Daenerys is driven by the need to protect her *khalasar*, especially since she has been left with those too weak to leave her for a more powerful *khal*. She also has little choice: failing in her new position of leadership means a certain death for her and for her people. And Dany, too, has her own prophecy from a *maegi*, cursing her to a life of childlessness.

Magical women are very common in ancient literature, especially among women of the lower social orders. And unlike in the Middle Ages, when magic was often associated with the devil, magical practice was rife across the ancient world in largely legitimate forms. We have surviving curse tablets, on which people ask one of the infernal gods and goddesses to, for instance, sabotage someone who stole or damaged their possessions, or to pray that the litigant on the opposing side of a trial perform badly, that someone might be compelled to fall in love with them, or that a rival for a

20. Roman curse tablet

lover's affection might meet some horrible end. And while none of the great ladies of Westeros practices magic, some of the great mythological women of the ancient world were notorious for their supernatural powers. Cersei Lannister's own namesake, the witch Circe, is the daughter of the Sun, and has the power to turn men into animals. When Odysseus arrives on her island, she turns all his men into pigs, while he stays with her for two long years and enjoys the delights of her palace. Medea, a princess from the Black Sea, whom Jason brings home as his wife when he returns from his quest for the Golden Fleece, is also descended from the Sun, is powerful enough to brew an immortality potion, and is cruel enough to kill those who get in her way, from her brother to her children. At the end of the play named after her, she leaves the stage in a chariot drawn by dragons, clasping to her bosom the bodies of the sons she has just killed.

Medea and Circe both have something quite important in common with Helen of Troy in addition to their abilities with cauldrons and magic: they are all descended from divine beings. Medea and Circe both descend from the Sun, and Helen, who also seems to be a dab hand at potions, is the daughter of Zeus, the great god of the Greek pantheon. This divine connection partly explains their affinity with the supernatural: like their parents, they can do more than mere mortals; and perhaps also like the gods, they have less care for ethical scruples. The same semidivine sangfroid and reputation for supernatural ability is not the province of any Westerosi woman, but rather comes from the exotic East. This foreignness has always been a property of magic: Medea comes from the Black Sea, a region considered exotic in most of fifth-century Greece and renowned for its witchy ways well into the Roman empire. The magical nymphs Odysseus encounters

21. Mithraic relief from Fiano Romano

are not only not entirely human, but also live on lonely islands in a very sketchy mythical Mediterranean, an environment beyond sure human knowledge, where really anything might happen (on another island, Odysseus meets a Cyclops, a one-eyed monster who feasts on Odysseus' men but is tenderly protective of his herd of sheep – he, too, is the son of a god). Coming from somewhere far away and unknown inspires easy fear and easier admiration, and from there the road to supernatural powers is short. In Westeros, the further away the better in terms of supernatural ability, and the furthest away is beyond doubt Melisandre of Asshai, a place so distant none of the characters ever reach it, which nobody can really describe, and which even the maps show only on their very edges.

Melisandre, or the Red Woman, as she is also known, is a priestess of R'hllor, a god of light who is worshipped by the burning of great fires. The Greco-Roman world worshipped the sun in many guises, including as Helios, an anthropomorphic deity, and as part of an eastern cult called Mithraism, which was popular among soldiers and whose main hero, Mithras, was regularly featured as feasting with the sun god Sol. In its association with the sun and concern with rebirth, Mithraism is often seen as a precursor of Christianity, but the Romans thought its origins were Persian and Zoroastrian.[14] Across Persia, the god of the empire and its great king was Ahura Mazda (Ormazd), the supreme spirit of goodness locked in battle with the agents of evil. Zoroastrian worship centers around fire: prayers are said in the presence of light (either the sun or fire), and during the Achaemenid and Sassanian empires, great sacred fires burned day and night across the realm.

This immortal tension between light and darkness makes Melisandre all the more interesting: a priestess of light and worshipper of fire, she nevertheless comes from Asshai-by-the-Shadow, and she herself preaches the interconnectedness of light and shadow, a tenet of a version of Zoroastrianism called Zurvanism.[15] Her main mission, however, is to find Azor Ahai, the 'prince that was promised,' whom she finds, of all people, in the dour Stannis Baratheon. What exactly the reborn Azor Ahai is meant to accomplish is not yet clear, but her focus on him is messianic and mysterious, and the methods she is willing to resort to show a familiar indifference to moral scruple. Women with seemingly supernatural powers could certainly serve a cult in ancient myth: the female followers of Dionysus or Bacchus could be imagined as exotic, potent, frenzied, and dangerous, like their god. But the witches and sorceresses, like Medea, were generally viewed differently, as independent agents who were threatening precisely because they were able to divorce themselves from the normal bonds of human society and interdependence. In this way, Melisandre straddles two different conceptions of the supernaturally gifted woman: on the one hand, a powerfully autonomous figure, separate from the community around her but holding great authority; on the other hand, a representative of a religion that by its nature demands worship from all and, aptly, spreads like wildfire.

When we first encounter Melisandre, she has already established herself in Stannis' court. She advises the king, sits next to him at banquets, and has infiltrated the queen's inner circle, so that she has a growing following of the queen's men. Her influence is so great that she even convinces Stannis to abolish the worship of the Seven and burn their effigies, taking up the worship of R'hllor instead. Even Stannis' banner now proclaims his new faith, with the prancing stag of House Baratheon trapped within the flaming heart of the Lord of Light. The worship of R'hllor is spreading in the Free Cities as well, so we know that Melisandre isn't alone in preaching the faith, but she has succeeded in attaching her cult to political power and her iconoclasm suggests that her purpose isn't only to find Azor Ahai, but also to proselytize for her god, to bring his worship to more and more people. Meanwhile, the hardship caused by civil war, widespread destruction, and the coming of winter means that Westeros is ripe both for adopting new faiths, but also for re-entrenching old ones, as Cersei finds out when she attempts to use the newly resurgent church of the Seven. As a growing number of farmers, merchants, hedge knights, and other small folk become destitute, the rift between the wealth of the Church and the poverty of the people becomes untenable, until violence removes one High Septon and replaces him with another. The new leader of the Church is much more willing to engage in hard-nosed politics. Like Melisandre, he aims to control the royal family, first by promising them what they need (Melisandre offers power, the septon money), and then by accruing enough power and influence to become a mover and shaker in his own right.

The process by which religions ebb and flow is well documented in antiquity, especially in the rise of Christianity. The Roman empire comprised people of various religions, including multiple versions of polytheism, and Rome itself in consequence was home to many forms of worship. For the Romans what mattered was maintaining the cosmic balance in their favor, which meant that they had to ensure the gods were pleased with Rome and its doings at all times. In order to establish this, every public action started with the taking of the auspices, which involved guessing divine disposition through a set of techniques: finding clues in animal entrails, or in the flight patterns of birds, or the feeding patterns of sacred chickens, and so on. Divine displeasure stopped all action until whatever problems the gods indicated could be corrected and the balance restored. As long as nobody did anything to upset this precarious balance, the Romans were happy for most faiths to exist side by side. Suppression was political in its aims, by and large, since the Romans were well aware that religion bolstered the political cohesion of a people and also that religious association could be convenient cover for all sorts of clandestine plotting, not to mention other immoral behaviors.

Early Christians ran up precisely against two of these hot-button issues. They refused to acknowledge the Roman gods (which by this point also included the Roman emperor) as powers to be propitiated and kept on their side. They also convened in private places, men and women together, and did all sorts of unspeakable things like eat the body of their god – or, at least, that is what it would have looked like to the average Roman, who tended to interpret the world in terms he was already familiar with. As Christianity spread and grew, so did Roman aversion to it: suspicion became savage persecution, especially as emperors understood that Christians made a convenient target for populist fears and aggression. The situation became better when two things changed: first, when an increasing number of the senatorial elite took up Christianity, thus adding political weight and voice, and second, when the emperor Constantine took up a version of Christianity and made it the state religion. A Stannis victory might well have spelled the same fate for Westeros, with the Red God trampling over the Faith of the Seven, just as a Lannister entrenchment might yet bring out more of the church militant. But Westeros' religious history shows that, as in Rome, the old and the new could exist side by side, albeit not without tensions. If religion is to play a large role in the development and potential resolution of affairs in Westeros – and at this stage that certainly appears to be the case – then it is female agency of one kind or another, magical or political, that will be instrumental in determining the specific contours of the outcome.

Despite her stature, Cersei Lannister is not the only model for women's political behavior in Westeros. Although young women like Sansa and Margaery aspire to imitate her – indeed, to become her – their view of womanhood is limited in important ways. Most significantly, their power is restricted in that it can rarely be exercised officially. This does not mean that they subscribe to a traditionalist view of a woman's role: despite the fact that Cersei, Catelyn Stark, Sansa, or Margaery all conform to societal expectations, including that of the men in their lives, their roles are hardly apolitical. They serve as castellans of their husbands' keeps, as regents and stewards in their absence, and have a pervasive

22. Cornelia Africana and the Gracchi

influence on the goings-on at court. Catelyn even serves as her son's ambassador to Renly and reports back on his death – but even she is reconciled to having to wait endlessly behind the lines while the menfolk, and those few women who dare to buck expectations, do the fighting.

In this they take after the great noble ladies of Republican and Imperial Rome, who, though their power might be termed 'soft,' were far from excluded from the affairs of state. For instance, Cornelia, the daughter of the great Scipio Africanus who saved Rome from Hannibal, raised two sons. Both turned out to be radical politicians who spent their career fighting against rising inequality following Rome's rapid expansion into empire. Both died for their political beliefs, and both owed much of their ideology to their mother's upbringing: she was the one who chose their teachers, who exposed them to Greek ideas about democracy, and

23. Julia Domna

who remained an object of adoration in Rome long after her sons'
death. Her granddaughter Fulvia, meanwhile, married three men
of similarly radical flair, including a young Mark Antony. Cicero's
wife Terentia controlled the household purse, while Hortensia,
the daughter of a great public speaker, led an all-female appeal
to the Senate.[16] When the republic changed to the autocracy of
the Caesars, the women of the imperial family connived with the
best of them. Augustus' wife Livia was said to have poisoned her
stepsons and all other contenders, the better to ensure her own
son's path to the throne. Agrippina the Younger, mother of the
emperor Nero, kept her son alive long enough to inherit, and then
advised him as fledgling emperor. One of the earliest signs of his
madness was his repeated attempts – eventually successful – to have
her murdered. Much later on, the empress Julia Domna wielded
enough power to be accused of treason and adultery, though neither

charge stuck. She toured the military camps with her husband the emperor, and later on acted as mediator between her feuding sons. What these women all had in common was their determination to make a mark, to be part of the world and the society in which they lived. If they couldn't do it openly like their menfolk, or like exotic witch-women, they nevertheless did it within the confines of their gender roles.

THE UNLIKELY HERO

Westeros, it seems, faces not only a brutal civil war, but also a severe crisis of heroism. Jaime Lannister, and the other young men like him, struggle with the generational gap: neither as heroic as their fathers, nor as the heroes of old, they cannot convert their education at the jousting fields into glory on the battlefields. The women of Westeros, meanwhile, find themselves hemmed in not only by the horrors of civil war, but also by the restrictions of gender and a host of menfolk who expect them to conform to gender norms rather than fill the leadership vacuum on the throne. Those who try might either face odium like Cersei, ridicule like Brienne, or find their fortunes elsewhere, like Daenerys. In this strange situation, hope, it seems, must come from unlikely sources: whether from outside (again like either Daenerys or Melisandre), or from among the ranks of the men at home who are not deemed fit for heroic service.

A cross-sectional view of the heroes at Troy, and indeed in most other epic stories, will reveal a fairly broad distribution of ages and talents. Some are old, some are young. Some have the loveliness of youth still upon their cheeks, while others are scarred with old wounds. Almost all are fierce warriors, but some excel in hand-to-hand combat while others fight better with the spear or the bow, and others still speak well and counsel wisely; this range of specialties is celebrated regularly in the heroic athletic competitions held to commemorate fallen comrades. But of all the epic wars fought in antiquity, one participant stands out for being ugly and deformed, the bow-legged and lame Thersites. He appears exactly once in the *Iliad*, when he rails against Agamemnon and the other Greek leaders and is sharply rebuked by Odysseus, who promises to drive him naked from the Greek camp if he catches him again speaking out against his betters. Thersites is meant to be an example of the simple soldier who came to Troy at his king's behest, and is now, after nine long years, starting to grow restless for either home or victory. He is singled out by name from among the mass of soldiers (some of whom also receive a stern talking-to from Odysseus, but not of the same vitriol, nor with the shame Odysseus dishes out to Thersites). He is also the ugliest of all the men who come to Troy, not only limping and bow-legged, but also stooped in the shoulders and with few hairs on his narrow head, and he cannot, it seems, keep his mouth shut, always baiting and railing against the leaders to get a laugh out of his fellow foot soldiers. Thersites' insubordination is swiftly and harshly dealt with, and it's clear that Odysseus allows himself to do this because Thersites is drawn as a perfectly inferior being in looks, martial ability, and social class. Everything about him marks him out as unfit for epic performance, and he is only there to be taught a richly deserved lesson.

His character doesn't seem to improve in other versions: he is said to meet his end at Achilles' hands because he rips out the eyes of the dead Amazon Penthesileia, and in another version he mocks Achilles for crying, to similar results. But Thersites is also there to expose or capture the class hypocrisy that pervades epic: Achilles kills Thersites because he violated a corpse, but Achilles himself had done exactly the same thing and worse, dragging the corpse of Hector round and round the walls of Troy and leaving it unburied for the dogs and birds to prey on. Odysseus allows himself to threaten and shame Thersites into tears, but Odysseus himself is also described as short and bow-legged, and his main prowess is in cunning and speech more than in outright fighting (though he's no slouch in battle). What is allowed to a noble is punished in the common man, and there are even some famous readers of the *Iliad* who have interpreted the critical treatment of Thersites to be Homer's way of deflecting from a view that would otherwise have been too disruptive to contemporary social norms, too incendiary. Thersites' punishment allows the audience to be exposed to the biting lessons of his speech, while not leaving them so incensed at his presumption that they find fault with Homer's presentation.[17]

Westeros has its own Thersites, and one who would have immediately recognized in his own life many of the indignities Thersites suffers in his brief moment of fame. Tyrion Lannister, although not a bastard, does not enjoy his father's affection and barely receives his recognition as a legitimate son. As a dwarf he is mocked, faces difficulties in access and credibility, and has to rely on his native cunning to make his path in the world. However, unlike Thersites, Tyrion cannot even fade into anonymity: when he tries to settle down with a commonfolk girl, his father finds out and via Jaime deceives Tyrion into thinking she's a whore, before forcing his son (and all of his guardsmen) to rape and abandon her. Nor is Tyrion allowed recognition for his prodigious intelligence: his management of King's Landing is barely acknowledged by his father or sister, nor his crucial role in neutralizing Stannis' fleet. When he gives his nephew a rare book, chosen to provide young Joffrey some historical examples he might follow, Joffrey uses his new sword to hack the book into pieces. And during the Purple Wedding the guests are treated to an entertainment of dwarves riding pigs, a show calculated to offend and humiliate – and if Tyrion should somehow have missed the clues, Joffrey then demands that Tyrion ride the pig himself for his guests' amusement.

Despite all this, Tyrion is without doubt one of the more beloved characters in the vast cast of *Game of Thrones*. George R. R. Martin has published a book of his sayings and witticisms, and network analyses have shown him to be the most important of the characters, at least in terms of how many other characters he engages with.[18] This distinction alone would certainly make him a serious, if unlikely, contender to that all-important title to the heroic economy: the best of the heroes. But does that suffice to make Tyrion a hero? He is, after all, almost Jaime's diametric opposite: ugly while Jaime is beautiful, weak while Jaime is strong, bookish while Jaime is equipped for the work of battle. And unlike Jaime, whose heart and body is given to only one woman (albeit his own twin sister), Tyrion is a womanizer of some renown, especially given to frequenting whorehouses wherever he goes. Tyrion is also given to drink, blunt speech, and myriad other vices – none of which characterizes the average strapping knight of Westeros. These characteristics were, however, normally assigned to sufferers of dwarfism and other deformities in the ancient world, since the Greeks and Romans generally took deformity or disability as markers of barbarism or other types of inferiority. Although representations of dwarves are frequent, much of their appeal is owed to a fetishizing interest in grotesquerie, and we often see, for instance, dwarves depicted with a disproportionately sized phallus, possibly to indicate abnormal lustfulness.

And yet, it is only Tyrion, of all the people involved in the War of the Five Kings, who actually manages to accomplish anything: he fights in a real battle and runs a city through famine and siege. He has real relationships with real people, as well as political allegiances with both high and low. And Tyrion is also by far the best traveled of the *Game of Thrones* cast: from the Wall to Slaver's Bay, he makes journeys in which he sees the wonders of the world, gets himself into and out of various kinds of trouble, and makes new allies into the bargain. Even the womanizing is part and parcel of a heroic lifestyle. The heroes of the *Iliad*, after all, are only in Troy because of a woman, and the great quarrel that divides Achilles and Agamemnon, and drives the entire plot of the poem, is likewise over a woman. In the *Aeneid*, Aeneas comes very close to abandoning his divine mission over his love affair with Queen Dido of Carthage, and when he finally sneaks away in the night and eventually makes it to

Italy, one of the points of contention between him and the native inhabitants of Italy is over another woman: the daughter of the king, Lavinia, who was already as good as promised to another. In the *Iliad*, when Hector fears for his wife's fate after his death and the fall of Troy, he imagines her, a princess of Troy, as a maidservant to a haughty Greek woman. Epic heroes traffic in women in the same way they traffic in spoils: as an inalienable part of the rewards of martial performance on the battlefield. For Tyrion, women are a compensation for the hardships of his life rather than a reward for accomplishment, but they are part of the hedonism that attends the lifestyle of the heroic.

To be properly heroic, however, one must perform acts of heroism, and here a hero has two options. One could either be the swashbuckling type who fights for king and country and usually perishes (or comes very close to perishing) in a blaze of glory. Or, if one has survived one's warlike urges, one could embark on a quest, whether one to return home, to find a special object, or to embark on exploration. If these types seem familiar, it is because they rank among the most familiar plot types humanity possesses. The war narrative runs continuously from the *Iliad* to *Great Wall*, while the quest narrative runs equally continuously from the *Odyssey* to *Lost*. Some stories combine the two. The *Aeneid* starts out as a quest plot, and switches to a war narrative once it gets to where it's going. The *Harry Potter* series likewise incorporates both quests (usually for objects) and heroic fighting, whether on or off the screen, and much the same can be said of *Lord of the Rings* and *Star Wars*. *Game of Thrones*, for its part, contains a lot of fighting and a lot of voyaging, and many characters participate in both: Jaime and Brienne, for instance, journey together from Riverrun to King's Landing, and Brienne continues from there on a quest for Sansa while Jaime stays behind to take up his duty to the Kingsguard and his family.

We've already seen some of the features that make Tyrion a remarkably Odyssean hero: his penchant for taking long trips, his intellectual curiosity, and his ability to present different faces and facets of his personality to different people. All these are emblematic of Odysseus *polytropos*, Odysseus of the many turns, angles, faces, and wiles. But although Odysseus is mostly famous as the protagonist of the *Odyssey*, he is one of the more important heroes of the *Iliad* as well. In fact, he is responsible for ending the war in Troy, a feat that all the heroes of Greece could not accomplish in ten years of fighting. When it becomes clear that Troy is impregnable, Odysseus turns his mind to finding a strategy that could breach the walls instead of sheer fighting. With the aid of the goddess Athena, he oversees the building of the Trojan horse, an enormous and hollow wooden horse whose belly contains a troop of Greek soldiers. The Greeks themselves retreat, leaving only the horse on the shore, along with an informant, Sinon, whose task is to convince the Trojans that the horse is a gift to Athena, and that they should therefore bring it within the city walls. Rejoicing at the war's end, the Trojans drag the horse into the city square, offering gifts of thanks to all the gods and especially to Athena. When night falls, the Greek soldiers emerge from the horse's belly and open the gates to the waiting Greek army. Within one night, the city is taken, its king killed, and the war brought to an end. What is particularly striking about the story, other than the daring subterfuge, is Odysseus' use of technology to outsmart the enemy, a trait he has in common with some of the great generals of antiquity. Julius Caesar, for instance, was famous for building immense siege works in all kinds of terrain in order to nullify any city's topographical advantage. For Odysseus in particular, the Trojan horse is another *tropos*, another turn and shift in the course of the fighting: he not only brings victory, but also a new way of winning. Cunning wins where epic brawn has failed.

Tyrion Lannister, too, has to contend with fighting through cunning and clever use of technology, since it is clear that the only way King's Landing can survive is by amplifying what topographical advantage it has. Here, then, Tyrion is a Trojan Odysseus, and he has two great tricks at the Battle of the Blackwater Rush to Odysseus' one: wildfire, and the great chain that blocks the mouth of the harbor. Wildfire, the mysterious substance developed by the alchemists and produced in excess for the Mad King, Aerys, might here descend from so-called Greek fire, a highly combustible compound which continued to burn while floating on water.

Greek fire was developed in the seventh century AD by the Byzantines (Byzantium is modern Istanbul), and was a key ingredient in many of their naval battles thereafter. Types of fire-based weapons were used in the ancient world for almost a thousand years, though their use, usually against ships, was sporadic and not always technologically advanced or successful. It wasn't until 672 AD that a more durable and combustible substance was developed and used against enemy ships. The debut made quite an impression on the historical record, not least because its first recorded use was during a battle which effectively saved the capital of the Christian Roman empire from a sure invasion by Muslim forces, who were at the time in such ascendance that they conquered the Persian empire and then stripped the Roman empire of most of its Asian possessions almost within a single generation.

24. Greek fire, from a twelfth-century manuscript

The key to Tyrion's success, however, is the double ruse of the fire and the chain. It relies on luring Stannis' ships to a narrow harbor where they cannot use their numerical superiority to quash the meager Royal fleet. Once the ships are committed, Tyrion can unleash the fire, and once that is done and chaos reigns, the chain blocks off any route of escape, thus ensuring Stannis' fleet is doomed. The basic maneuver of drawing a larger force to a narrow pass is a military classic, made most famous perhaps by the 300 Spartans King Leonidas led in Thermopylae during the Greek war with Persia. Fighting in harbors, however, had its own history. With Thermopylae lost and the Persians in full advance, the Greeks fought two great battles to win the war. The first, and more important of the two, was fought near Salamis, an island not far from Athens, now burnt and held by a Persian garrison. The Greeks by this point were heavily outnumbered, and some were already talking of surrender. But an Athenian general named Themistocles, known, like Odysseus of old, for his wily cunning, convinced the allied forces to do battle one more time.

They faced the Persians in the straits of Salamis, where the king of Persia set himself up on a golden throne to see his forces annihilate the pesky Greeks once and for all. (Similarly, the Blackwater Rush has two kings watching it – one, Joffrey, from the walls of King's Landing; the other, Stannis, from his camp on the other side of the river. Neither, we might presume, especially likes what he sees.) What Xerxes didn't know, however, was that he was operating on false information. At some point before the battle, Themistocles sent his enemy an envoy to tell the king that the Greeks were riven with infighting, that Themistocles himself was on the king's own side, and that Athens would be willing to break away from the rest of Greece if Xerxes sent his ships to blockade the straits of Salamis. The king believed this welcome news, and the Persian fleet was sent into the straits and blockaded both entrances to the harbor. What this meant, however, was that conditions were suddenly much too cramped for the Persian ships, which could neither turn nor maneuver. In the ensuing mayhem, the Greeks, who had spent the night preparing, could form up their lines and defeat the Persians. All Xerxes saw from his golden throne that day was his own ships sinking into the depths of the Aegean. The next day, he began the march home to Persia, leaving his lieutenant Mardonius to do what he could. The Persian forces in Greece were still formidable, but the tide had turned, and in a few years those too were driven out.

But in order to really conform to the Odyssean type, one must adventure, which for Tyrion is difficult both because of his physical limitations and because he has a very Odyssean tendency to get into trouble and deviate from the straight path of the Kingsroad. This is exactly what happens to him when he runs across Catelyn Stark on the way back from the Wall, and he must charm his way to safety several times before finally arriving triumphantly at King's Landing. This arrival, and the taste of power he gets as acting Hand of the King, does not spell the end of his voyaging, and he is forced to embark on another journey, the end of which is not yet in sight. Tyrion's departure from King's Landing and from Westeros, however, is not completely Odyssean. The chain of events that leads to it begins at the Purple Wedding, which, as it turns out, was an even more eventful occasion than planned. Tyrion is implicated in it up to his ears. Not only has he helped to plan the wedding, but he finds himself at the end of it accused of the murder of his king, as well as without his wife, who has left King's Landing under the cover of night to start her own voyage home. Having lost both king and wife, his own family then turns on him, with sister and father orchestrating a trial Tyrion cannot hope to win.

Odysseus leaves home out of a political obligation: having been one of Helen's suitors and sworn to aid her husband in a time of need, he has little choice but to join the expedition to Troy, despite an unsuccessful attempt to feign madness to avoid his duty. Aeneas, by contrast, must leave his home in Troy as a matter of survival, to avoid the wrath of the victorious Greeks and ensure the continuation of his people. Even Jason, the leader of the Argonauts, leaves home to find the Golden Fleece partly at the instigation of his wicked uncle and partly in order to prove his worth and win himself a throne. Tyrion, on the other hand, leaves Westeros simply to avoid retribution: having lost a trial of champions, he has been sentenced to death by his own father. And the last thing Tyrion does in Westeros is to kill his father, thus giving his voyaging a strong taint of expiation and self-discovery rather than just epic adventuring.

In the ancient world, murder, especially within the family, brought sacred pollution upon the perpetrator and upon everything he touched, used, or interacted with. In the *Oresteia*, a trilogy of plays from fifth-century Athens telling the story of the House of Atreus, Agamemnon's son Orestes kills his mother. He is then forced to leave his home and wander about Greece, hounded by the Furies, repulsive deities who drive men to madness and represent in vivid form the tainted pollution that surrounds anyone who has broken the bonds of society. More commonly, young aristocratic men who committed murder had to leave their homes to seek expiation, usually by spending time at a foreign court, where the king could perform the necessary religious rituals. An interesting comparison for Tyrion's case is that of Achilles' mentor, Phoenix, who was also a product of these expiation-exiles, having arrived at the court of Achilles' father to seek purification when Achilles was young. Phoenix stayed in Phthia and helped educate the young hero, and then joined the expedition to Troy along with his protégé. The relationship between Achilles and Phoenix is clearly one of great affection, but the position of elder counselor to a young and hotheaded hero has relevant applications for Tyrion. Joining the mercenary troops before Meereen, Tyrion's goal isn't obviously expiation as much as help in recapturing Casterly Rock, and in this, at least, he is a perfect parallel to Daenerys, who is likewise seeking assistance for all and sundry to recapture the Seven Kingdoms. But if – as may well be the case – Tyrion and Daenerys were to join forces in the books, would Tyrion play the role of mentor and counselor to the inexperienced queen, as he does in the show by becoming the Hand of the queen? Daenerys herself already has two mentors: Barristan the Bold and Jorah Mormont both act as cultural conduits, teaching her what they can about the customs of her homeland. Neither, however, is her social equal, and neither has the experience of politics Tyrion can offer. Like them, Tyrion's service might be offered in expiation of his and his family's crimes against the Targaryen dynasty, but whether he becomes the Phoenix to her Achilles remains to be seen. Of course, there is an inherent danger for Dany in imitating Achilles too closely: his choice of glory over long life meant he never saw his family or homeland again, nor saw the war in Troy end. Phoenix, for his part, fades from the pages of epic, while Odysseus is doomed to endless voyaging, too restless to settle in one place with the patient woman who has waited for him for 20 years. Whatever we make of Tyrion, he fits the quintessential epic requirement: striving endlessly for glory, and achieving it only in fame and memory.

What we have seen over the course of the chapter, however, is George R. R. Martin's blending of an already composite epic heroism with the heroism of classical tragedy, a genre that uses the same characters as epic but typically subjects them to extraordinary dilemmas and personal disaster. The battlefield and the voyage are thus complemented with palace intrigue and intrafamilial violence, and women are moved from a supporting cast to center stage, often taking on great and disturbing power along the way. Tyrion, another figure outside the mainstream of epic protagonists, likewise moves to the center in part through his tragic characterization, an unloved monstrosity whose innocence has been stolen in an act of betrayal and violence, and whose trajectory has led him to become a murderer and parricide. As Martin himself has said, 'The act of killing his father is something of enormous consequence that would be forever beyond the pale, for no man is as cursed as a kinslayer.'[19] Tyrion, the perpetrator of sexual deviancy and father-killing, is an Oedipus as much as an Odysseus. It's this capacious embrace of multiple heroic roles that gives his character such complexity and justifies the numerous chapters told from his point of view, his ambivalent perspective marked yet enriched by the many experiences enjoyed and suffered. The introduction to this chapter ended by claiming that an insight into a work's heroes is an insight into how the work itself should be judged, and Tyrion, like the mutilated Jaime and embittered Cersei, represents a central tenet of Martin's creation: that beauty is superficial, and that the path to self-understanding must have its moments of ugliness.

25. Dracarys

CHAPTER 4

POLITICS

Man is a political animal.

ARISTOTLE, *POLITICS* 1.1253A

I f *Game of Thrones* can be said to be about anything, it is about politics. Clausewitz famously stated that war is the continuation of politics by other means, and indeed in the war-torn world of Westeros politics generally represents not a hope for a brighter future but merely another way to obtain and maintain power, using all available means. Some figures – Ned Stark, Jon Snow, Daenerys Targaryen, for instance – seem at times to have higher motives and more admirable ambitions than others, such as Cersei Lannister, Walder Frey, or Roose Bolton. But no one emerges from the world of politics with entirely clean hands: compromises have to be made, principles have to be sacrificed. For a fantasy world, Westeros' political goings-on are remarkably realistic and familiar.

But before we look at the various manifestations of politics in *Game of Thrones*, we need to understand the range of activities that we're talking about, the kinds of thing people have in mind when they refer to 'politics' or 'the political,' and how those ideas and definitions can change from one context to another. In common speech, politics means, strictly speaking, the arena in which politicians operate. We also maintain a distinction between elected politicians and unelected public officials (public servants in the UK, state employees in the US), the first of which we perceive as fundamentally chasing after power, while the latter are doing a job, however influential. In both Westeros and the ancient world this distinction did not exist, or at least not in the same way it does for us; anyone who performed a task on behalf of the state did so by a power vested in him or her through the sovereign entity, whether people or king. Politics in the ancient world de facto meant engaging actively in the governance and ordering the public life of the *polis* – the Greek city-state – and by extension any self-governing entity, right up to and including the Roman empire. From this idea of politics we get our modern, more popular sense of 'office politics' and other expressions like it, which assume that politics means simply the organization of a group or, even more basically, an involvement in what other people do (indeed the Athenians prided themselves on their 'busybodiness,' a quality they felt drove each citizen to involve himself in public life, and the city-state of Athens to involve itself in more global politics). Politics, therefore, at least inasmuch as it is understood as a deliberate involvement in the workings of power, exists at multiple levels and in many forms: at the level of the state, of the family, or of the individual, as well as between states, nations, and even continents.

Despite its considerable complexity, politics in the world of *Game of Thrones* can by and large be thought of as running along two main axes. The first axis runs from authoritarianism to populism, or between power as vested in one person and power as vested in the sovereign people, which we also call tyranny and democracy, respectively. Along that axis we have many models to consider, from Joffrey's outright tyranny to the benevolent feudalism of the Starks, as well as many other examples. The second axis is geographical, and it moves from Westeros proper to the continents and islands surrounding it. For while the Seven Kingdoms offer models of autocratic rule, its neighbors practice various models of popular rule, from the anarchy of the wildlings to the various forms of rulership by committee in Essos and among the Dothraki. It is no coincidence, therefore, that the two characters most invested in events outside Westeros, Jon Snow and Daenerys Targaryen, both experiment with types of leadership that bring them into closer engagement with both autocracy and democracy: experimentation is seen to occur on the margins, set off from a center that has fallen into a predictably repetitive cycle. This view is inherently Westeros-centric, to be sure – one can imagine an alternate account that places Westeros on the periphery and Essos or the region beyond the Wall in the center, and we do indeed get some glimpses of this perspective; but the view from Westeros is the principal one that Martin encourages us to take from his representation of events and their political coloring. Among these tensions between types of polity and different geographical contexts are also others: the growing identification of political power and political violence with religion; the inefficacy of ethics and morality; the responsibilities of a good king; what constitutes a good courtier; and what role women can have in a domain often unthinkingly associated with men. Most of these questions find immediate parallels in classical antiquity, which likewise had a wide variety of political forms as well as a robust theoretical apparatus pertaining to political ideologies and relationships.

Any discussion of political life in Westeros must begin with the Targaryen dynasty, the ruling family of the Seven Kingdoms since Aegon first came to Dragonstone after the Doom of Valyria. Legend has it that every Targaryen king flirted with madness (SS 987), and indeed Robert's Rebellion finally comes about when, generations later, Aerys' madness leads to arbitrary and often perverse violence committed on the members of the court, leaving no room for civility, which is the bedrock of all stable society but especially of courtly culture. Yet Robert's Rebellion, however successful, does not bring about a stable new government, and indeed effects only a change in personnel, not in the form of the regime. Robert may not be mad, but he is often drunk and imprudent – in fact, a little of Aerys' paranoia might actually have served Robert well in warding off the machinations of the Lannisters. With the line of succession disturbed by allegations surrounding the legitimacy of Robert's children, the Seven Kingdoms are plunged into a protracted civil war, with five separate contenders, and with elements outside Westeros agitating for the throne as well. The cruelty of Joffrey and the wine-fueled rage of his mother Cersei are likewise implicit criticisms of a regime that is fundamentally flawed – a superficial improvement, if that, from Aerys' reign.

This narrative of political change (and lack of change) in Westeros captures, at a general level, several important strands of ancient political thought. The deterioration and ultimate over-throw of a ruling dynasty is a familiar narrative in antiquity, and the Targaryens in particular seem to combine two separate stock ideas: the arrival of a foreign dynasty and the corruption of good monarchy into capricious tyranny. Both the Ptolemies in Egypt and the Tarquins in Rome offer good ancient parallels. The lack of stability brought on by political change is likewise consistent across the ancient world, where states often experienced periods of intense turmoil before the situation could be settled down by good administration, the emergence of a strong king, or a combination of both. More often than not, however, disputed inheritances were settled by long and bloody civil wars, of which the Roman civil war of 69 A D, which saw four emperors come to power (and, therefore, three deposed), stands as a tempting parallel to Westeros' War of the Five Kings.

Putting the story of *Game of Thrones* in these terms is itself an ancient conceit, since it focuses the story not on the human suffering or economic motivations or supernatural concerns like dragons or the White Walkers, but strictly in terms of constitutional evolution. Ancient historical narratives were often organized around political structures; for instance, the basic unit of Roman history was the consular year, the period of office of the two highest public officials. In monarchies, history could be organized by regnal years, while political upheavals, like the expulsion of a dynasty or the foundation of a republic, provided a convenient benchmark for chronological reference. Westeros by and large measures time in summers and winters, and lacks any real sense of historical record-keeping other than noting the era before and after Aegon's conquest (note Sam's difficulties in finding reliable information about the White Walkers), but to the extent history does exist in the Seven Kingdoms, it is organized around the reigns of the Targaryen kings and queens, and notable events from their reign.

But the transformations that Westeros undergoes likewise conform to an ancient political theory about the way societies grow and change. This theory, formulated by the Greek historian Polybius, who was in turn influenced by Plato and Aristotle, held that societies naturally went through a cyclical pattern of constitutional change, for which the Greek word was *anacyclosis*. The pattern consisted of three 'good' types of constitution, monarchy, aristocracy, and democracy, each of which had a corresponding 'bad' type, into which the constitution naturally degenerated – tyranny, oligarchy, and ochlocracy (mob rule). Overall, then, a society could expect to go through the pattern as follows: monarchy, tyranny, aristocracy, oligarchy, democracy, ochlocracy. The story would begin with a good king (*monarchy*), who would bring the people together under a wise and benign rule. In time, power would pass to the king's descendants, who would eventually start exercising power for their own ends, at which point abuses of power would become characteristic, and monarchy would become tyrannical. In due course, the *aristocracy* ('the best people') would grow tired of the abuses of the tyrant and would expel him. From here the cycle repeats: power eventually corrupts the aristocracy, so their rule becomes that of a clique made up of the few (*oligarchy*) rather than the best. The people expel the few and set up a *democracy*, until they too succumb and the state comes to be ruled by a mob (*ochlocracy*).

Here, notionally at least, we come to where we started, as society
deteriorates into a primitive state of lawlessness, from which it can
be saved by a wise and noble king, and so the *anacyclosis* pattern
can repeat again and again.[1]

In this most elaborate version of the pattern, Polybius has in
mind the growth of the Roman republic, which, after going through
the first part of the pattern (monarchy to tyranny to aristocracy)
has managed to avoid the subsequent tribulations by developing
a form of mixed government. This mixed type begins to look
like the modern version of representative democracy, albeit with
important differences: the monarchical element is represented by
the two consuls, who have what we would call executive power;
the aristocratic element is represented by the senate, who advise
the consuls and other officials of the executive, and who hold also
the power to declare war and approve legislation, thus serving as a
check against popular or consular excess; the democratic element,
finally, is represented by the assemblies of the people, who pass
laws, elect officials, and form part of the judiciary branch of the
state. This mixture, Polybius thought, was what kept the republic
stable for its 500 years of existence.

However familiar Polybius' Roman outline might be, super-
imposing it on Westerosi politics is a more complicated matter.
As I noted above, many of the aristocracies and polities in *Game
of Thrones* exist outside Westeros: in Braavos, Pentos, Slaver's Bay,
and even, to some extent, among the Dothraki and in the societies
of the wildlings, who clearly have their own systems of hierarchy
and single-rulership. Westeros itself is very much in the medieval
feudal mode traditional to the fantasy genre, with a king presiding over a layer of squabbling barons, each with his own holdings,
resources, and bannermen. Nevertheless, we can usefully see some
of the Polybian pattern in action. The Targaryens arrive from a
doomed eastern state, bringing with them its secrets and advanced
technologies. After initial tumult, they rule well for many years – a
typical enough monarchy – until either power or madness begins

to creep into the line. The ultimate madness of Aerys brings us squarely into tyranny, which is in due course expelled by a coalition of the aristocracy: Ned Stark, Robert Baratheon, Jon Arryn, and eventually the other Great Houses. But this phase too cannot last, and as the Lannisters insinuate themselves further and further into the nooks and crannies of power, their rule becomes oligarchic, with Joffrey and Tommen vacillating between a return to outright tyranny and a puppet king: it's the unelected Small Council that often seems to be determining what should happen in the state. Democracy proper is difficult to find in Westeros, but the Sparrows, rising against (yet also with the connivance of) aristocratic excesses, more than hint at the ochlocratic element. During long years of war, *A Song of Ice and Fire* tracks the collapse of Westeros from a society unified under a just king into a mess of warring factions and shifting alliances, some focused on individuals, others on political beliefs and mass movements. The next step, on this view, is a return to just monarchy, or perhaps a more brutal dictatorship, depending on who ultimately wins the war and asserts their dominance.

The ancient technical terms, especially ones that have survived to the present day, do not overlap completely with modern usage, and they have little parallel in Westeros. For instance, aristocracy for us connotes a social class rather than moral worth, and has mostly to do with descent and relation to the Crown (or by metaphoric extension, another source of power). When we say democracy, we mean by and large that executive decisions are made by a set of elected officials, as well as those appointed and approved by those officials. In either case, we expect a certain set of rules to be operating: that an elected government step down at the end of its office; that it steward the state's wealth well; and that it be responsive to popular feelings, whether by referendum, the media, or free protest. We expect also the freedom to speak truth to power, or be otherwise protected from political, legal, and financial abuse. Above all, we expect to exist in what the Greeks

called *isonomia*: an equality before the law. For the Greeks, however, these conditions pertained only partially: democracy meant
the direct representation of the people by the people, with public
offices sometimes decided by lot, with mandatory participation in
public affairs, including decisions on fiscal policy, military intervention, or religious worship. Republicanism, which the ancients
would have understood as aristocracy, imposes the layers of elected
officials working on behalf of the people, while tyranny entailed
only a single ruler, who had convinced the people to invest in him
their sovereign power (though in ancient characterizations the
tyrant typically has henchmen and other nefarious agents, as well
as a layer of fearful and obedient courtiers). In other words, unlike
in the established first world of the twenty-first century, ancient
states had no expectation of stability, and therefore also show an
ongoing concern with solidifying and ensuring some permanence
to the best of their ability. The Roman empire, in fact, is remarkable
exactly for its longevity, having undergone only two fundamental
regime changes in its millennium-long history.

Polybius' view of constitutional change is certainly not value-
neutral, and even his idealized view of the Roman republic as a
'mixed' constitution doesn't hide a marked preference for what is
effectively aristocratic rule. Indeed, the very name 'aristocracy,' or
'the rule of the best people,' already betrays a bias toward the dominance of the educated well-to-dos. But the ancients often debated,
in more or less stylized formats, the merits of various systems of
government. The earliest debate is in Herodotus' account of the
background to the Persian Wars, wherein he delves deep into the
origins of the Persian empire to illustrate its defining differences
from Greek culture. In this constitutional debate, the Persians find
themselves with an opportunity to choose for themselves the type
of new regime. Herodotus gives us three points of view, one each
on monarchy, aristocracy, and democracy. Monarchy offers the
best ruler, aristocracy the greatest bolster against corruption, and
democracy offers equality before the law – but in the end monarchy

wins out because monarchy is the traditional form of rule in Persia, and, as Darius asks, why ought the Persians change from what has worked so well for them before?[2] Indeed, monarchy tends to come out tops in many of these debates, even in surprising contexts; Scipio Aemilianus, for instance, admits to thinking monarchy the ideal form of rule, despite being deeply committed to the monarchy-averse ideology of the republic.

What was it about kingship that exercised such admiration, then, especially in a world where kings again and again could be seen to abuse their power? The same question might well be asked of the people of Westeros, who never really seem to consider a systemic change in form of government, despite some experimentation from the Church and some more sustained explorations abroad. In antiquity, at least, the reason was partly moral and partly philosophical. A king connoted not only absolute political power, but also a commitment to wielding it well and wisely. Monarchy also offered some protection against corruption, which was the pervasive fault of republican regimes, and against popular excesses and fickleness, the pervasive fault of democracy. Obviously political reality and even political mythology rarely fulfilled this heroic ideal, and the tradition that has come to dominate part of the Western tradition – that of Rome and Athens – is accordingly heavily slanted toward rule by the few or the many, but never the one. Nevertheless, kingship continued to act as a foil and as a real political presence in the sprawling Eastern kingdoms. To ambitious men, kingship, whether idealized or in the form of a real court, offered a tantalizing hope for advancement, a way of measuring one's power, or of shielding oneself from one's enemies. In Westeros, however, kingship is an aspiration, and much of the game of thrones is in fact a series of competing models of kingship: cruel, benevolent, immature, legitimate, and so forth. Kingship also came with a court, a set of courtiers, and the expectation of legitimate issue, so that autocratic societies in fact offer a better and more visible view of women's role in political life than ancient republics and democracies, which privileged only the male and free elements of society. Kingship, in its various permutations, therefore, is the root and core of this chapter, and where better to start than with Westeros' oldest ruling dynasty, the Targaryens?

QUEEN OF BEASTS, MOTHER OF DRAGONS

Alexander the Great died in 323 BC, in far-off Babylon, leaving behind a vast empire and a big question over who should inherit it. There was no direct male issue, but there was a large group of advisors, generals, and relatives, all of whom wanted a share. Legend has it that Alexander meant to leave his empire to his advisor Krateros, whose name conveniently meant 'the strongest man,' a desire misinterpreted on Alexander's deathbed as an invitation for the inheritors to fight it out for the spoils of empire. Over the next four decades, Alexander's inheritors pulled apart his empire, until it was finally settled into three main kingdoms: the Antigonids in the homelands of Macedon, the Seleucids, whose holdings stretched from the Syrian coast to the Persian hinterlands, and (the longest-lasting of all) the Ptolemies in Egypt. Each of the new realms faced enormous challenges, but one that was common to all was the challenge of managing a native population over which a foreign ruling house had been superimposed. For the Ptolemies, the problem was most acute; their capital in Alexandria was a new and artificial settlement, benefiting from proximity to the Nile Delta and a natural harbor but dissociated almost entirely from the rhythms and culture of the local Egyptian populace. Like its kings and queens, Alexandria was a city of foreigners, opinionated, volatile, and consumerist, while the wealth of the kingdom, both in coin and in grain, derived from the fertile fields along the Nile, worked by Egyptian peasants. The differences were social, economic, ethnic, and religious. But the Ptolemies lasted, not least because they implemented a successful mixture of syncretism and segregation: when they could, they took on the title of pharaoh, and kept Alexandria prosperous by aligning the Egyptian economy toward Alexandria. But it was all too easy to starve the city out and incite the crowds to overthrow their king, which meant that the Ptolemies were also constantly on the lookout for international allies to bolster their rule, trade interests, and in times of need, offer a place of refuge.

The Ptolemies presided over one of the most impressive flourishings of culture and learning the world has known, building and patronizing the library of Alexandria and the scholars who worked in it. Those librarians, in turn, codified ancient literature and shaped literary aesthetics for decades (if not centuries) to come, and the Roman poets who inherited those aesthetics made in turn an indelible impact on the vernacular literatures of Europe and the Americas. But while the Romans were happy to take on Alexandrian culture, and happier still to pocket Ptolemaic money in exchange for political and military meddling in the affairs of Egypt, they remained fundamentally inimical to the Ptolemaic habit of marriage between siblings. Incest, or the practice of intercourse between too-near kin, is associated with the Ptolemies from early on in the dynasty, and while they did not practice it absolutely (some married into or from foreign dynasties, and most had mistresses), the existence of names like 'philadelphos' or 'philopater' ('brother-lover' and 'father-lover' respectively) demonstrate that incest was the marital norm. Given that incest between too-near kin was taboo across the Mediterranean, there remains an open question as to why the Ptolemies chose to practice it. One reason might be that it assimilated them to the pharaohs of ancient Egypt, though the extent to which incest existed in pharaonic dynasties is unclear.[3] Another reason has been so-called 'blood purity,' or the desire to keep the royal family free of any taint of the local population and maintain their ethnic difference from the people they governed. In fact, the two reasons needn't be separated: the Ptolemies benefited both from assimilation to the pharaohs *and* from remaining a distinct ethnic identity, which connected them to Alexander the Great and his empire. Above all, however, incest was practiced as part of a dynastic brand, and was a behavior that went hand in hand with Alexandrian culture, learning, cosmopolitanism, and wealth (in Greek, *truphe*).[4] Incest was a way to mark the Ptolemies out from other dynasties, from local Egyptians, and indeed from mere mortals, since sibling-marriage was part and parcel of Greek mythology. The gods on Olympus were all too-nearly related, and so were the Ptolemies in their Alexandrian palaces.

A Song of Ice and Fire gives little enough information about the Targaryens, starting as it does 15 years after their expulsion. What it does give us, however, is a tantalizingly close-to-Ptolemaic image. We know, for instance, that the Targaryens had a distinctive look to them: blond and purple-eyed; and we know also that such looks stood them apart even from the other aristocratic houses of Westeros. Ancient physiognomy is nearly impossible to recover, and we cannot know how different or distinctive the Ptolemies would have looked from the people they ruled (especially since even that population was extremely diverse), but ancient royal dynasties across the board worked hard to make their special status easily visible in their dress, conduct, and so forth. The population at large rarely saw their ruling families, with the Romans being an unusual exception to which we'll return shortly. Indeed, the Romans found the separation of the Ptolemaic monarch from his people curious, and when they visited Alexandria and were shown around by a hugely out-of-shape Ptolemy, Scipio Aemilianus was said to have whispered: 'Well, the Alexandrian people have already benefited by our visit, for it was thanks to us that they saw their king.'[5] However unnatural the Romans thought this separation (an opinion produced by long-standing republican traditions), such separation between royals and the rest was the standard across the eastern Mediterranean, and was a means of establishing the basic precept that the monarch was unique, and therefore entitled to rule.

This royal seclusion was supported and made possible partially by the practice of royal incest, another defining Targaryen characteristic. There seems to be little obstacle to applying much of the same rationale for the Ptolemaic version to the Westerosi royal line, and in particular the desire to keep intact the Targaryen blood purity. After all, unlike the local population of Westeros, the Andals and Rhoynar and the First Men, the Targaryens are the remnants of Valyria, a mythical empire to the east, whose language and infrastructure still dominates much of the landscape of Essos. That Valyria has more than a shade of Rome to it seems clear, lying as it does in the mythical past of a pseudo-medieval world, but mythologics of foreign origin were common. The Romans had their own version, where the mother-empire was Troy, also to the east, while the Hellenistic world after Alexander the Great had kingdoms whose royal families – like the Ptolemies in Egypt – hailed from elsewhere. Marriages within the family helped maintain the distinction between the ruling house and the populace, because it kept the bloodline old and pure, or at least strong enough to produce family resemblances where needed. But incest was also important for reasons of culture and power (the Ptolemaic *truphe*), and incest for the Targaryens was a way of demonstrating how much better they were than anyone else around them. This was a lesson well learned by the people of Westeros. When the truth of Cersei and Jaime Lannister's affair begins to emerge, Cersei justifies it to herself by pointing to the Targaryens: they did it all the time, she says, and what is good for the Targaryens is surely good enough also for the Lannisters (S1, E7). The fact that the Lannister case is still treated as breaching a significant taboo, however, is also a sign that the uniqueness of the Targaryens has likewise become naturalized: the distinctive property of the Targaryens cannot be translated over to other families, just as Lannister blond looks could not be transmuted into Targaryen elfish silver (Martin seems be playing on the familiar hierarchy here by making silver more unusual than – and possibly more beautiful than – gold).

Truphe comes up in other aspects as well. Although they are by and large not a bookish family, we know that Prince Rhaegar played the lute and composed poems, and at least one Targaryen we know of had turned to the life of a maester. Further, the marvelous Targaryen technological skills used to build the Red Keep are rivaled only by the mythical people of the North, like Brandon the Builder of Winterfell. More importantly, however, is that they have – or used to have – dragons and the secrets of dragon-rearing. Now we might think of the distinction between dragons and walls as a distinction between art and innate skill, a difference with which the ancients were much preoccupied. On that analogy, the dragons represent the innate ability of the Targaryen dynasty, their inherent affinity toward and mastery of dragons and dragonlore. The Stark wall-building project, by contrast, underscores their stability and solidity. Unlike dragons, walls cannot fly and have little mystique about them, though the scale of the Wall and its supposed building by giants does render it somewhat less prosaic than any ordinary fortification; nevertheless, it remains less fantastical than dragons. We might note as well that Maegor has his architects killed when the construction of Maegor's Keep is complete, so that its secrets cannot be revealed. As a king, Maegor can command and dispose of life and labor, but he cannot build for himself. Dragonlore, therefore, represents not only the key Targaryen claim to Valyrian descent – proof of their origin, which incest works to maintain and reinforce – but also the particular style of the dynasty. Their words, banner, architecture, and mythical history are all built around the image of the dragon, even after the dragons themselves become extinct.

One of the recurring conceits of the aristocracy in Westeros is that they are, or possess qualities of, the totems of their houses. Indeed, Viserys and Daenerys both repeat that they are the 'blood of the dragon,' and Viserys bullies his sister by warning her 'not to wake the dragon.' This is a logical extension of the heraldic metaphor, but it brings up another important tension at the heart of the Targaryen dynasty. Part of the reason the dragons became extinct, we are told, is that they were kept in captivity, a situation which caused them to grow smaller and less robust with the generations. Metaphorically as well as genetically, this applies to the line of monarchs they represent: the Targaryen kings and queens deteriorate over the years, with madness creeping further into the line. The walls of the Red Keep, which symbolize the temporal power of the Targaryens, become also the walls of a prison, which keeps the dragons, real and metaphorical, captive and eventually leads them into extinction. It is no mistake, therefore, that Daenerys receives her dragon eggs from an Eastern merchant, and that she and they become stronger the further they move away from Westeros and its restrictions. The walls, symbolic throughout antiquity of the political cohesion and martial integrity of the city-state, become also a marker of the tension between nature and captivity, between regulation and excess. For the Targaryens to be reinvigorated, they must escape the prisons of paranoia and physical constriction and embrace altruism and liberty – yet another reason why the family's fortunes are more prosperous with Daenerys than Viserys.

Of all the Targaryens since Aegon the Dragon, Daenerys seems to have the closest link to her dragons. She nurses and raises them, and comes to be known as the Mother of Dragons, having cracked their eggs on the pyre of her dead husband. As Daenerys finds out, however, the dragons become increasingly hard to control, and especially difficult to contain within the urban environment of Meereen. Like her legendary predecessor, she builds her hopes of a triumphant return on her possession of dragons, but she also knows that the dragons are a double-edged sword: they are as much a danger to her rule as they are crucial to her triumph. This tension is part and parcel of a broader tension between the supernatural and the mundane which is being waged across Westeros: Jon Snow's defense of the Wall against a wildling army supplied with giants and other creatures of legend, as well as the menace of the White

Walkers, is of exactly the same coin as the Targaryen domestica-
tion of dragons, and equally as politically loaded. The defense of
the realm against hostile or uncontrollable supernatural forces is
the purview of the kings – it is in that implicit capacity that the
Starks defend the North, having once ruled it themselves – but the
Targaryens defend the realm by capturing within it a force that
could bring it to destruction (the civil war known as the Dance of
Dragons is a good example).

In the end, of course, the Targaryens bring about their own
ruin. Whether through genetic deterioration, the loss of dragons
and dragonlore, or the idiosyncrasy of individual kings, madness
(and especially pyromania) eventually spells doom for the dynasty.
Both Aerys and Daenerys are dragon-obsessed, and Aerys' madness manifests itself most clearly not just through his pyromania,
but through a specific compulsion to become more dragon-like
through the use of fire. In essence, Aerys finds himself insufficiently
Targaryen, and his tyranny is therefore in the classical mode of excess
and overcompensation. Daenerys, however, is almost superfluously
Targaryen, in possession of dragons, but without a kingdom to rule
or brothers to marry. She is thus free of some of the trappings of her
family, but the ones she does have – the dragons – come to define
her, as she becomes known as the Mother of Dragons. The title, while
meant honorifically, is not without problems. Mother of Dragons
suggests a relationship with these animals that is deeper, both
physically and emotionally, than might be expected: Dany nurses
them, and consistently treats them as her children, replacement to
the monstrous baby she lost in the attempt to revive Drogo. As the
series currently stands, there is serious doubt cast over whether or
not she can in fact control the dragons, and at some level that doubt
extends also to her ability to achieve and maintain the Iron Throne.
Nor are dragons the only options; the most recent entrant into the
game of thrones is none other than Dany's nephew, Prince Aegon,
the son of Rhaegar and Elia, who is in many ways the mirror image
to Daenerys. He has no dragons, but has been raised to believe in

his own role as future king, and he both knows Westeros and has troops willing to take him there. His aunt, by contrast, languishes in Slaver's Bay, having expended her energies on the liberation of the slaves – a defining concern of a young woman once herself bought and sold. Although the two remaining Targaryens, Aegon and Daenerys, might profitably join forces, indeed even marry, nevertheless the Ptolemaic template leaves other avenues open, not least the prospect of a bloody civil war.

WOMEN AND MONARCHIC OVERTHROW

Strong women are at the heart of *Game of Thrones*, and none, perhaps, stronger than Cersei Lannister, scheming queen, devoted mother, and resident villain. Two things drive Cersei: her love for her children, and her love of power – and often the two are impossible to separate, since her children are also her surest route to power. These two qualities, along with her gender, are also what separates her from her twin brother, Jaime. Whereas he has no political ambition, or love for the ones he turns out to have fathered (*SS* 855, 843–4, respectively), Cersei's life by contrast revolves around her position in court: as queen and mother of the king. Jaime cockily asserts that there are no men like him, and in the unusual discrepancy between his elevated position and his lack of aspirations there may be more truth to his claim than even he himself recognizes, but there certainly are other women like Cersei. Sansa Stark and Margaery Tyrell, each in their own way, dream of inheriting Cersei's position, complete with loveless marriage and dubious comforts in court. Catelyn Stark, on the other hand, is almost a precise mirror image of Cersei. Catelyn thrives in her marriage, whereas Cersei loathes hers; Catelyn's children are legitimate, for all that they take after their mother in complexion, whereas Cersei's children's coloring gives away their bastardy; Catelyn teaches Robb kindness, and loses him to his own and the Lannisters' trickery, whereas Cersei teaches her son cruelty, and loses him to Tyrell ambition and poison. But Cersei is above all the inheritor of a long literary and historical tradition of strong women at court, stretching from Helen's need to survive in Troy, and continuing through Roman legend to the historical figures of Livia and Agrippina and Messalina, the imperial women of the Roman empire.[6]

But it is not only the strong woman at the helm of power who can effect political change, and in fact it was a commonplace in antiquity that great changes were wrought from small beginnings, often from domestic disputes and the manipulations of wives and mothers who would otherwise have no presence on the stage. Whatever else we might think of the Targaryens and their madness, what brings their long dynasty to an end is not simply Aerys' madness, but also Jon Arryn's stubborn refusal to kowtow, and the righteous indignation of Robert Baratheon. For in the end, and whatever the truth of the stories, Robert's Rebellion is fought over a woman and, more tellingly, over alleged sexual violence against that woman. That Robert fails to gain his beloved Lyanna is, perhaps, tragic, but as his rule matures under Lannister influence, it becomes clear that whatever noble morals might have driven the rebellion, they did not extend to the culture of the new dispensation.

The corruption of power is an old idea. Ancient political theory generally held that it took three generations for power to corrupt. Another ancient idea was that revolutions usually took place over the body of a sexually violated woman, vengeance for whom provided cause and impetus for political change. Two acts of sexual violence against women become iconic of the Rebellion: Prince Rhaegar's alleged kidnapping and rape of Lyanna Stark, and the rape and murder of Princess Elia by Gregor Clegane. Violence against women is, of course, prevalent in Westeros, but its main victims (at least out in the open) are the wives and daughters of the lowly and the poor, and in the show also prostitutes, whose profession is deemed to deprive them of any legal or moral protection. One of the striking features of the failed society after Robert's death, however, is that noble women, too, come to feel less and less secure as regards their bodily integrity. Sansa is stripped before the court, Lady Lollys raped on the streets of King's Landing, and even Cersei is forced to parade naked through the streets. Different agents cause all these outrages, but they are all fundamentally related to the absence of legality or morality caused by the new unstable climate of tyranny and its associated cruelty.

The idea that sexual violence against women is a driver of political change finds expression as early as Herodotus, the first writer of extended historical prose in the Western tradition. Seeking to explain the long-standing enmity of East and West, or more specifically of Greeks and Persians, Herodotus mines mythological stories to point out that reciprocal kidnapping of women has shaped generations of conflict between the two peoples. The quintessential example is Helen of Troy, whose kidnapping by/elopement with Paris, the prince of Troy, models in many ways the uncertain history of Rhaegar and Lyanna's affair. Famously, Lyanna is remembered as a great beauty, with whom Rhaegar is smitten despite being already married, and for whom he is willing to bring the kingdom to ruin. Heavy hints throughout the series suggest that Lyanna went willingly with her alleged kidnapper, and that theirs was a story of elopement rather than rape, but it is hardly a surprise that neither Robert nor Ned is willing to set much store by that version of events. And being the victor, Robert's version comes to dominate the record, while Rhaegar's remains a shadowy suspicion of truth for the reader to affirm or debate.

Famously, Helen was promised to Paris by the goddess Aphrodite, as a reward for choosing her as the most beautiful of the Olympian goddesses. Helen, however, was already married to Menelaus, king of Sparta and brother to the powerful Agamemnon, king of Mycenae (both cities are in the Peloponnesus in southern Greece). Seduced by Paris, Helen comes to Troy with him as his wife, and the armies of Greece (with the proverbial thousand ships) duly follow. Through the ten years of the war, Helen remains

the sole Greek woman in the city, and the *Iliad*, the fullest story
of the war in Troy, brims with little moments where she comes
to terms with the consequences of her choice. One of the more
poignant ones comes early in the *Iliad*, when Helen stands on
the walls of the city, pointing out to her Trojan father-in-law the
various heroes:

> And Helen in all her radiance, her long robes, replied,
> 'Why, that's the giant Ajax, bulwark of the Achaeans.
> And Idomeneus over there – standing with his Cretans –
> like a god, you see? And the Cretan captains
> form a ring around him. How often Menelaus,
> my good soldier, would host him in our halls,
> in the old days, when he'd sail across from Crete.
> And now I see them all, the fiery-eyed Achaeans,
> I know them all by heart, and I could tell their names [...]
> but two I cannot find, and they're captains of the armies,
> Castor, breaker of horses and the hardy boxer Polydeuces.
> My blood brothers. Mother bore them both. Perhaps
> they never crossed over from Lacedaemon's lovely hills
> or come they did, sailing here in the deep-sea ships,
> but now they refuse to join the men in battle,
> dreading the scorn, the curses hurled at me...'
> So she wavered, but the earth already held them fast,
> long dead in the life-giving earth of Lacedaemon,
> the dear land of their fathers.[7]

The descriptions Helen uses are typical of epic diction: 'like a god,'
'breaker of horses,' and so forth are the standard terms of description
used by Homer to illustrate the poem, as is the habit of providing
further information on how any two people in the poem know
each other. As a woman, Helen knows Idomeneus as a guest in her
husband's house, but beyond the standard method of description,
she is also recalling her former life as a Greek queen and wife,

and the life she knew before Paris came. But the most poignant moment here is her searching out her famous brothers, Castor and Pollux, and the shame she imagines them to feel for her, unaware that since she has left Sparta with her new lover her brothers have died and been buried.

Nor does she find much consolation in her new marriage, for Paris falls rather short of the expectations of heroic manly conduct in the Homeric poems. He lacks prowess in battle, escapes a duel with Menelaus, and is given more to pleasure and leisure than the serious business of defending his native city. Helen, for her part, is torn between a set of contradictory emotions: affection, lust, and crushing disappointment. All this is captured brilliantly in one scene in particular, where, following a fight between the lovers, the goddess Aphrodite appears to Helen and compels her to sleep with Paris. It is difficult to know quite how to read the scene: is the goddess a reflection of the lust Helen feels, or an excuse for the rape Paris commits in his own marriage bed? This question remains constant for Helen: is she a victim of other people's lusts or a perpetrator of her own desires? Antiquity has a range of answers: in the *Odyssey*, for instance, her marriage is restored, though rich seams of mutual suspicion remain between husband and wife. Stesichorus, one of the nine great lyric poets of Greece, likewise wrote a poem portraying Helen as a bad character. Legend has it that he was struck with blindness for this affront, and in consequence wrote a poem retracting his previous work, claiming instead that Helen never went to Troy; either she never left Sparta, or she took refuge in Egypt for the duration of the war while only a phantom copy of her arrived in Troy, rendering the war there an even more pointless waste of life. The tragic playwright Euripides elaborates the version that had Helen arrive in Egypt, including Menelaus meeting his (real) wife after the war, only to change his mind about her, and then change it again after a heartfelt declaration on her part.

Thus Lyanna Stark has something of Helen about her: she is a willing victim and a reason for a war that changes the course of a kingdom and a dynasty. But whatever the truth of her story, Lyanna does not survive the Rebellion, and Robert Baratheon, despite playing the cavalier hero, does not get the girl or the happy ending. Instead he marries Cersei Lannister for political reasons, and their marriage is afflicted almost from the start. Cersei, of course, is the new beauty of the court, and her resentment at her husband's continued devotion to Lyanna simmers over long years and into the opening scenes of *Game of Thrones*. Nor is Cersei without her own internal turmoil: in one scene invented entirely for the HBO adaptation (S1, E7), she confesses to Ned that she loved Robert once, early in their marriage, but that this love has turned to hate instead. Is Cersei, therefore, a victim of male machinations in the same way as Lyanna Stark was, or does her relentless ambition and incestuous desire make her responsible for the unhappiness she feels throughout her marriage? Cersei and Lyanna, Robert's women both, thus capture the Helen dilemma perfectly: are they strong women or weak? Are they the victim of rape, manipulation, and male dominance, or are they rather cunning seductresses, themselves complicit in their own ruin? Cersei is, of course, much easier to judge: we know her better, or at least we think we do, and she has much more scope to perpetrate all sorts of atrocities. Lyanna remains shadowy and mysterious, and the atrocities of the Rebellion are instead committed by the men around her, Targaryen and Baratheon both.

But Helen of Troy, and the reciprocal kidnapping of women that Herodotus discusses, are not the only way in which women drive political change. The Romans had another model, which saw in the exploitation of a virtuous woman's body an extreme embodiment of tyrannical rule. The most famous instance of this is perhaps the rape of Lucretia, a story which gained some currency in the Augustan age, when Rome was reverting back to an autocracy, but one keen to emphasize its credentials as benevolent, protective of old Roman values, and as far away as possible from the excesses of Eastern monarchy (as modeled by the Ptolemaic queen Cleopatra, whose reputation bore the brunt of Augustan propaganda). As Livy and Ovid both tell the story, Lucretia was the wife of a man named Collatinus, a cousin to the Tarquins, Rome's royal family. By this point, the Tarquins were faced with rising popular unrest, caused by an increased military burden and the consequent growing poverty among men who spent too long on mandatory service to provide for their families. The king had decided to treat this unrest by increasing public works, keeping the citizenry occupied in the building both of a great temple to Rome's tutelary deity, Jupiter Optimus Maximus, and – in stark contrast – of Rome's great sewage system, the *cloaca Maxima*. (These monumental works are not a coincidence; they represent monuments very much on the mind of the Augustan reader: both religion and infrastructure were left in tatters by the civil wars that ushered Augustus to power, and both were in the process of being restored and repaired by the new regime.)

Against this background, the prince, Sextus Tarquinius, was laying siege to a neighboring city. He was accompanied by the flower of Rome's aristocratic youth, including his cousin Collatinus, and as officers do, they turned talk at the mess into reminiscences of home, with each of the men boasting that his particular wife was the very embodiment of wifely virtues. The talk must have been lively and getting livelier, because prince and retinue decided to settle this dispute empirically: they would ride through the night and see for themselves what their wives got up to when there were no men to see. First they went to Rome, where the royal women were found enjoying their leisure and generally behaving indecorously, much to their husbands' embarrassment. Unseen by their womenfolk, the men pressed on to Collatia, and to the home of Collatinus. There, they were greeted by Lucretia, who had been sitting up with her handmaidens, all preoccupied with their weaving and sewing, and Ovid even specifies that Lucretia was weaving a cloak for her husband to wear into battle. After such a display, Collatinus naturally collected bragging rights, and the next day the men returned to camp, with the matter seemingly settled.

Obviously, such a simple division of women into virtuous and immoral foreshadows the political changes to come: the royal women are immoral and excessive at home just as their menfolk are immoral and excessive in the public realm. Further, the royal women are duplicitous: they do one thing when their husbands are home, and another when they are away, while Lucretia is good and honest through and through. But even this division already guides us to read women's morality as a function of their male relations' suitability for rule; in other words, they are an index for how well a regime is doing. Applying this to Westeros is easy enough: Sansa's imagination of a virtuous court and her struggle to understand that things in King's Landing are not always as they seem mark her as moral in herself, but she is also an ornament to Northern virtue, and especially to the Stark code of honor (and perhaps their naivety). Margaery Tyrell's flirtatiousness, on the other hand, signals Tyrell duplicity and hunger for power, while Cersei's incest leaves no doubt about the morality of House Lannister.

Lucretia's modesty, however, spells a bad end for her. Smitten with her beauty and character, Sextus Tarquin determines to have her for himself. The next night, he sneaks back to Collatia from the army camp, and demands that Lucretia submit to his sexual advances. When she fights him off, he threatens to kill her and arrange for a dead slave's body to be found in her bed along with her, so that people, including her husband, will think she debased herself with a slave. Lucretia submits, but when Sextus leaves she immediately sends for her father and husband, urging them to bring a witness each to her home. When they come, they find Lucretia with knife in hand, preparing to kill herself over her ruined honor. 'Never shall Lucretia provide a precedent for unchaste women to escape what they deserve,' she proclaims, and refuses to listen even when told that rape cannot vitiate her honor, since she neither wished for nor consented to the act.[8] Nothing avails. As father and husband mourn, Brutus, another cousin brought along by Collatinus, pries the bloody dagger from

Lucretia's dead fingers and swears vengeance on her rapist. In short order, Collatia is in open revolt against the king and his family, and seemingly overnight the Tarquins are expelled and Rome becomes a republic.

Lucretia's story is of a type; ancient Athens had a similar version, where a pair of lovers, Harmodius and Aristogeiton, overthrow the tyrant Peisistratus for a slight to Aristogeiton's sister, and the Romans told variations of the Lucretia story whenever the people's sovereign rights seemed to be trampled. And Lyanna Stark, over whom the Rebellion was started, was not the only victim: Princess Elia Martell of Dorne, too, was raped and murdered when King's Landing was taken, and Elia remains just as much in the background of this saga as Lyanna. Oberyn Martell – indeed, the whole of Dorne – still seeks justice for Elia's death, a grievance that will become more important as the new Targaryen generation closes in on Westeros. The theme of female modesty likewise continues to be important, and it structures some preconceptions we have of these characters. For instance, how are we meant to 'read' Elia? She at first appears to be simply the wronged woman, another victim of Rhaegar's lust for Lyanna, same as Robert Baratheon. Further, her gruesome death and the long-standing vengeance sworn by her family make her appear even more like Lucretia, a rallying figure for toppling a dynasty, but here against the usurping Lannisters rather than the Targaryens. However, if Rhaegar is meant to play Sextus Tarquin, is Elia his 'bad' royal wife to Lyanna's chaste Lucretia? Neither woman lives to tell her tale, but both are beatified as paragons of some kind of wounded femininity, and as justification for long grievances against the ruling dynasty. The Lucretia story was one of Rome's more successful cultural memes: it repeats and replicates. Will Elia prove to be a new Lyanna, a new Lucretia? As so often, Martin expands upon and further complicates a traditional idea: the rapist may not be a rapist at all, and vengeance for both real and alleged sexual violence is multiple and disparate.

Shades of Freedom

Democracy is by and large considered to be one of the great inventions of ancient Athens, and one of the greater legacies bequeathed to us by the ancients. For most of us living in Western democracies, however, our experience of political participation is drastically different from anything the Athenians might have recognized as their own. For example, we do not, as the Athenians did, draw lots to elect our office-holders, but vote for them instead out of a small slate of self-selecting candidates who have been preapproved by their own party protocols. Though we might choose Conservative or Labour, Democrat or Republican, we are never at the mercy of chance: it isn't just any Democrat who would suffice, nor even any random citizen, but rather a political operative who works within party systems. In fact, even those who would purport to work outside such systems can't escape it entirely, or don't in practice distance themselves all that much. For the Athenians, by contrast, all citizens were considered equal, and therefore any of them would do as an office-holder. Further, the only way to ensure that the exercise of power was spread out evenly among all the citizens was to draw lots from within regularly rotating groups, so that any one citizen would have the same chance at power, and for the same duration, as anyone else. This seeming equity is, of course, misleading, because when the Athenians said 'all citizens' they meant only men, and only those born to other Athenian citizens. Women, migrants, slaves, or other residents had no direct political participation: they had no say in making the rules that regulated and controlled their lives. The Roman view of citizenship was altogether more flexible: freed slaves, Italian allies, and those foreigners who rendered the Roman state particularly meritorious service could all expect to be given some gradation of the citizenship, and either full or partial protection of Roman law. But both Greece and Rome were slave-owning societies, and whatever conditions those slaves lived under, or whatever opportunities they could look forward to at

Rome, there was no escaping this clear and sharp contrast: there were those who were free, and those who, in the most absolute of terms, were not.

The distinction between slave and free is the foundation of ancient ideas of freedom, and it sits at a complicated intersection of politics, law, ethics, and ideology. All types of political regime were, by some definition, free. Absolute monarchies were sovereign, so that even kingdoms like Persia or Egypt, the quintessential examples of autocracy, were to some extent free in the sense that they were not conquered by an external force. For the Greeks and Romans, however, that was cold comfort: in an absolute monarchy, the only genuinely free man was the king. Everyone else was de facto his slave, and therefore not free. Free states, by contrast, are characterized by the rule of law, by the distribution of limited power among the citizens, and by open, extensive, and frank face-to-face interaction in the senate or assemblies, as well as in the public sphere more generally. That, despite substantial differences from antiquity, is what we today colloquially call democracy and the Romans would have called a republic (*res publica*, literally 'the common concern'), and that is also where we locate our basic freedom, in the ability to act free from political retaliation.[9]

Does such freedom exist in the Seven Kingdoms? By a strict political definition, any ancient man would say no. Ned Stark's trial is a perfect example: arrested for an alleged coup, even though he was operating perfectly within his legal rights as regent, Ned is persuaded to confess. As soon as he does, he relies entirely on the king's caprice, and Joffrey signals his tyrannical disposition with this first act of his reign. Rather than do what he has been coached to do by his mother and advisors, he decides instead to execute Ned, whether as a show of force or simply to hurt Sansa, who is standing at his side. Indeed, the Westerosi court has all the hallmarks of corrupt power, as the ancients would have seen it: little birds spy and whisper, eunuchs and women run the country, and everyone can be bought and sold for the right amount – though whether they stay bought is another matter. Still, just because Westeros is authoritarian does not mean it lacks ideas of freedom or decency: for instance, across the Seven Kingdoms slavery is forbidden and engaging in the slave trade is an abomination, as Jorah Mormont finds out to his cost. Since Westeros is heavily modeled on the English Middle Ages, this attitude might recall the much later doctrine of the free air of England, which, in theory, turned every slave who arrived on English soil into a free person (but which didn't stop English participation in the Atlantic slave trade). But whatever its historical source, Westeros' status as a non-slave society throws into sharp relief the existence of slaves elsewhere in the Known World, against which the Westerosi can feel themselves ethical and superior, whatever their crimes or attitudes at home.

Still, there are other examples of freedom on the Westerosi landmass, though it is striking to note that they are all located in the geographical periphery. So, for example, women, even those of low or illegitimate status, have much greater political power in Dorne, where primogeniture does not exclude female offspring, and where Oberyn Martell's mistress and illegitimate daughters are neither shamed nor excluded for their status. On the other end of the continent, Asha Greyjoy carves for herself a genuine place among the powerful on the Iron Islands, right down to captaining her own ship and undertaking her own voyages and military assignments. But just like the rest of the Seven Kingdoms, neither Dorne nor the Iron Islands are truly free: whether or not they remain under the authority of King's Landing, they are still ruled by a single hereditary ruler whose word is law. The only real example Westeros knows of the kind of freedom that recognizes no mastery is that of the wildlings across the Wall, a people they see as savage and threatening, and who are very much locked in perpetual antagonism with the 'kneelers' south of the Wall and all they represent. Before we look further at both the wildlings and Slaver's Bay, we might observe a point of structure: both environments are ones of controlled chaos, experimentation, and education; and both Dany and Jon Snow learn leadership by immersing themselves in hierarchical autocracy and in embracing various degrees of freedom. Dany frees the slaves, Jon lives with the wildlings – but neither explicitly intends to transform Westeros itself into anything other than it is. The headiness of unfettered freedom remains strictly outside Westeros proper.

Mother: Dany in Slaver's Bay

Daenerys' sweep of the cities of Slaver's Bay combines what should appear as two opposite phenomena: the intrinsic authoritarianism of a Targaryen queen and *khaleesi* and her passionate commitment to the freeing of the slaves, and in particular of the Unsullied, troops of slaves raised and trained as perfect war machines. According to modern sensibilities, there should be an almost irreconcilable difference between freedom on the one hand and the autocratic rule of one person on the other. Freedom, after all, is something the West, at least, has come to associate deeply with democracy. This idea, however, is the product of certain cultures, times, and places. The ancients, who did not believe that all men were created equal, saw no problem with being free from autocracy and holding slaves at the same time. Nor, it seems, does Daenerys; her freeing of the Unsullied merely transfers them from being owned to being in her service: on the one hand a deeply meaningful change in status, but on the other hand making little real difference to their purpose and lives. Freedom cannot undo what the Unsullied have already been through: a loss of personhood, names, individual identities, or a choice in what they do and how they do it.

Notwithstanding the dramatics made possible by having a dragon breathing fire on the scene, a Roman would have recognized the procedure Dany enacts with the Unsullied as that of manumission: the legal transition from a slave to a freed man (I say 'freed' and not 'free' because the Romans recognized a real difference between being a former slave and being born free, although both could enjoy the same Roman citizenship). Roman masters often manumitted slaves in their wills as a reward for faithful service during the owner's lifetime. Much more rarely, a slave might save enough of his or her meager allowance to buy their freedom. When a Roman man deemed one of his slaves deserving, he could choose to enact proceedings to change the slave's legal status, and confer on him Roman citizenship as well as (usually) his patron's Roman name. Thus, a Greek slave named Andronicus might be freed by his Roman master, Livius, and become himself the Roman citizen Livius Andronicus (a historical, and famous, poet). But the new citizen, although free, still had obligations toward his former master; rather than slave, he would become a client, one of the throng of men who waited upon the Roman rich and famous to perform any number of services. Clients might do odd jobs for their patron, or accompany him as he went about his daily business in the Roman forum, showing by their numbers the popularity and clout of the patron. Above all, clients might vote for their patron, canvass for him as he ran for important public office, and generally be at the ready to show themselves their patron's man. In exchange, patrons offered a powerful network of connections and benefactions: sons might be placed in useful jobs or given postings in the army; the patron might serve as his client's legal representation in a trial, or provide local muscle to keep racketeers away from shops and other businesses. And, if nothing else, patrons handed out gifts of cash, food, and other utilities as surety against future service. Clients needn't have been former slaves – indeed, they could come from all walks of life. But while a former master lived, a freed slave could expect to continue his service, albeit in a different capacity.

Some freedmen opened businesses and left behind them great monuments of their success and prosperity. Others, especially those lucky enough to have been freed by or associated with those who rose to the highest power, could achieve great status and success. Lucius Cornelius Chrysogonus, the freedman of the dictator Sulla, was the overseer of Sulla's proscriptions, a process which entailed the loss of citizenship, life, and property for all those designated as public enemies by the dictator. Chrysogonus controlled the list, oversaw the auctions of confiscated properties, and handed out the prize money for those who showed up with the head of any proscribed person. He also sold places on those lists to people who offered rich enough bribes to proscribe their enemies, and ensured that those who enjoyed his favor got the best deals on any sold property. Whether Chrysogonus really was the one to introduce corruption to proceedings or was simply the scapegoat for his even more powerful master is unknown, but when he was found out the dictator claimed ignorance, and ordered his former slave executed.

Later on, powerful freedmen ran the imperial bureaucracy, influenced emperors and generals, and de facto ran the court, its archives, and accounts. The emperor Claudius, already mocked for his limp and his stutter, was also mocked for being controlled by women and former slaves, and the social importance of freedmen only grew as the empire became bigger and more complicated to govern. This is not surprising: slaves who were manumitted were often those who served close to their masters, positions which they reached by being competent and highly skilled in the tasks they were assigned. They were often literate, better educated than their masters, and in charge of the high-level operations of the great houses of Rome. For all that, however, freedmen were still looked down on and mocked as a consequence of their servile origin. A satirical work from the reign of Nero shows freedmen sitting down to a symposium which works very hard to imitate the lifestyle of the aristocracy, but succeeds only in exposing them as crass, excessive, tasteless, and unable to appreciate the finer aspects of high culture – an unfair description, to be sure, but there were worse things than mockery, since all this of course applied only to the very luckiest of slaves. Moreover, the bad rap suffered by freedmen can in part be attributed to the authors of our sources, almost all of whom were free aristocrats. The authority of these men – often of senatorial rank, like Seneca, Tacitus, and Pliny – was threatened by the ascendant freedmen, and in imperial times they saw the emperor's close reliance on freedmen as dubious and supplanting the proper influence and role of the senatorial elite. In other words, whether reading ancient historical texts or contemporary fiction, we have to be alert to the class tensions that underlie and subtly affect the perspectives and representations on show.[10]

Slavery across the ancient world had its own hierarchies, and these came along with severe differences in quality of life, length of survival, and opportunities for improvement or freedom. All slaves shared a legal status: they were the property of someone else, and as such were excluded from any of the protections of the law. Roman religion illustrates this starkly: during the Compitalia, a holiday dedicated to the Lares Compitales, household gods of crossroads, worshippers hung little dolls from tree branches. Free Roman citizens hung little human-shaped dolls made of wool. Slaves, however, hung woolen balls, since they had no legal rights or protections even over their own persons. Slaves were vulnerable to

26. Roman slave shackles

sexual or physical violence by their master, and slaves' families could be broken up at will. Slave evidence in trial was only admissible if it was extracted by torture, and slave jokes (for instance on the comic stage) were often focused on torture and other forms of violence. If they worked outdoors, slaves wore collars stating that they were the runaway slaves of so-and-so, and that whoever captured them ought to send them back for punishment.

Slaves performed an enormous range of tasks, and were present in nearly every waking moment of the master's and family's daily lives, but their presence is hardly ever mentioned in the vast majority of our sources: slaves cooked and cleaned, kept the house, served meals, fetched items, helped their masters dress themselves, and did up their hair. Less fortunate slaves did all sorts of menial labor, and the more physical the task the less likely was the slaves' chance of survival. Perhaps the most punishing assignment was work in the mines: slaves mined the silver that financed Athens' trade, empire, and artistic culture. In Roman Spain, slaves mined lead and harvested the mineral wealth of the province for the benefit of aristocratic generals like Gaius Marius and later on Caesar. Equally punishing work was done in the fields, whether on smaller private farms, where slaves and masters might toil together, or vast agricultural holdings, where slave gangs worked under the supervision of an overseer. And though the practice of manumission might suggest that the Romans, at least, had a softer approach to their slaves, Cato the Elder shows the much more prevalent attitude when he advises his readers to sell their slaves as soon as they get too old to work: to do otherwise would be, for the entrepreneurial gentleman-farmer, nothing more than a waste of scarce resources.

The slaver cities of Slaver's Bay acquire their stock not from going out to war themselves, but from a slave trade fed heavily by wars between Dothraki *khalasars* and incursions into the lands of the so-called 'Lamb People' who live between Slaver's Bay and the lands of the Dothraki. Other slaves, we assume, come from further east, as well as from across the lands that used to be the Valyrian empire. The Summer Islands, too, are a source of slave resources, but it isn't quite clear what kind of interaction these islands have with the rest of the Known World. The ancient slave trade, too, stretched across a vast geographic area, and most of the slaves came from selling into slavery the women and children of conquered cities and even whole nations. As early as the Homeric epics it is understood that slavery was the fate that awaited any Trojan who survived the war, and this practice lasted long past antiquity. After a military defeat, surviving men of fighting age would be put to the sword, while everyone else was sold to slave traders who swarmed after the Roman legions. Some of the new slaves were then sold at home, whether to serve in private homes – slave ownership ran deep in Roman society, and many low-income households could still keep one or two slaves – or in the fields and mines. Others were sold further afield, whether to other places across the Mediterranean or to the Persian empire. The only aspect of ancient life forbidden to slaves was military service: that was the province of free citizens, and theirs alone. Only once in Roman history, in the darkest of days during Hannibal's invasion, were slaves drafted for the legions, and so well did they fight that they were awarded their freedom. The occasion was deemed so unusual that it was commemorated in a mural in the Roman forum, a testament to the importance of slaves in Roman life.

Daenerys frees the slaves by executive fiat – she simply announces that they are free, and enforces this by her own presence and new position as queen. The Unsullied, for their part, go into her service, just as Roman freedmen would have remained obligated to their master or mistress. The slaves, and especially the Unsullied, respond by hailing her as 'Mother,' an honorific that already resonates with her informal title as Mother of Dragons. It is poignant as well because Daenerys herself cannot bear children – or, at least, she thinks she cannot, having been cursed by the *maegi* Mirri Maz Duur. All she has instead is her dragons, and now too the former slaves. Viewers of the liberation scenes in the HBO adaptations have expressed some discomfort with the image of a white woman being worshipped by a group of dark-skinned people, and the scene is indeed uncomfortable not only from a racial perspective but because calling Daenerys 'Mother' puts the ex-slaves in the position of children. The power dynamic in effect has changed very little, although it now has a strong dimension of affection attached to it, maternalism in place of the more customary paternalism. In Rome, too, slaves were in a similar legal position to children, in the sense that sons and daughters were also subject to the will of the *paterfamilias*, the master of the household. The *paterfamilias* in turn had considerable power over his family members, from his wife on down to the least valuable of the slaves. He could, for instance, beat both the free and the enslaved members of his household, and even sell them into slavery, a practice that must have been common enough that a law survives specifying that after a son had been sold into slavery three times, he was considered a free man and out of his father's power.[11]

Perhaps the most controversial power the *paterfamilias* had, however, was the power of life and death over his family members. It is not entirely clear what exactly the law meant by this right, but at the very least it allowed the master to decide whether or not to acknowledge as his own any children born to his wife, or indeed to any woman in the household with whom he had sexual relations. A household might contain, therefore, in addition to legitimate children, also slave children called *uernae* – children born to a slave woman and a free man within the household. These children received their mother's servile status but were often raised alongside the rest of the family, a situation Jon Snow would have been deeply familiar with. For children born to the *materfamilias* (the master's wife), the husband could decide whether to recognize the child as his own, in which case the child was accepted into the household, or reject it as either deformed or illegitimate, in which case the child was often left to die or given away. This custom is horrific enough, but ancient Rome knew many stories in which fathers ordered the death of their adult sons as well: one father was rumored to be so depraved that he ordered his son killed so he could marry the son's beautiful bride instead. Since the father happened also to be a conspirator against the state, the story is very unlikely to be true, but it shows both the Roman revulsion at paternal filicide and the readiness with which they could attribute it to someone. Another father, during a military campaign, ordered his son executed for disobeying an order – this despite the fact that the son gained an important victory by disobeying the order, and despite his impassioned pleas. And as early as the first year of the republic its founder, Brutus, executed his own sons, who had conspired to restore the kings that the citizens of Rome had only just succeeded in overthrowing. In short, the Roman family was legally and ethically a highly complex environment, where fathers had extensive rights over their children, rights that ran parallel to the rights the same fathers had over their slaves.

Although women in Rome could own slaves in their own right, and therefore probably had the same rights in relation to their slaves as their husbands did, mothers did not seem to have the same legal powers over their children, and were in fact equally in the power of the *paterfamilias*. However, the ancient imagination was full of women able and willing to kill and plot against any who tried to thwart them: Clytemnestra kills her husband, Medea both her sons in order to spite their father. According to rumor, Livia, the wife of the emperor Augustus, poisoned anyone who stood in her own son's way to inherit the throne. Dany herself exercises an informal version of the right to determine life or death when she decides both to revive Khal Drogo and then later on when she decides to kill the soulless golem he has become. Only life can pay for life, says the *maegi*, and Dany chooses which life is more precious to her. The loss of her unborn child proves devastating, but she chooses it nevertheless, albeit unknowingly.

The maternal relationship, though not as endorsed by the state and the force of law and institution, nevertheless had its fair share of terrible precedents. So when the Unsullied call Daenerys 'Mother,' the honorific packs a lot of punch. It connotes the affection of a mother, as well as the idea of manumission as rebirth, of freedom as a kind of life following the social death of slavery. But it also hints at turbulent power dynamics beneath the surface: though they are no longer chattel, they are also not entirely free. They are unwilling to abandon her who freed them, and unable, perhaps, to undo the training of years of forced service. The noblemen of Meereen, for their part, undergo the same process, but in reverse: they pretend to acquiesce in the new order, but are unwilling and unable to really learn to live without slaves. Insurrection and unrest is all around Dany, as well as the effect of unleashing people who are unused to civic life into the city: vengeance and freedom mix together to produce difficult conditions within and outside the city.

Outside the city converge mercenary bands of all stripes and colors, paid by Dany's enemies as well as her friends to make war against the foreign queen. In sharp contrast to the slaving culture of Slaver's Bay, mercenaries offer an example of a more mobile type of freedom. Bound by choice to the leader of the mercenary companies, mercenaries are soldiers for hire, selling their services to whomever they like – a degree of freedom rarely enjoyed within the city-states of the ancient world. There, although citizens might participate in voting for or against a war, recruitment was by and large mandatory, and done by sending officers into the countryside to draft any able-bodied man of eligible age, provided he had not already served the legally mandated number of campaigns. In times of dire need, as when Rome was fighting Carthage on multiple fronts, or after the heavy loss of life in the early years of the Hannibalic War, the last two conditions were often overlooked. Rome and Athens could also rely on the military strength of their allies, who were bound by treaty to contribute men, officers, ships, or other equipment to the war effort. These foreign forces were often commanded by their own officers, and provided their own maintenance and armor in the field. But even these were not always enough. Rome, for instance, lacked a good cavalry, despite the notional role of the aristocracy as mounted troops. The answer, rather than train at home, was simply to hire abroad: both the Gauls and Numidians excelled in cavalry warfare, and rented out their skills and troops to Rome or any other forces. Carthage, in contrast to Rome, hired the majority of both its cavalry and its infantry, and paid a very heavy price when all these long-term hires defected and turned on them after the Hannibalic War.

But the situation outside Meereen recalls above all the convergence of mercenary bands in the Persian hinterlands around the fourth century BC. Athens, Sparta, and the rest of the Greek world had been aware of and involved in Persian affairs from very early on. Athenian grandees used the Persian court as a last refuge if they were exiled from home, despite the wary relationship between Persia and Greece through the classical period. But in the late fourth century, 10,000 Greek mercenaries were brought together to fight for a Persian prince, Cyrus the Younger, who aimed to seize the throne from his elder brother. This mercenary army marched far inland toward Babylon, where they fought and won the Battle of Cunaxa. The victory proved empty, however. Cyrus was killed in the fighting, and the Greeks found themselves stranded alone in a strange and hostile land. What happened next was one of the great adventure stories of antiquity. Banding together despite their different nationalities and allegiances, the Greeks managed to fight their way back toward the sea and home. The *Anabasis*, as the story of the 10,000 is known, makes for a great yarn, but it is also a story of Greek political cohesion in the face of adversity.[12] Although they come from many of the city-states of Greece, all the mercenaries are united by the necessity of survival in a hostile environment, and they begin to work together as a unified group – a political vision of Greece realized only in the heyday of the Persian War, and not to be repeated until Greek independence.

The situation outside Meereen raises interesting questions, therefore. Greek companies tended to divide along national lines: Spartan, Theban, Athenian, and so on. This meant that they had many things in common, and made them also miniature versions of the city-states they came from. The idea of an army as a mobile city is old, going back to the Greek army in Troy, another instance of a general Greek mobilization made up of smaller regional units. Despite the fact that the mercenary companies around Meereen are not based on nationality, they do by and large conform to the same social hierarchies one might find in a functioning city: someone is in charge overall, there is a layer of leadership which advises the leader but also has its own interests, and the rest of the company combine personal interests with loyalty to the entire group. Like the roving *khalasar*, where riders are able to challenge a weak *khal* or defect to another *khalasar*, so too the mercenary companies are an image of a free city on the move, picking and choosing what it will do and why based on its own interests and opportunities. What will happen next with the companies is unclear – the Golden Company has declared for Aegon Targaryen and begun marching for Dorne. Dany, for her part, has chosen to move away from the mercenary model to practice queenship, while Aegon and Tyrion have adopted the companies wholeheartedly. How different the two approaches are, or how successful, is in many ways the big question in the fortunes of House Targaryen.

THE WILDLINGS

While Daenerys finds her feet as *khaleesi* and queen in Essos, Jon Snow explores the furthest reaches of Westeros, the cold climes that stretch beyond the Wall. It is a strange world, populated by wild tribes, mammoths and giants, Old Gods and White Walkers, and as we learn when Bran makes the same voyage, also sentient trees and talking crows. In this, at least, it forms a parallel with the mystical world of the far East, from where Melisandre draws her magic, and with Daenerys' dragons. All are manifestations of the supernatural, a stock element of fantasy which is here kept to the margins rather than taking center stage as is more often the case in the genre. This demarcation of the supernatural follows in the tradition of Roman ethnography, a commonplace of writing wherein the author deviates from the regular plot to describe a particular place, its geography, and its inhabitants. The ancients believed that the geography and weather patterns of a place influenced the character and physical build of its inhabitants, so it was important to know the lay of the land in order to know what kind of people lived there. For the Romans, Italy was an earthly paradise, the perfect place to nurture an imperial people: bountiful in crops, but not so lush as to encourage softness, equally distant from the excessive cold of the north and heat of the south; it produced men of medium build, used to hard work but not drained by extreme or unnecessary hardship.[13] The hot east, on the other hand, with its wealth in spices and gold, produced men who were too soft to be proper fighters, although prodigious in the arts and in philosophy. In the north, by contrast, you might encounter hulking giants of great physical prowess but without much mental agility, so that the Romans could always win by being nimbler and lighter on their feet. Geography is thus a convenient justification for the Romans' own sense of superiority, and Westeros by and large maps itself along similar lines: Dorne is sensuous and soft, the Starks in the North are harsh and proud, and the middle of the kingdom, from Highgarden to Lannisport, combines wealth and fecundity with the center of political power.

Ethnographic writing has a set of conventions and interests which shaped how these texts worked and what they described. Oddly, one of these conventions was that ethnographies were distinct from travel memoirs, even when authors were describing places they had actually lived in or visited. Ethnographies were not a faithful description of what travelers saw on their journey, but rather a combination of convention, local tradition, outright invention, and previous accounts of the same places. Another common convention was that ethnographies always proceeded from civilization into the wild, so that they became less and less 'normal' as they went. Herodotus' description of Egypt, for instance, starts out in the Nile Delta on the Mediterranean shore, which was where most Greeks who went to Egypt might disembark. Traveling up the Nile away from the Mediterranean (i.e., south) would see our traveler encounter stranger and stranger things, from the growing prominence of the animal-headed gods worshipped in the local religion to outright fantasies like winged serpents and the phoenix that lives for 500 years.[14]

The Romans were even more explicit: in Gaul (modern-day France) near the border with Rome you'd find the most civilized of the Gauls, masters of rhetoric and participants in all the rituals of civilization, like the drinking of wine. As you moved further away, however, civilization (by which the Romans meant only what they would approve as civilization) quickly faded away. The seemingly civilized Gauls would turn out to worship trees and practice human sacrifice, as well as polygamy and other sorts of lewd and strange behavior. Still, the Gauls had some redeeming features in the eyes of the Romans, since they practiced much of their politics in ways the Romans could recognize: an organized religion, a code of honor that demanded warriors stood their ground, elaborate funerals, a political structure that had rotating magistrates, proper marriages, and a deep cultural memory that included reading, writing, and rhetoric. But beyond the Gauls lay an even less civilized people: the Germans, who ran around naked, had no system of permanent agriculture or law, and worshipped no gods, not even the kind that required human sacrifice, but instead only what they could see – the sun, the moon, and fire. And the wildness of Germany is truly confirmed by its geography. While the Gauls have some semblance of city living, the Germans rotate their people in randomly allocated plots of land. Further, the environment itself is strange: the rivers are exceptionally deep and foggy, and the place is bounded by a vast forest, so massive that no living German could claim to have ever reached the other side. And still stranger creatures live there: rams with only one horn growing between their eyes, enormous bears, and elks with no knees who lean against trees to sleep in the night, or at least try, since the forest is also full of unusual birds who shine brightly in the dark.[15]

The Germans continued to fascinate the Romans even as the Roman empire encroached further on their lands, and as Romans came to know more and more about them. Tacitus, for instance, the great historian on the Julio-Claudian house, wrote a potted history of the Germans, called the *Germania*, which still holds some of the earliest accounts of what is today the nation of Germany. Other peoples which fascinated the Romans were those of Britain, the Iceni, the Picts, and others whom the Romans had never encountered before Caesar crossed the channel in 55 BC. Indeed, the more the empire grew, the more fascinated were the Romans with the people who lay just beyond their borders, and the stronger their desire to conquer and domesticate them. Of course, they met strong resistance, for instance the rebellion of Boudicca, and they always responded with swift and unrelenting brutality. Even the Romans themselves were aware of the brutality of their conquest, and used ethnographic works to put criticisms of the Roman empire in the mouth of those who most directly resisted it. These speeches were often a figment of the author's invention, but they are no less stirring for it. One of the more trenchant ones is 'given' by the Caledonian leader Calgacus, rousing his people before the battle at Mount Graupius:

> As often as I consider the causes of war and our dire straits, I have great confidence that this day and your union will be the beginning of freedom for all Britain; for you have all joined together, you who have not experienced slavery, for whom there are no lands further on and not even the sea is safe, with the Roman fleet threatening us. Thus battle and weapons, which are honorable for the brave, are likewise the greatest source of safety even for cowards. Earlier struggles, in which we fought against the Romans with varying success, had a hope of assistance at our hands, since we, the noblest people of all Britain

and for that reason living in its innermost sanctuary and not gazing upon any shores of those in slavery, kept our eyes also free from the contagion of conquest. Us, the most distant people of the earth and of liberty, our very isolation and the obscurity of our renown have protected up to this day: now the farthest boundary of Britain lies open, and everything unknown is considered marvelous, but now there are no people further on, nothing except waves and rocks, and the Romans more hostile than these, whose arrogance you would in vain try to avoid by obedience and submission. Plunderers of the world, after they, laying everything waste, ran out of land, they search out the sea: if the enemy is wealthy, they are greedy, if he is poor, they seek prestige, men whom neither the East nor the West has sated: they alone of all men desire wealth and poverty with equal enthusiasm. Robbery, butchery, rapine they call empire by euphemisms, and when they produce a wasteland, they call it peace.[16]

Faced with eloquence of such fervor, Roman readers themselves must have found it difficult to resist shaking their own fist against the oppressor – themselves. And indeed, one of the key tricks ethnography plays on the reader is to blur the boundaries between the self and the other – Romans see some of themselves in the barbaric Gauls and even more barbaric Germans, and feel some of the indignation of being on the wrong side of a legionary advance. This creates a kind of affective dissonance: the foreign is brought closer in, but without actually stopping or undermining the imperial project, and without outright suggesting that the Romans are doing something wrong in pushing their empire's boundaries further and further.

Westeros is not, by and large, an imperialist nation; or more precisely, the days of expanding its borders are long past. Instead, the Wall is a defensive measure, and the Night's Watch hold fervently to the belief that their task is of paramount importance. This belief, however, seems to be something they share less and less with anyone beyond the Watch itself, barring only the Starks at Winterfell, who remain sympathetic to the Watch and its travails. The further south one goes, however, the less convinced the king and lords become of the urgency or national importance of the Watch's task. They therefore increasingly use the Wall as a dumping spot for the criminal and the poor, a combination of murderers and rapists as well as perpetrators of small-time crimes driven by hunger and desperation. Arya travels in the company of just such a group from King's Landing, and they make for quite a change from the more dignified members of the Watch we meet earlier. It is no coincidence that the very first scene of the whole saga features one of the aristocratic members of the Watch dying during a ranging mission beyond the Wall, and that Ben Stark goes missing shortly thereafter. Inasmuch as this frontier zone is a microcosm of Westeros itself, the aristocratic elements of the Watch dwindle and the Watch is overstretched; just so, the Southern court cannot hold onto the stability and prosperity of peace, as the very people who might have held things together fall victim to plot and intrigue. But there is still some hope: the success of the Watch, after all, is predicated not on the pedigree of its watchmen, but on their devotion to the cause, as their awful oath spells out. And although even the Watch is not free from class distinctions (Jon Snow suffers twice, once on account of being a bastard, and once on account of being the bastard of Winterfell and therefore as good as one of the upper crust), on the Wall anyone can rise to a position of authority if they are good enough and survive to serve long enough. The same cannot quite be said of the war-torn South, although people like Varys and Littlefinger suggest that even here hard work and survival skills can still produce advancement – whether that advancement is used for the greater good, however, is anyone's guess.

A more interesting question, however, is who exactly it is that the Watch is meant to protect against. Their oath does not specify; they simply 'guard the realms of men' (*GT* 522) from any and all unspecified dangers coming from the North. As the series develops,

we are clearly meant to suspect, together with Sam and Jon, that
the real enemies that the Wall is meant to stop are the Others, the
mysterious White Walkers, against whom so far the only defense
is obsidian, or perhaps Valyrian steel. This suggestion makes ample
sense within the programmatic tension between ice and fire, since
obsidian and Valyrian steel are both associated with dragons and
fire – in other words, with some type of Targaryen return to old and
forgotten origins. Sam attempts to shortcut the process by delving
deep into the library at the Wall, and it cannot be a coincidence that
the maester of the Night's Watch turns out to be himself a Targaryen,
a living repository of dragon lore. But until the White Walkers make
a definitive advance against the kingdoms of Westeros, the enemy
on the ground is not the Others but the wildlings, a loose collec-
tion of tribes and people, who seem to have no more in common
than a hatred for the men of the Watch, as well as a fierce sense of
freedom ('kneelers,' they call the people south of the Wall, and 'we
do not kneel' is Mance Rayder's refrain to Stannis Baratheon when
he demands allegiance).

Like the tribes of Gaul and Germany, the various groupings
of the wildlings normally recognize no single overlord – indeed,
to do so would be anathema to their way of living, in which sense
they are not very dissimilar from the Romans (and to a lesser
extent the Greeks), who also abhorred monarchy and the loss of
political freedom. However, under the growing threat from the
White Walkers, the wildlings come together under the leadership
of Mance Rayder, a former Night's Watch man gone rogue, who is
meant to lead them south of the Wall, where they can live in some
safety from the threats that exist beyond. The whole situation is
reminiscent of the one Caesar finds in Gaul when he arrives on the
scene: the Gallic tribe of the Helvetii has been pushed south from
its homelands toward southern Gaul and the Roman province by
a German migration coming from further north. But the Gauls
nearer the Roman province neither want nor can afford their presence, and send to Rome for help. Caesar, in turn, tells the Germans

to go back where they came from, since Rome would permit them neither to live in nor travel through the Roman sphere of influence. The Germans, however, seem to have little choice, and inevitably Caesar must face them in battle.

This kind of tribal migration was common in the ancient world, especially beyond the borders of the established powers around the Mediterranean and in the Fertile Crescent. The Greeks and Romans, of course, often could not really know the ultimate reasons why a barbarian tribe might have suddenly come knocking on their borders – perhaps they were driven away by another tribe, as was the case with the Goths in the fourth century AD, who were displaced by the Huns, a fact of which the Romans were aware. Whatever the cause, however, the Romans inevitably had to deal with the consequences. In Caesar's case, he used the Helvetian invasion as the pretext for a ten-year campaign in Gaul, which ended only when the entire province was brought to heel, together with parts of Germany, Belgium, and southern Britain. The reason it took ten long years, however, was not simply the original Gallic tribe of the Helvetii – they are swiftly dispensed with and rarely heard from again – but rather that the tribes of Gaul are brought together by necessity and common hatred of the new oppressor. Like Mance Rayder, a single figure, the chieftain Vercingetorix eventually brought together what were normally disparate and sometimes hostile tribes. It is just such a diversity of tribes – Goths and Visigoths and their various subgroups – that is often associated with the so-called collapse of the Roman empire in the fourth century AD and onwards. Whereas the example of Vercingetorix suggests the pacification of the wildlings, then, the later examples of Fritigern and Alaric, tribal leaders both, suggest the existential threat felt – rightly or wrongly – by those south of the Wall.

The term 'wildlings' covers a diverse group of people. The Magnar of Thenn, Mance Rayder, and the old man Craster are all, technically speaking, wildlings, but they could not be more different from each other. Their leader knows this better than anyone: 'They

27. Vercingetorix

speak seven different languages in my army' (S3, E2), he informs Jon
Snow, and the only reason he can keep them together is to convince
them that it is more dangerous on the north side of the Wall than
on the southern one. This, too, is a classical marker of the 'other'
or the enemy in Greek and Roman thought: the Trojan forces at
Troy, consisting of various allies, speak many languages, as does the
vast force raised by the great king Xerxes to march on Greece, and
as does Hannibal's army fighting against Rome. Even the Roman
general Pompey the Great's army, with its Eastern allies, speaks
many languages, a sure sign that it is inferior to Caesar's thoroughly
Latin-speaking army. To this common detail is added a further layer
of linguistic presentation: Caesar's Gauls and Homer's Trojans speak
correct Latin and Greek, respectively, although Caesar's text makes

occasional mention of interpreters. So too do Martin's wildlings: for all their linguistic variety, they speak the Common Tongue of Westeros, so that neither Jon Snow nor anyone else ever needs an interpreter to speak with any of the wildlings that they encounter. This is partially a requirement of convenience and consistency, the same way we all know that Nazis in Hollywood movies would have spoken German among themselves, rather than English with a heavy German accent. But this is also partly a matter of focalization, of establishing a specific point of view – the wildlings are only wildlings, as opposed to distinct Thenns and Hornfoots and Moon Worshippers, if one insists on remaining willfully ignorant of the differences between them, just as they all speak the Common Tongue because of a fundamental power asymmetry: not only are they excluded from the Seven Kingdoms by the force of many swords, they are not even given their own voice to tell their own actions, histories, or, in the case of Rayder and Calgacus, the stories of their own resistance. They exist only inasmuch as someone from the center of power comes to see them for their own purpose. Jon is beyond the Wall to spy, not to mingle, and Caesar comes to Gaul as a conqueror, not an anthropologist.

Even Bran, the most likely candidate for genuine immersion in life beyond the Wall, comes out of necessity. Homeless, controlled by his emerging warg powers, and led by dreams of a mysterious three-eyed raven, his voyage to the North seems a world apart from anything else that might be happening across the land. Whether his voyage proves fruitful is uncertain, but even he comes looking for something he cannot quite name. None of the Westerosi voyagers in the lands beyond the Wall have any genuine claim to understanding that wild and mysterious place. Like the Hercynian Forest, it has fabulous animals and sights, and like the Gallic tribes, the wildlings practice strange religions and have strange ways of conducting their affairs. Long years of exposure to the Wall and the Watch have conditioned them in certain ways, so that they know where safety lies, what code the world south of the Wall lives by, and what political ideologies they espouse. But above all, the wildlings stand for what Westeros is not: untamed, radically free, and still immersed in the paranormal.

And yet through that ostensible contrast our attention is also drawn to the ways in which Westeros is closer to the wildlings than at first glance: individuals can exemplify 'wildness' in the most extreme terms (consider Gregor Clegane or Ramsay Bolton), its people can cherish freedom (the character of the ironborn or the motto of House Martell, 'Unbowed, Unbent, Unbroken'), and strange forces can be seen at work (the magic of R'hllor has come to Westeros, and the necromantic powers of Qyburn originated in Westeros' very own Citadel). This doubleness – at once differentiating and assimilating two groups – is characteristic of ancient ethnography. As much as it alternately alienates and normalizes the other, it does the same for the reader's view of their own culture. And this is perhaps the clearest overarching lesson for how we ourselves should interpret *Game of Thrones* as a work of art: its fantasy world has its more and less familiar parts, to be sure, but it's the implicit comparisons with our own world, and the ways in which our self-conceptions are constructed and undermined, that emerge illuminated by the mirror of fiction.

28. Watcher on the Wall

EPILOGUE

There is one question that every reader or viewer of *Game of Thrones* wants answered: what happens at the end? All sorts of speculation have been floated: a military victory by one of the contenders, a complete collapse of Westerosi society, a cosmic encounter between good and evil as the screen fades to black on one last 'Hodor.' What is in store, then, for war-torn Westeros, and can the classics, in all their manifold presence, help us predict it? As far as definitive prediction goes, the answer, I'm afraid, is a categorical no. Even ancient literature, with its generic conventions, cannot predetermine what any single author will do; and anyway, a single myth could have very different endings in different retellings. What I *can* do, however, is to follow a few threads to a logical conclusion, and offer some options for what ending this story might be heading for.

The closest parallel antiquity offers to the situation in Westeros is the civil war in 69 AD, the year known as the Year of the Four Emperors, since four different emperors claimed the throne in the span of a single year, concluding in the coming to power of the emperor Vespasian, founder of the Flavian dynasty.[1] Although the Year of the Four Emperors conformed to the type established by the century of civil wars that destroyed the Roman republic and ushered in the Augustan regime, it nevertheless had one distinguishing characteristic, at least according to the Roman historian Tacitus, who provides us with our most detailed account of events. As in all civil wars, this war too saw the destruction of bonds of loyalty, as fathers turned on sons, brothers against brothers, and

slaves against their masters. Just as in other wars, fortunes were
made and cast down, and people found within themselves depths
of brutality and compassion of which they were previously unaware.
But unlike earlier civil wars, which were fought between the leading
figures of Roman politics (even if the actual battles took place far
away from the city), *this* civil war revealed an important truth about
the political order – that emperors could be made and undone by
armies far away from the center of power, on the far-flung borders
of the empire, in Spain and Gaul, in Germany and Judaea.

This shift in emphasis had tremendous consequences, because
it all but nullified the idea that legitimacy resided in the city of
Rome, its buildings, and its institutions. In earlier wars, holding
the city itself had important symbolic value, both for propaganda
and for control of the treasury or, even more crucially, the senate
and the people's voting assemblies. Rome's politics were from the
moment of its foundation irrevocably connected to the city and to
the civic bodies that met, made decisions, and passed laws within
its boundaries – a pretense that lasted even as Rome moved toward
an ever-increasing autocracy within an ever-expanding empire. The
Year of the Four Emperors showed the purported status of the city
to be just that, a mere pretense, since for all the legitimacy Rome
conferred, emperorship could be conferred by the will and swords
of loyal troops. And so one contender after another was declared
emperor by his armies, and they met each other in epic battles across
Italy. The clearest and most tragic sign of the change in Rome's
status was the harm done both to the city and to its inhabitants
by the troops of Vitellius, one of the claimants to the throne, as
they entered the city – damage that was further compounded later
that same year in the urban fighting between Vitellian and Flavian
soldiers. Even the temple of Jupiter on the Capitoline was burned
down: what no enemy had managed to do, says Tacitus, Rome had
done to itself. Yet the pretense was not completely empty: in order
truly to be emperor, one had to have both the support of the troops
and the city of Rome – both or nothing at all, even if the city might

lag behind the army in importance. This fundamental truth lasted until the empire became too great to manage; only then did the center of power begin to be recognized as the body of the emperor himself as he traveled across his empire.

Westeros has no senate house, and no real civic institutions to confer legitimacy on any king. What it does have, however, is the macabre Iron Throne, and that resides only in King's Landing. Like all of Rome's civil wars until the fourth century A D, the War of the Five Kings has its own centripetal motion, pulling all participants inexorably toward King's Landing. Even Renly Baratheon, waylaid and murdered in Storm's End, makes his way to the capital city, albeit as a ghost in green armor. His brother Stannis, too, comes to the capital to suffer defeat, and after that must seek his fortunes far to the north, from where Robb Stark had already tried and failed to mount a successful bid for the throne. The southern reaches of Westeros seem, at the moment, a more promising venue, as the Targaryens strive toward Dorne, a region historically sympathetic to their interests. Will a pincer movement begin, pressing the Lannisters from both directions? Whatever else happens, it seems crucial, at this juncture, to keep an eye not on the center at King's Landing, which is going through its own set of upheavals, but rather on the edges of the map. There, indeed, be dragons.

Besides the locus of authority, another question which the Year of the Four Emperors brings up is that of legitimacy – what is it that makes a man or a woman a true king or queen? Westeros again has limited mechanisms to establish this, as, for that matter, did ancient Rome: a senatorial proclamation or people's decree has limited value, after all, when obtained at the end of a sword. In both cases, it would seem, might is right, and the contender who suppresses all competition will gain victory. This, to some extent, characterizes the ascendancy of the first Roman emperor, Augustus, who simply eliminated by war, murder, or threats all who opposed him until there was no significant opposition left. Still, some other mechanisms besides force pertain. The reign of Robert Baratheon shows us that inheritance is an important factor – even as he rose against Targaryen tyranny, stories were circulated about his family relationship to the ruling family. (Recall, too, that Augustus' great-uncle and adoptive father was none other than Julius Caesar, who was dictator at the time of his assassination.) History, too, makes some kings legitimate: Robb Stark is proclaimed King in the North by the acclamation of his bannermen, and they do so on the strength of the Starks' historical kingship of the North, a kingship that they had forsaken but which was never forgotten (not least in the crypts of Winterfell, where the old kings were brought to rest). Finally, the Tyrell queen Margaery is loved because she brings with her the promise of prosperity and of full bellies for the hungry people of King's Landing, and they embrace her as such. Against all this, the Lannisters have little claim: they have neither a history of kingship, nor are they loved for their generosity, nor do they have genuine connections to either the Targaryens or the Baratheons. All they have is wealth and ambition, and these seem to be wearing down fast. By contrast, both Stannis and the Targaryen contenders have legitimate, if mutually exclusive, claims of inheritance, and both have troops, albeit foreign troops, to proclaim them rightful king.

Here, it seems, history offers a tantalizing choice. The war of 69 AD was won by the emperor Vespasian, and long before he even set foot on Italian soil. His great advantage lay in beginning his campaign not with a march on Rome, but with a march on Egypt, the better to secure Rome's grain supply for himself. Once he secured the loyalty of the Eastern armies, he could allow the other contenders to exhaust themselves against each other before coming onto the scene. Food, in Westeros, inevitably comes from the south, flowing up the roseroad from Highgarden. The fate of the Tyrells has diverged from books to series, but whoever manages to fill that void will have strong claim to make to a starved capital and starving nation. One of the other advantages Vespasian had was that his son was like him a capable and competent general, and could stand in for his father in crucial moments. Stannis, by contrast, stands alone, while the Lannisters and Targaryens each field a slightly dysfunctional brother–sister set. We mentioned already the Targaryen incestual practices and their relationship to the Egyptian Ptolemaic kings, and family indeed can prove decisive as the plot develops, whether as a bulwark of support or as a source of a new civil war, pitting families against each other again. Once again we might look to Rome, whose very beginnings sprang from a conflict between two brothers, Romulus and Remus, and whose penchant for familial and civil war didn't prevent it from also achieving new, and ever-renewed, heights of greatness.

NOTES

INTRODUCTION

1   Pliny, *Natural History* 34.18.
2   For more on the Greek city-state, see Mogens Herman Hansen, *Polis: An Introduction to the Ancient Greek City-State* (Oxford: Oxford University Press, 2006).
3   'The Wall predates anything else. I can trace back the inspiration for that to 1981. I was in England visiting a friend, and as we approached the border of England and Scotland, we stopped to see Hadrian's Wall. I stood up there and I tried to imagine what it was like to be a Roman legionary, standing on this wall, looking at these distant hills. It was a very profound feeling. For the Romans at that time, this was the end of civilization; it was the end of the world. We know that there were Scots beyond the hills, but they didn't know that. It could have been any kind of monster. It was the sense of this barrier against dark forces – it planted something in me. But when you write fantasy, everything is bigger and more colorful, so I took the Wall and made it three times as long and 700 feet high, and made it out of ice.' *Rolling Stone*, available at http://www.rollingstone.com/tv/news/george-r-r-martin-the-rolling-stone-interview-20140423.
4   Cornelius Nepos, *Themistocles* 2 (*Cornelius Nepos*, trans. J. C. Rolfe (Cambridge, MA: Harvard University Press, 1929)); Plutarch, *Themistocles* 11.4 (*The Rise and Fall of Athens: Nine Greek Lives*, trans. Ian Scott-Kilvert (London: Penguin Classics, 1960)).
5   Troy: *Iliad* 7.540–1 (*The Iliad*, trans. Robert Fitzgerald (New York: Farrar, Straus and Giroux, 2004); Thebes: Pausanias, *Description of Greece* 6.20.18, trans. W. H. S. Jones (Cambridge, MA: Harvard University Press, 1933); Rome: Livy 1.7 (*Livy: The Early History of Rome*, trans. Aubrey de Sélincourt (New York: Penguin Classics, 1971)); Dionysius of Halicarnassus, *Roman Antiquities* 87.4.
6   Livy 1.7.
7   'We were strangers lost in our own city until your books played the role of hosts, leading us home so we could at last recognize ourselves and where we were.' Cicero, *On Academic Scepticism* 1.9, trans. Charles Brittain (Indianapolis, IN, and Cambridge: Hackett Publishing, 2006).

8   Lucan, *Civil War* 3.437–45, trans. Susan H. Braund (Oxford: Oxford University Press, 1992).

9   Standard-bearer charging forth with the standard, and all the soldiers feeling compelled to follow: Caesar, *The Gallic War* 4.25, trans. Carolyn Hammond (Oxford: Oxford World's Classics, 2008); standard-bearer throwing the standard over the walls of the Roman fort to safety, ibid. 5.37; Caesar ordering the standards to be brought wherever the Romans are struggling, ibid. 7.67; Caesar grabbing a shield from a soldier and running to the front line himself, ibid. 2.25.

10   Lucan, *Civil War* 3.635–41, trans. Braund.

CHAPTER 1: FEASTS AND FAMILIES

1   For a global history of salt, see Mark Kurlansky, *Salt: A World History* (New York: Penguin, 2003).

2   Valerius Maximus 6.3.9 (*Valerius Maximus: Memorable Doings and Sayings, Vol. II*, trans. David R. Shackleton Bailey (Cambridge, MA: Harvard University Press, 2000)). Gellius, *Attic Nights* 10.23, trans. John C. Rolfe (London: William Heinemann, 1927); see also Stuart J. Fleming, *Vinum: The Story of Roman Wine* (Glen Mills, PA: Art Flair, 2001).

3   'Behind them came a great dish and on it lay a wild boar of the largest possible size […] [the butcher] pulled out a hunting knife and made a great stab at the boar's side and as he struck, out flew a flock of thrushes.' *Petronius: The Satyricon and the Fragments*, trans. John P. Sullivan (Harmondsworth: Penguin Classics, 1965). For more Roman recipes, see *Apicius*, trans. Christopher Grocock and Sally Grainger (London: Prospect Books, 2006). And for those interested in preparing the Roman recipes themselves, see Sally Grainger, *Cooking Apicius: Roman Recipes for Today* (London: Prospect Books, 2001).

4   Juvenal, *The Sixteen Satires* 4.44, trans. Peter Green (Harmondsworth: Penguin Classics, 1967).

5   For more on food and politics in Roman satire, see Emily Gowers, *The Loaded Table: Representations of Food in Roman Literature* (New York: Oxford University Press, 1993).

6   Plato, *Republic* 3.404bc: 'For you know that, during the campaign, at the feasts of the heroes, he doesn't feast them on fish,' trans. Allan Bloom (Ithaca, NY: Basic Books, 1968). Athenaeus, *The Learned Banqueters*, 1.25: 'Where does Homer refer to any Achaean as eating fish?,' trans. S. Douglas Olson (Cambridge, MA: Harvard University Press, 2006).

7   Suetonius, *Vitellius* 13, in *Suetonius: The Twelve Caesars*, trans. Robert Graves (Harmondsworth: Penguin Classics, 1957).

8   *Aeneid* 1.288–99 (*The Aeneid*, trans. Robert Fitzgerald (New York: Vintage Classics, 1990)).

9   Ovid, *Metamorphoses* 1.216–39, trans. Mary M. Innes (London: Penguin Classics, 1955).

10 Pindar, *Nemean Odes* 10.55–9 (*The Odes of Pindar*, trans. Cecil M. Bowra (Harmondsworth: Penguin Classics, 1969)) and Ovid, *Fasti* 5.715–20 (*Ovid: Fasti*, trans. Anthony J. Boyle and Roger D. Woodard (London: Penguin Classics, 2000) both describe Pollux, the immortal twin, as having specifically asked Zeus to split his immortality with his recently deceased twin, Castor.

11 For the recipe, see http://innatthecrossroads.com/jellied-calves-brains-2/. Or, if you prefer your recipes in Latin, try Book 4 of Apicius' cookbook from the fourth century A D, where you'll find plenty of ways to prepare your calves' brains!

12 The Romans, like Jordin Sparks and Pat Benatar, thought love was a battlefield. They called it *militia amoris*, though, and it's one of the important themes of their love poetry.

13 *Odyssey* 4.599–602 (*The Odyssey*, trans. Robert Fagles; introduction and notes by Bernard Knox (London: Penguin Classics, 1996)).

CHAPTER 2: THE KNIGHTS OF SUMMER

1 Looping Wor(l)d,'Wordcount of (un)popular (and hefty) Epics,' available at http://loopingworld.com/2009/03/06/wordcount/http://loopingworld.com/2009/03/06/wordcount/.

2 For what survives of the other poems of the so-called 'epic cycle,' see *Greek Epic Fragments: From the Seventh to the Fifth Centuries BC*, trans. Martin L. West (Cambridge, MA: Harvard University Press, 2003).

3 The story of how the Homeric poems came to be, and then came down to us, is fascinating, controversial, and sometimes highly technical. A good starting point is Bernard Knox's introduction in Fagles' translations of the *Iliad* and the *Odyssey*.

4 In the show: Tyrion whistles it (S2, E1), Bronn and his fellow pubmates sing it (S2, E9), Thoros of Myr sings it (S3, E2), it's at the Red Wedding (S3, E9), and the Purple Wedding (S4, E2); it's also in the end credits of S2, E9 and S4, E2 by The National (https://www.youtube.com/watch?v=ozVcbIc5yWI) and Sigur Rós (https://www.youtube.com/watch?v=w3QW8PVyyNM), respectively. In the novels: Red Wedding (*SS* 701–5), Purple Wedding (*SS* 820, 821), Tom of Sevenstreams singing it to Edmure so he knows not to cross the Lannisters (*FC* 817–18).

5 For more on the death of beautiful young men in the *Aeneid*, see James D. Reed, *Virgil's Gaze: Nation and Poetry in the Aeneid* (Princeton, NJ: Princeton University Press, 2015).

6 Suetonius, *Life of Virgil* 32, trans. John C. Rolfe (Cambridge, MA: Harvard University Press, 1998); Servius, *Commentaries on the Aeneid* 6.861.

7 *Iliad* 2.250–5, trans. Robert Fagles (London: Penguin, 1990).

8 Ibid., 2.248–9.

9 Ibid., 2.310–17.

10 On epic games: Helen Lovatt, *Statius and Epic Games: Sport, Politics and Poetics in the* Thebaid (Cambridge: Cambridge University Press, 2005). On 'real' games: David Goldblatt, *The Games: A Global History of the Olympics* (New York: W. W. Norton & Company, 2016).

11 Frederick Ahl, *Virgil: Aeneid* (Oxford: Oxford University Press, 2007), p. 358, note 360.

12 *Iliad* 23.745–50, trans. Robert Fagles (Harmondsworth: Penguin, 1990).

13 The ancients, too, were fascinated with the effects of snake venom: see the catalogue in Lucan, *Civil War* 9.700–838, trans. Susan H. Braund (Oxford: Oxford University Press, 1992), which is based on a Hellenistic predecessor.

14 *Aeneid* 9.613–20 (*The Aeneid*, trans. Robert Fitzgerald (New York: Vintage Classics, 1990)).

15 'To be Continued (Chicago, IL; May 6–8),' *The Citadel* (http://www.westeros. org/Citadel/SSM/Entry/To_Be_Continued_Chicago_IL_May_6_8).

16 Marco Fantuzzi, *Achilles in Love: Intertextual Studies* (Oxford: Oxford University Press, 2013).

17 For examples of this, see Suetonius, *Life of Julius Caesar* 49–52, in which Suetonius provides the laundry list of insults that were heaped upon Caesar for his alleged bisexuality, culminating with his being titled "every woman's husband, every man's wife." (*Suetonius: The Twelve Caesars*, trans. Robert Graves (London: Penguin Classics, 1957.)

18 Achilles in *Iliad* 19–22; Odysseus in *Odyssey* 22; Aeneas at the very end of *Aeneid* 12.

19 *Iliad* 19.429–56, trans. Fagles.

CHAPTER 3: EPIC HEROES

1 For more on how this dynamic works, see Gregory Nagy, *The Best of the Achaeans: Concepts of the Hero in Archaic Greek Poetry* (Baltimore, MD: Johns Hopkins University Press, 1981).

2 For more related to these topics, see Jonathan Shay, *Odysseus in America: Combat Trauma and the Trials of Homecoming* (New York: Scribner, 2003).

3 Nagy, *The Best of the Achaeans*.

4 For how this works in historical context, see W. Jeffrey Tatum, *Always I Am Caesar* (Hoboken, NJ: Wiley-Blackwell, 2008), especially Chapter 7 on precisely this generational tension and the murder of Caesar.

5 Oedipus, abandoned as a young child because of a prophecy made about his future, eventually comes to murder his biological father and marry (and have children with) his biological mother, thereby fulfilling the prophecy that had caused them to abandon him in the first place. Polyneices and Eteocles are two of the offspring from this incestuous union. (For their story, see Sophocles' trilogy *Oedipus the King*, trans. David Grene (Chicago, IL: University of Chicago Press, 2010), and Statius' epic *Thebaid: A Song of Thebes*, trans. Jane Wilson Joyce (Ithaca, NY: Cornell University Press, 2008)).

6   *Iliad* 4.488–95: 'We say we are far better men than our fathers were. Not they, but we, took Thebes of the seven gates, leading a smaller force against a heavier wall – but heeding signs the gods had shown, and helped by Zeus. Our fathers? Their own recklessness destroyed our fathers! Rate them less than equal to ourselves!' (*The Iliad*, trans. Robert Fitzgerald (New York: Farrar, Straus and Giroux, 2004)).

7   Horace, *Ode* 1.37 (in *The Complete Odes and Epodes*, trans. David West (Oxford: Oxford World's Classics, 2008).

8   Herodotus, *The Histories* 7.99, trans. Aubrey de Sélincourt (London: Penguin, 1954).

9   For the sacrifice: Euripides, *Iphigenia in Aulis* (in *Euripides: Orestes and Other Plays*, trans. Philip Vellacott (Harmondsworth: Penguin Classics, 1972)); for the aftermath: Aeschylus, *Agamemnon* (in *Aeschylus: The Oresteia*, trans. Robert Fagles (London: Penguin Classics, 1975)). The scene has its own parallel in the *Game of Thrones* world, when Stannis is asked to do the same with his own daughter, Shireen. The spoiler-happy can learn more about the classical connection in Amanda Marcotte's piece for *Slate*: http://www.slate.com/blogs/browbeat/2015/06/09/game_of_thrones_is_a_classical_tragedy_don_t_be_so_shocked_my_the_deaths.html.

10 Athenaeus, *The Learned Banqueters* 8.347, trans. S. Douglas Olson (Cambridge, MA: Harvard University Press, 2008).

11 *Iliad* 6.504–11: 'Draw up your troops by the wild fig tree; that way the city lies most open, men most easily could swarm the wall where it is low: three times, at least, their best men tried it there [...] whether someone who had it from oracles had told them, or their own hearts urged them on' (*The Iliad*, trans. Fitzgerald).

12 Stesichorus 192: 'This tale they tell's not true: / you did not sail in those benched ships / or come to the towers of Troy' (in *Greek Lyric Poetry*, trans. Martin L. West (Oxford: Oxford World's Classics, 1994)); and also Euripides, *Helen* 31–6.

13 Odyssey 4.307–13: 'When along *you* came, Helen – roused, no doubt, by a dark power bent on giving Troy some glory [...] Three times you sauntered around our hollow ambush, feeling, stroking its flanks, challenging all our fighters, calling each by name – yours was the voice of all our long-lost wives!' (*The Odyssey*, trans. Robert Fagles (New York: Penguin Classics, 1996).

14 Dio 63.5.2 has Tiridates saying that he revered Nero as Mithras. Porphyry (*de antro Nympharum* 2) associates Zoroaster and Mithras specifically.

15 For more, see Mary Boyce, *Zoroastrians: Their Religious Beliefs and Practices* (London: Routledge, 1979).

16 For more on Terentia, see Susan Treggiari, *Terentia, Tullia and Publilia: The Women of Cicero's Family* (London and New York: Routledge, 2007).

17 *Iliad* 2.244–319 (*The Iliad*, trans. Fitzgerald).

18 George R. R. Martin, *The Wit and Wisdom of Tyrion Lannister* (New York: Bantam, 2013); http://www.blastr.com/2016-4-4/researchers-use-math-prove-tyrion-most-important-character-game-thrones.

19 James Hibberd, 'Game of Thrones: George R.R. Martin explains that murderous finale scene,' *Entertainment Weekly*, available at http://www.ew.com/article/2014/06/16/game-of-thrones-finale-martin (16 June 2014).

CHAPTER 4: POLITICS

1 To see his full discussion of this, see Polybius 6.4–9. (*Polybius: The Rise of the Roman Empire*, trans. Ian Scott-Kilvert (New York: Penguin Classics, 1980)).
2 For the full passage, see Herodotus, *The Histories* 3.80–3, trans. Aubrey de Sélincourt (London: Penguin, 1954).
3 On incest in Egypt, see Paul John Frandsen, *Incestuous and Close-Kin Marriage in Ancient Egypt and Persia: An Examination of the Evidence* (Carsten Niebuhr Institute of Ancient Near East Studies, Book 34) (Copenhagen: Museum Tusculanum Press, 2009).
4 For discussion of the Ptolemies and their court, I'm indebted to Sheila L. Ager, 'Familiarity Breeds: Incest and the Ptolemaic Dynasty,' *The Journal of Hellenistic Studies* 125 (2005), pp. 1–34.
5 Plutarch, *Moralia*, 200f–201a.
6 The imperial women are one of the more fascinating aspects of the Roman empire. For Livia, see Anthony A. Barrett, *Livia: First Lady of Imperial Rome* (New Haven, CT: Yale University Press, 2004). For Agrippina, see Anthony A. Barrett, *Agrippina: Sex, Power, and Politics in the Early Empire* (New Haven, CT: Yale University Press, 1999). For women in the Roman empire, see Annelise Freisenbruch, *Caesars' Wives: Sex, Power, and Politics in the Roman Empire* (New York: Simon and Schuster, 2010).
7 *Iliad* 3.273–91 (*The Iliad*, trans. Robert Fagles (New York: Penguin, 1990)).
8 Livy 1.58 (*Livy: The Early History of Rome*, trans. Aubrey de Sélincourt (New York: Penguin, 2002)).
9 The overlap between ancient and modern usages of words like 'democracy' and 'republic' was difficult to manage, especially for Rome, which has a mixed constitution. For thoughts on how the Romans did manage this, see Fergus Millar, *The Crowd in Rome in the Late Republic* (Ann Arbor: University of Michigan Press, 1998).
10 For more on Rome's freedmen, see Henrik Mouritsen, *The Freedman in the Roman World* (Cambridge and New York: Cambridge University Press, 2011). For the experience of freedwomen, see Matthew J. Perry, *Gender, Manumission, and the Roman Freedwoman* (New York: Cambridge University Press, 2013).
11 This of course raised questions about whether the Greeks and Romans had the same (or similar) family feelings to what we have today. For some more answers, and a view of family life and the challenges facing families in antiquity, dip into Blackwell's *Companion to Families in the Greek and Roman Worlds*, ed. Beryl Rawson (Malden, MA, Oxford, and Chichester: Wiley-Blackwell, 2011).

12   *Xenophon: The Expedition of Cyrus*, trans. Robin Waterfield (Oxford: Oxford University Press, 2009).

13   For a specific source for this, see the passage from Vergil's *Georgics* (2.136–76, trans. Janet Lembke (New Haven, CT: Yale University Press, 2005)) which is commonly referred to as the 'praises of Italy' (*laudes Italiae*).

14   For the strange creatures of Egypt, see Herodotus, *The Histories*, 2.73–6, trans. de Sélincourt; note that Herodotus himself doesn't mention Egypt's gods.

15   Pliny, *Natural History* 10.132, trans. Harris Rackham (Cambridge, MA: Harvard University Press, 1940); Caesar, *Gallic War* 6.25–8, trans. Carolyn Hammond (Oxford: Oxford World's Classics, 2008).

16   Tacitus, *Agricola* 30, trans. Herbert W. Benario (Indianapolis, IN: The Bobbs-Merrill Company, Inc., 1967).

EPILOGUE

1   The war is narrated in Tacitus' *Histories*, trans. Rhiannon Ash (London: Penguin Classics, 2009), as well as in the lives of the relevant emperors composed by Suetonius (*Lives of the Caesars*, trans. Catharine Edwards (Oxford: Oxford World's Classics, 2009)): Galba, Otho, Vitellius, and Vespasian.

FURTHER READING

The ancient world has been an object of study for over two millennia; as a result, there is a bewildering amount of information out there for any curious readers. The best starting point, however, is Greek and Roman literature itself. Oxford World's Classics and Penguin both have extensive catalogues of classical works in English translation, all of them with concise introductions and notes. Many of the most famous texts have been translated multiple times, and everyone has their favorites. The *Iliad* and *Odyssey* in particular have many options to choose from, including Robert Fagles' 1990 deluxe edition from Penguin, with Derek Jacobi reading an abridged *Iliad* for the audiobook. The Homeric poems were meant to be sung, and hearing them spoken out loud can transform the experience. Anyone interested in the wordplay and soundscapes of Vergil's *Aeneid* can dip into Frederick Ahl's 2007 translation for Oxford World's Classics, which keeps both the original meter and many of the puns and sound effects.

The classical world has been enjoying a particularly popular moment in the last few years, and there's a slew of new accessible books about numerous facets of Greco-Roman culture. For an overview of the Romans, you might try Mary Beard's *SPQR: A History of Ancient Rome* (New York: Liveright, 2016). For the Greeks, try Edith Hall's *Introducing the Ancient Greeks* (London: W. W. Norton, 2014). On the history of Roman expansion, there's Adrian Goldsworthy's *Pax Romana: War, Peace and Conquest in the Roman World* (New Haven, CT: Yale University Press, 2016), and for Greek democracy and its long afterlife, there's Paul Cartledge's

Democracy: A Life (Oxford: Oxford University Press, 2016). This is only the most recent crop, and there are many more out there to choose from, including academic studies designed for a specialized readership, which I've omitted here.

If you're after a snappier read, the Oxford *Very Short Introductions* handily live up to their name. For classics, we have *Classics* by Mary Beard and John Henderson (2000); *Ancient Greece* by Paul Cartledge (2011); *Ancient Warfare* by Harry Sidebottom (2005); *Classical Literature* by William Allan (2014); *Classical Mythology* by Helen Morales (2007); *The Trojan War* by Eric Cline (2013); and *The Roman Empire* by Christopher Kelly (2006). This is only a selection.

The best one-stop resource is the *Oxford Classical Dictionary*, 4th ed. (Oxford: Oxford University Press, 2012), with a regularly updated online edition to appear soon. A standard textbook for classical myth is the co-authored *Classical Mythology*, 10th ed. (Oxford: Oxford University Press, 2013). There's lots of good information on Wikipedia, though it should be consulted with the usual caveats about checking and evaluating sources. A huge amount of content relating to classical myth, especially English translations of the sources, can be found at http://www.theoi.com.

Besides source material, the classics likewise have a strong showing on the web when it comes to news and cultural commentary. *Eidolon* is a web magazine publishing short pieces on all matters classical and especially classical–modern relations (https://eidolon. pub). Sarah Bond, whose pieces on various points of classical interest are always worth reading, has also collected a list of links to blogs, resources, and other useful tidbits (https://sarahemilybond. wordpress.com/links/), as has the website *Rogue Classicism* (https:// rogueclassicism.com). And if you've always wanted to speak Latin and Greek, the Paideia Institute offers a range of online courses in conversational Greek and Latin: http://www.paideiainstitute. org/online_classes. The ancient world is not nearly as dead as it might seem!

Finally, there is the vibrant community of *Game of Thrones* forums, websites and wikis, which between them report, dissect, and explain any question or theory you might have about this sprawling world: http://winteriscoming.net, http://asoiaf.westeros. org, http://gameofthrones.wikia.com, and a series of very detailed Wikipedia articles.

Happy reading!

INDEX